HERE, THERE, AND ELSEWHERE

---

# Here, There, and Elsewhere

*The Making of Immigrant Identities
in a Globalized World*

**TAHSEEN SHAMS**

STANFORD UNIVERSITY PRESS
*Stanford, California*

STANFORD UNIVERSITY PRESS

Stanford, California

Printed in the United States of America on acid-free, archival-quality paper

Library of Congress Cataloging-in-Publication Data

Names: Shams, Tahseen, author.

Title: Here, there, and elsewhere : the making of immigrant identities in a globalized world / Tahseen Shams.

Other titles: Globalization in everyday life.

Description: Stanford, California : Stanford University Press, [2020] | Series: Globalization in everyday life | Includes bibliographical references and index.

Identifiers: LCCN 2019046794 (print) | LCCN 2019046795 (ebook) | ISBN 9781503610699 (cloth) | ISBN 9781503612839 (paperback) | ISBN 9781503612846 (ebook)

Subjects: LCSH: South Asian Americans—Ethnic identity. | Muslims—United States—Ethnic identity. | South Asian Americans—Social conditions. | Muslims—United States—Social conditions. | South Asian Americans—Politics and government. | Muslims—Political activity—United States. | Immigrants—United States—Social conditions. | United States—Ethnic relations.

Classification: LCC E184.S69 S528 2020 (print) | LCC E184.S69 (ebook) | DDC 305.800973—dc23

LC record available at https://lccn.loc.gov/2019046794

LC ebook record available at https://lccn.loc.gov/2019046795

Cover design: Brad Norris

Typeset by Westchester Publishing Services in 10/14.4 Minion Pro

*To my family here, there, and elsewhere*

# Contents

# Acknowledgments

Writing this book has been deeply humbling. I am humbled by the generosity of the South Asian Muslim Americans who have shared their lives with me and whose stories are now woven with mine throughout this book. I am grateful to each and every one of them.

This book was written over the course of five years, a journey that took me from Mississippi to California, and now to Toronto. I feel blessed to have met people who inspired me along the way. In Mississippi, being a first-generation immigrant from a Bangladeshi Muslim background often meant I was the only nonwhite, nonblack person in any situation. My experiences on the margins of a predominantly white, Christian, conservative milieu opened my mind to sociological imagination, sparking questions that I sought to answer through my research in California. There, at the University of California, Los Angeles, I was extremely fortunate to learn from Roger Waldinger and Rubén Hernández-León, who both instilled in me a deep appreciation for intellectual rigor. Their enthusiastic encouragement of my pursuit of the questions I longed to explore, their mentorship, and their joy when I found answers made research for this book an immensely gratifying endeavor. They have read various iterations of this book multiple times, and each time their comments have led me to sharpen my writing and discover new dimensions of my own ideas.

At the University of Toronto, my colleagues have made the Department of Sociology an exciting place for intellectual pursuits. For creating a supportive environment in which I was able to immerse myself in writing this book, I thank Scott Schieman and Christian Caron. Monica Boyd and Jeff Reitz helped brainstorm ideas for the book's subtitle and have been a source of encouragement and wisdom. Zaheer Baber and Bonnie Erickson regularly checked in to see how I was acclimating to life in Toronto and were readily available to provide advice. I also thank Blair Wheaton, Vanina Leschziner, Anna Korteweg, Ron Levi, Patricia Landolt, Luisa Schwartzman, Bob Brym, and Judy Taylor for their support and mentorship. I am grateful to Neda Maghbouleh for our conversations on research, academia, and public sociology. My warm thanks to Geoff Wodke for planning happy hours that regularly reminded me to step away from the work desk. For their camaraderie, my thanks to Angelina Grigoryeva, Rania Salem, Hae Yeon Choo, Yoonkyung Lee, and Clayton Childress. I also thank Melissa Milkie, Cynthia Cranford, Irene Boeckmann, Fedor Dokshin, Bonnie Fox, Dan Silver, Kim Pernell-Gallagher, Alexandra Marin, Rachel La Touche, Jerry Flores, Zach Richer, Phil Goodman, Paula Maurutto, Jack Veugelers, Fidan Elcioglu, and Akwasi Owusu-Bempeh. My sincere gratitude to Sherri Klassen, Grace Ramirez, Tina Colomvakos, Jeremy Nichols, Donna Ragbir, and John Manalo for providing vital support to our department. For stimulating conversations and encouragement, I give thanks also to my colleagues outside University of Toronto Sociology: Kate Choi, Filiz Kahraman, Donna Gabaccia, Joseph Carens, Abdie Kazemipur, Phil Triadafilopoulos, Amelie Barras, Thomas Soehl, Randall Hansen, Pallavi Banerjee, Rupa Banerjee, Anna Triandafyllidou, Rina Cohen, Anver Emon, and Miglena Todorova.

As exciting as it was to share what I learned through fieldwork, the writing process was a journey in and of itself, mired in conundrums that, at times, led to wild goose chases and blank pages, not to mention one too many existential crises. As such, I am immensely grateful to the people who read drafts and shared their feedback, giving me much-needed assurance that I was, in fact, making sense. Rogers Brubaker's sharp insight at various stages was extremely meaningful in developing the book's theoretical framework. Nile Green's comments on transnational organizations helped address elements missing from earlier drafts. David FitzGerald's suggestions, rooted in his deep knowledge of immigration history, and his excitement for the book were a wonderful source of inspiration in the revision stages. I also give my sincere thanks to Steve Gold for his words of support and thoughts on the book's key chapters. Careful comments from the anonymous reviewers at Stanford University Press and from Rhacel Salazar Parreñas, the series editor of *Globalization in Everyday Life*, strengthened and added nuance to the book's arguments. My monthly accountability sessions with Phi Hong Su made writing this book a much less isolating experience than it otherwise would have been. I thank her for her detailed comments and friendship.

I have been deeply inspired by the works of many scholars over the course of writing this book. For their important contribution to scholarship, their advice, and their encouragement, I am indebted to Peggy Levitt, Phil Kasinitz, Rubén Rumbaut, Nancy Foner, and Nazli Kibria. I also thank Louise Cainkar, Sunaina Maira, Pawan Dhingra, Erik Love, John O'Brien, David Cook-Martín, and Saher Selod, among others. For shaping my outlook on conducting research, I am grateful to C. K. Lee, Rebecca Emigh, Bill Roy, Gail Kligman, and Vilma Ortiz. Gail continues to be someone I turn to for advice on navigating fieldwork and life as a female academic. For their constructive comments on engaging with the sociology of religion and Islam, I thank Jeff Guhin and Kevan Harris.

Research for this book was made possible due to generous grants from the National Science Foundation [DGE—1144087], the UCLA Institute of American Cultures and Asian Studies Program, and the UCLA Graduate Division. Some parts of chapters 1, 4, and 5 were published in article form in "Mirrored Boundaries: How Homeland-Hostland Contexts Shape Bangladeshi Immigrant Collective Identity Formation," in *Ethnic and Racial Studies* 40(4): 713–31, and in "Visibility as Resistance by Muslim Americans in a Surveillance and Security Atmosphere," *Sociological Forum* 33(1): 73–94 and "Successful Yet Precarious: South Asian Muslim Americans, Islamophobia, and the Model Minority Myth," *Sociological Perspectives* (forthcoming). I am grateful to these journals for allowing me to republish my work in this book with additional data and new interpretations. I am also grateful to BUFLA (Bangladesh Unity Federation of Los Angeles) for opening up their photo gallery to the public. Figure 1.1 has been republished with permission from their archive. I especially thank Zia Islam for his help and cooperation.

I give my thanks also to Janna Shadduck-Hernández for her feedback on the book's cover.

For helping me bring the book to the finish line, I thank my editor, Marcela Christina Maxfield, at Stanford University Press. Marcela believed in the book from our very first meeting and has been the best editor I could have possibly asked for. I am very grateful to her, Sunna Juhn, John Donohue, Stephanie Adams, Gigi Mark, Greta Lindquist, Lynn Everett, and the incredible team at Stanford for looking after my book with such care.

Like many immigrant families, mine too is a small diaspora spread out in different corners of the world. Yet my family's love and encouragement have been a constant presence in my life—a reminder that my immigrant story is just part of the next chapter in a broader anthology of all those who have traversed these paths before me, and a gift from all those to whom I have said goodbye. I thank Boro Chacha, Boro Ma, and Waseem Bhaiya. My thanks also to Chhoto Chachi, Sumaiya, Mejo Fupi, Khalamoni, Boro Khalu, Nanu, Bappu, Chhoto Khalu, Monna, Dada, Poonam Bhabi, Joyee, Jeeyon, and Baby Aunty. I wish Chhoto Chacha was still alive to see my book. And I wish I could have thanked him for his unconditional love, countless quiet sacrifices, and fierce pride in our family, all of which have made where I am today possible. I am lucky to have a second set of parents in my Chhoto Fupa-Fupi. I recuperated from the long months of writing with a trip to Bangladesh, where I stayed with them in their loving home. As short as the days were, with the bittersweet note of goodbye never too far away, I cherished every second I got to spend with them. They have been eagerly anticipating this book since I first told them about it. I can't wait to send them my first copies.

I am also grateful to my Hattiesburg family—Arif Uncle, Noverra Aunty, Ratna Aunty, and Amal Uncle—for their warm support. I thank Julie Reid for her mentorship and friendship over the years.

Finally, I thank the four who give greater meaning to all my scholarly ambitions: Maa, Baba, Reevu, and Dadu. My grandmother instilled in her children and grandkids her love for knowledge, and my parents left the country of their birth and the people they love so I could thrive in the pursuit of it. My brother has been my companion and a continuing source of love and support in that adventure. This book is a testament to our family's story.

# HERE, THERE, AND ELSEWHERE

# 1 | SOCIETIES INTERCONNECTED

**THE PERIOD FROM 2015 THROUGH 2017** was a turning point for the world. ISIS was on the rise, having conducted terror attacks both on U.S. soil and in places as wide-ranging as France, Belgium, Turkey, Lebanon, and Bangladesh. Great Britain shocked the world with its vote to "Brexit" from the European Union—a decision analysts have explained was a reaction against immigration and globalization. And the world could no longer turn a blind eye to the horrors of the Syrian refugee crisis as photographs of the dead body of a three-year-old boy named Aylan Kurdi lying face down on a beach in Turkey circulated across newspapers and social media.

The tremors of these global events were felt in the United States, where the 2016 presidential election was in full swing, with several candidates campaigning on the same kinds of nativist and anti-Muslim platforms that were driving the resurgence of right-wing populism around the world—from France, Germany, and the Netherlands in Europe to India and the Philippines in Asia. Donald Trump famously called for a wall on the U.S.-Mexico border. Not to be outdone, Ted Cruz, ostensibly in reaction to ISIS terror attacks in Paris, proposed a religious test for Syrian refugees, showing willingness to grant asylum to those who were Christian but not to those who were Muslim. But perhaps what most prominently reestablished Muslim immigrants at the center of national politics after 9/11 was Trump calling for a "total and complete shutdown of Muslims entering the United States."[1]

Although not everyone in America condoned these narratives, the nativist and Islamophobic platforms were met with widespread public support from many segments of U.S. society. Islamophobia rose throughout the election cycle,[2] with the number of anti-Muslim assaults reaching the 9/11-era level in just 2015 alone.[3] And national discourse about Muslims centered on debates over which of them—if any—could be considered "good Muslims" and whether any Muslim could ever be deemed "American." This discourse arguably determined the election cycle for both political parties. While the Republican Party largely played into the Islamophobic fears of many Americans, Democrats emphasized the "American-ness" of Muslims in the United States, inviting Khizr and Ghazala Khan, the Gold Star Pakistani immigrant parents of a Muslim American soldier killed in Iraq, to speak at the Democratic National Convention.

While these events showcase the centrality of immigration-related debates in the current global consciousness, there is another, bigger story at play, which is going unnoticed. Immigrants are vectors of globalization, who both produce and experience the interconnectedness of societies. When immigrants leave one country to settle in another, they do not forget the people and places they have left behind. Instead, they bring with them the beliefs, practices, conflicts, and histories from back "there" in the homeland to "here" in the host society. The contexts of their sending societies thus continue to influence these immigrants' worldviews, shaping who they identify as "we" as opposed to "them," even as they interact with various other immigrant and native groups and build new communities in the hostland. However, how the immigrants view themselves and where they draw the boundaries between "us" and "them" do not always converge with the receiving society's views. In fact, immigrants' views of themselves are quite unique, because in contrast to the lives of most people in the places of origin and destination, immigrants' lives straddle two or more national societies. Moreover, both processes of identification—that by the immigrants themselves and that by others—are located in a larger geopolitical tapestry that subverts territorial borders. As such, immigrants often face the immediate spillover effects of global events that occur *even* in places they are not from and to which they have never been, with contexts in seemingly faraway foreign lands coming to shape both how others view immigrants and how immigrants view themselves. I refer to these places as "elsewheres." "Elsewheres" are places that are neither the immigrants' homeland nor hostland but that are nonetheless important to immigrants' identity formation.[4]

Along those lines, this book introduces a broader, more comprehensive analytical design to study immigrant identities—the "multicentered relational framework"—which encompasses global geopolitics in the immigrants' sending and receiving countries, and in places beyond. In so doing, I show how contexts in the immigrants' homeland, hostland, and "elsewhere" *together* shape immigrants' lives.

This convergence of factors that construct an immigrant's identity can sometimes have tragic effects. For example, in the month after 9/11, Vasudev Patel, a Hindu Indian; Waqar Hasan, a Muslim from Pakistan; and Rais Bhuiyan, a Bangladeshi Muslim, were shot in Texas by Mark Stroman who called himself the "Arab slayer." Vasudev and Waqar died, whereas Rais survived but partially lost his vision. Stroman proudly admitted to the killing spree, claiming to be an American patriot avenging the 9/11 terrorist attacks by Arab Muslim extremists. None of his victims, however, were Arab—one of them was not even Muslim. Similarly, in February 2017, two Hindu immigrants from India, Srinivas Kuchibhotla and Alok Madasani, were shot in Kansas by Adam Purinton, who later bragged about killing "two Iranians." This incident took place just three weeks after President Trump had rolled out his first executive order to ban people coming from seven predominantly Muslim countries—including Iran—to keep out "radical Islamic terrorists." Neither Srinivas nor Alok, of course, were Iranian—nor did they identify as Muslim. Yet, how Vasudev, Waqar, Rais, Srinivas, and Alok had self-identified—whether based on religion, nationality, ethnicity, or politics—bore little effect. Instead, contexts stemming from the Middle East—a place *beyond* their homeland and hostland—determined how they were identified by others in America.

Conversely, immigrants can also *self*-identify with places beyond the sending and receiving countries, sometimes even prioritizing these connections over those oriented toward their homeland. For example, in late 2015, around the same time the Syrian refugee crisis caught the world's attention, another refugee crisis was unfolding in South Asia—that of Rohingya Muslims. Rohingyas are a Muslim ethnic minority in the Western Rakhine state of Myanmar. The Myanmar government views the Rohingyas as illegal Bangladeshi immigrants, although these people have lived in Myanmar for centuries. Fleeing violent persecution by the Myanmar government, Rohingyas have sought asylum in neighboring countries, mainly Bangladesh. Most now live in dire conditions in refugee camps. Although, unlike the Syrian refugee crisis, the Rohingya refugee crisis directly involves Bangladesh, many Bangladeshi Americans were still relatively unaware of who the Rohingyas are. Their unawareness was particularly remarkable given how avidly they had paid attention to the Syrian refugee crisis based on a sense of solidarity with fellow Muslims in the Middle East. Whereas the Syrian crisis had garnered the attention of Bangladeshi Americans as a whole—who responded by actively following news trends, engaging in social media posts and discussions, and raising and donating funds for Syrian refugees—the Rohingya crisis, although also involving Muslims in their homeland, went virtually unnoticed.

In the following pages, I tell the story of immigrants, as both agents and receptors of globalization, by exploring the lives and identities of South Asian Muslim Americans in California, as they struggle to merge into the religious, political, and racial contexts of both the United States and societies abroad. South Asians comprise the largest immigrant Muslim group in America,[5] with Pakistan and Bangladesh being the top two sending states of Muslim immigrants to the United States.[6] Most of the South Asian Muslim immigrants in this book come from these two countries, while a few others come from India, where, in contrast to Pakistan and Bangladesh, Muslims are the religious minority, despite being significantly large in number.[7] In fact, India, Pakistan, and Bangladesh have the second, third, and fourth largest Muslim populations in the world.[8] And immigration from these countries to the United States has steadily increased in recent years.[9]

The data for this book come from two main sources: First, they come from in-depth interviews of sixty South Asian Muslims across California, collected from 2015 to 2017. Second, they come from three years of ethnographic observations, made from 2012 to 2013 and then from 2015 to 2017, at various sites in Los Angeles—home to one of the highest concentrations of South

Asians in America. These two primary sources of data are complemented by content analysis of South Asian and Muslim Americans' Facebook activities and of selected organizational documents of the largest Muslim American organization in North America.

Although I began this research in 2012, before the rise of what is now popularly referred to as the "Trump phenomenon," my findings have since become extremely relevant in light of political developments in the United States and around the world. Many of these developments directly involve the sending countries of South Asia and their emigrants to the United States. Just some examples are the 2015 ISIS-inspired San Bernardino attacks by a married couple of Pakistani descent, the 2016 ISIS terror attacks in Bangladesh's capital, the 2017 low-tech bomb explosion in the New York City subway station by an ISIS-inspired Bangladeshi immigrant, and the ongoing Rohingya refugee crisis, involving Bangladesh and other neighboring countries in South Asia.

In telling this story about South Asian Muslim immigrants, this book fills a gap in what we know about immigrant identity-making. Although scholars have long theorized about how immigrants form new identities and build communities in their hostlands, the foundational frameworks they use—assimilation, panethnicity, transnationalism, and diaspora—focus exclusively on the contexts of the sending and receiving countries. Constrained within this dyadic homeland-hostland framework, what remains largely overlooked, then, is how sociopolitical dynamics in places *beyond*, but in relation to, the homeland and hostland also shape immigrants' identities. It is this question that this book seeks to answer, and it does so by using religion as an example of immigrants' global connections to trace how immigrants' sense of selves stretches over territorial borders. As immigrants arrive in their hostlands, they both produce and experience globalization through their interactions with other diverse immigrant and native groups, while also connecting societies that may have previously been distinct.[10] Through these interactions, they generate contacts not just across cultures but also across religions. As communities of believers, religions tie together people differently than migrations from "there" to "here" do. Rather, religions tend to transcend state boundaries and societal borders[11]—thus connecting "here," "there," and beyond.

Some world religions, like Islam, have structures and institutions built within them that connect believers from across the world in a bond of brotherhood. For Islam in particular, one such core notion is the *Ummah*—the imagined worldwide community of Muslims that transcends borders and connects all Muslims via shared beliefs, rituals, duties, and a sense of membership. A religious framework of this sort can invoke a sense of community and collective identity that people can then use to make sense of their world and relationships, to create group boundaries between an "us" and a "them" that transcend state borders.[12] Today these interconnections and group boundaries across state territories are facilitated by advanced telecommunications technologies, such as cable news and social media, and are shaped by global political dynamics. Consequently, the effects of religious conflicts reverberate across state borders, making themselves felt at opposite ends of the world. For instance, Muslims in the United States faced upticks of anti-Muslim sentiments following Islamist[13] attacks not just in America but also in Paris and Brussels, as indicated by spikes in Google searches for the terms "Kill Muslims" and "Islamophobia."[14] At the same time, as this book shows, telecommunications allows immigrants both to follow global events and to collectively interpret their meaning, which means Muslim Americans can anticipate and take precautions against the antagonism that these global conflicts may provoke.

Locating South Asian Muslim Americans in the multicentered relational model, this book shows how different dimensions of the immigrants' "Muslim" identity tie them to different "elsewhere" contexts in distinct yet overlapping ways. As Muslims, these immigrants are members of the *Ummah*. However, the heartland of that imagined global community is not found in South Asia but in the Middle East, in that part of the Muslim world that shares a contentious geopolitical relationship with the West, and particularly with the United States. As the birthplace of Islam and the Prophet Muhammad, and as the location of Islam's holiest sites, the Middle East is arguably the spiritual and political center of the Muslim world. And as self-identifying Muslims, these immigrants subscribe to the various histories, places, peoples, and conflicts in the Middle East that sustain their Muslim identity. In effect, many South Asian Muslim Americans engage in politics aimed at "elsewhere" places in the Middle East, such as in Palestine and Turkey. Yet, how these immigrants self-identify does not determine how they are identified by their hostland society at large. Despite the salience of the Middle East in these immigrants' self-identification, it is the Muslim-related contexts in "elsewhere" Europe that tend to shape how these Muslims are viewed in America and to trigger anti-Muslim backlash.

Thus, the multicentered relational framework captures three specific points of focus, or "centers," thereby expanding the homeland-hostland dyad: (1) "here," which refers to the hostland—in this case, the United States; (2) "there," which refers to the immigrants' homeland—in this case, Bangladesh, India, and Pakistan; and (3) "elsewhere," which refers to places beyond, such as the Middle East and Europe. Because each pole in this triad tugs at immigrants' sense of self, political conflicts in and between these places shape the immigrants' identity-making processes. Thus, this book tells the larger story of how the interconnectedness of societies at the global level shapes the everyday lives of immigrants and Muslims on the ground.

## ISLAM AS AN ANALYTICAL LENS

Located in what is popularly called the heart of Koreatown in Los Angeles, Little Bangladesh is a small, mostly residential neighborhood with around twenty thousand Bangladeshi residents and fewer than ten Bangladeshi-owned businesses. Although called Little Bangladesh, more businesses here are Korean and Mexican than Bangladeshi. Yet, for about a decade, this area has been the officially recognized enclave for Bangladeshis in Los Angeles. The residents here are working class—most of them Muslim. Not far from where the enclave begins is a prominent Islamic center where Muslims from diverse ethnic backgrounds congregate for prayers. Still, on Fridays, the Bangladeshi Muslim men in the area congregate in a small room alongside an ethnic grocery store to offer *Jummah*, or Friday afternoon prayers, by themselves. Given the very limited space, women are not allowed. However, on *Eid* (the main Islamic festival), the men—at least the ones who can afford to take the day off from work—dress up in their traditional kurta suits, called *payjama-panjabi* in Bangla, and with their families, they make the small trek to the Islamic center early in the morning to offer *Eid* prayers. The women also wear traditional Bangladeshi clothing like *saris* and *salwar kamiz*, usually bought just for this occasion. They carefully drape the *anchol* and *orna* to cover their hair, and many wear their prized gold bangles and other pieces of jewelry. After their prayers, they come home to share an elaborate breakfast with family and friends, which the women in the households have typically prepared the night before. In fact, the night before *Eid*, called *chaand raat,* or the night of the moon, is a time of celebration for the Bangladeshi Muslim residents in this area. As *Eid* is scheduled according to the lunar calendar, the moon sighting, which is typically done on *chaand raat,* is celebrated in many parts of the Muslim world. Many residents in Little Bangladesh, however, tend to schedule *Eid* according to the Saudi lunar calendar, which they deem to be the most Islamically authentic. Every year, the main Bangladeshi cultural organization in Los Angeles organizes a fair to celebrate *chaand raat,* where makeshift stalls sell *saris, salwar kamiz, kurta,* henna designs, *desi*[15] snacks, and jewelry on the grounds of a community center near the neighborhood. There are also dance and music performances, which Bangladeshis from other parts of Los Angeles drive to attend.

March or April usually marks another occasion for celebration for the residents of this enclave: the commemoration of Bangladesh's independence from Pakistan in 1971. Every year, the Los Angeles Bangladeshi organizations pay the city to block off the streets for the Bangladesh Day Parade, which marches through the neighborhood, transforming it into a space for celebrating Bangladeshi-ness (see figure 1.1).[16]

Those attending the parade wear traditional clothes in red and green—the colors of the Bangladeshi flag. Bangladeshi patriotic songs are played on loud speakers as parade participants carry their organizational banners, with words often scrawled in both Bangla and English. Many carry tiny Bangladeshi and American flags. Various Bangladeshi religious-political organizations also take part in the event, and many women from these organizations wear green or red *hijabs*. The non-Bangladeshis in the area also seem to find the parade amusing, as employees from the Mexican and Korean shops along the sidewalks come out to watch. An award ceremony recognizing the organizers marks the end of the parade. A regular but celebrated fixture at this ceremony is a brief speech by the Los Angeles city mayor.

My visits to Little Bangladesh, however, usually took place on the mundane, regular days, when I went either to pay house calls to a few families I knew in the neighborhood or to have lunch at a *deshi* (Bangla for *"desi"*)

FIGURE 1.1. Bangladesh Day Parade in Los Angeles, 2012. *Source*: Bangladesh Unity Federation of Los Angeles (BUFLA). Reprinted with permission.

grocery store/restaurant. The front of the restaurant looked a little run-down, with litter strewn here and there on the pavement and the small parking lot. A money transfer agent office conveniently stood on the same strip, for anyone wishing to remit money back home. The distinctly *deshi* smell of oil and spices engulfed me as soon as I walked into the store. The checkout counter, always laden with dates, tamarind, chutneys, and fruits, faced the entrance. On the left of the counter was a hot-plate bar with various Bangladeshi curries. On the right was a glass showcase with an assortment of popular *deshi* sweets, like *doi, chom chom, golap jaam, roshogolla,* and *shondesh.* The sweets, I learned, were sometimes made at the store and sometimes shipped from New York. The storeowner—a balding, unsmiling, middle-aged man—always greeted his customers from behind the counter with a small nod and the greeting "*Bhalo asen?*" (Are you well?).[17] Behind him, stacked high, stood a tower of white Styrofoam boxes. The customers pointed to the items they wanted from the hot bar, and he—with an air of grim authority—piled them into a box.

After getting my food, I usually walked over to the right side of the store, where there were a few booths and tables for diners. A television, which almost always played Bangladeshi channels, was placed high up on the back wall. I usually sat at the very back of the room to get a full view of the place. Past the booths in front of me was the grocery store with aisles of *desi* products imported all the way from Bangladesh and, in some cases, from India and Pakistan. In addition to the popular but hard-to-come-by *deshi* food products—like *shorishar tel* (mustard oil), *hilsha* and *kachki* fish, *shutki* (fermented fish jerky), *haleem* spice mix, and *chanachur* (fried snacks)—the store also carried prayer beads (called *tojbi*) and mats (*jaynamaj*), as well as traditional everyday clothing for men, like the *tupi* (a prayer cap) and the *lungi* (a kind of men's skirt). Women's clothing and accessories, like the *burqa*[18] and *salwar kamiz*, however, were not sold.

As a young Bangladeshi woman by myself, clad in a loose T-shirt and a pair of jeans, my presence at the restaurant invited curious looks and questions from the diners, who were almost always men. I can probably count on one hand the number of times I have seen women sit and dine by themselves at the store. Women diners were usually accompanied by their husbands, although a few times women from the enclave came in to do some quick grocery shopping and then promptly leave. The questions I usually received from male diners were whether I lived in the area, what my father's profession was, where my home in Bangladesh was, where I lived in Los Angeles, and how long I had been in the United States.

Indeed, the store was, by and large, a male—and Muslim—space. A big handwritten sign sat on a wall saying "*Halal* Meat" in English, with a smaller sign in Bangla advertising pre-orders for meat-shares for *Eid* celebrations. The customers and staff were co-ethnics—Bangladeshi Muslim. Usually the women who came in for grocery shopping or family dining covered their hair with a *hijab*, *burqa*, or *orna* (a long piece of fabric), indicating their Islamic faith. I remember seeing a Hindu couple only once—identifiable from the red vermillion in the wife's hair. The couple did not dine but left after buying their groceries. In contrast, it was easy to tell when customers were Muslim because of their frequent references to Islam in conversations with one another. For example, customers usually exchanged *salaam* with the storeowner upon entering the store. Even casual day-to-day interactions had

Islamic connotations. For instance, once, when the storeowner had asked his helper to carry a hot tray to the kitchen, he jokingly said, "If you are a true Muslim, you have no fear! You will not burn!" implying that Allah would protect him from the fire.

One day, I was waiting for my order when a family of seven entered the store. The family clearly looked religious. The father had a long beard and wore clothes traditional for Muslim men. The mother wore a *burqa*. Even though the restaurant was almost empty, with several booths unoccupied, the mother went all the way to the end of the store and sat at the last booth, with her back to the entrance, completely hidden from view. The three sons and two daughters sat with her. The father sat at the next booth all by himself. Although there was plenty of room in his booth, one of the sons borrowed a chair from another table to join the mother. The older daughter sat with her, facing the back wall, and the youngest daughter sat at the opposite corner, with only her head showing. Both daughters also wore *burqa*. The three sons were wearing the same kind of clothes as the father, who had an air of authority—he was clearly the head of the family. He placed orders for the whole family and had to walk by me several times to get napkins and ketchup, but he never looked at me directly. When he did look at me, to exchange pleasantries, he looked at my right arm, thus avoiding eye-contact, as per conservative Islamic gender norms.[19]

Several minutes later I left to go check on my food, and by the time I came back the father was having a lively conversation, in heavily accented English, with a young man having lunch by himself on the other side of the restaurant. I understood from their conversation that the young man was from Saudi Arabia. He too spoke with a heavy accent. Based on what I overheard from their conversation, the young man had been in America for four months and was attending a university in California. After complimenting the young man's English, the father told him that his oldest son was a *Quran Hafiz* (one who has memorized the Quran). He then turned to his son and told him to go sit next to the young man.

"He is from Medina! Allah has truly graced us," the father told his son in Bangla. However, the father had not asked the young man if he was religious. Upon hearing that the young man was from Medina, the father had assumed that he was Muslim and that the family had been "graced" by Allah to meet the man. The son, looking excited, did as told. The father then told the Arab to ask his son to recite his favorite verse from the Quran. The Arab asked the boy to recite anything. The boy started to recite Quranic verses loudly. Everyone in the restaurant stopped talking and turned to listen. They were all smiling. After the boy was done, the Arab turned to look at the father and said "MashaAllah," expressing his appreciation. One of the customers in the restaurant exclaimed, "Thank you!" The Bangladeshi boy smiled widely and smiled even wider when the Arab told him that he was good enough to go to a famous school in Medina for higher Islamic studies. The boy replied that he had heard about this school and wanted to go there to study.[20]

Day-to-day life in Little Bangladesh contains numerous such examples of how immigrants both experience and produce the interconnectedness of diverse societies through their interactions in the hostland, and how religion serves as a lens to capture those connections. The Bangladeshi Muslims at the restaurant interacted with someone who was not only a foreign national, but also a foreign coreligionist. The Bangladeshi and Arab immigrants in this instance actualized the abstract notion of the *Ummah* by physically connecting multiethnic Muslims and their societies with each other. The father very likely could not have met an Arab Muslim man from Medina had he remained in Bangladesh. Only after migrating could he, and other immigrants, be exposed to an expansive and diverse range of encounters with people and societies from across the globe.

Using religion to gain insight into social actors and how they interact with larger social processes,[21] this book uses Islam as an analytical lens to capture the myriad ties that immigrant coreligionists share both within and across various countries, even those countries from which they do not originate or to which they have never traveled. In so doing, it locates immigrants at the heart of a dialectical tension between transnationalism on the one hand and territorialization on the other. Whereas transnationalism highlights the ties and flows of information, people, and resources transcending state territories (i.e., deterritorialization), territorialization limits these trans-border connections by imposing state boundaries. To that effect, although immigrants can have global ties that are pertinent to their collective sense of self, they are nonetheless located within the jurisdiction of the host state and are thus subject to its legal, political, and social control. As such, state borders can still limit—and thereby, to some extent, reconstruct—immigrants' global memberships.

Islam has subsumed this dialectical tension between transnationalism and territorialization throughout much of its history. The emphasis on territorialization in Islam can be traced back to the pre-Arab era, when Meccan tribes imposed geopolitical boundaries around the *Ka'aba* as part of their sophisticated socioeconomic system.[22] Yet, based on its principle to refuse particularistic loyalties to ethnic and national groups, Islam prioritizes the creation and observance of the *Ummah*.[23] Although abstract in nature, this notion of an *Ummatic* or deterritorialized nation of Islam manifests itself in actions such as movements of people, flows of information, debates, interactions, community- and institution-building, political acts, financial correspondence, and exchanges of knowledge, thus serving as a strong unifying force despite "the continued fragmentation and pluralization of interpretations of the Islamic message."[24] With the creation of modern nation-states by the collapse of European imperial rule in many parts of the Muslim world, including the Middle East and South Asia, "Muslims have been struggling to reconcile their dual identities as both citizens of independent sovereign entities and members of a unified worldwide community."[25] For instance, although there is an overarching sense of solidarity based on the notion of *Ummah*, there are also local, national, and religious communities, such as "Muslim American" and "British Muslim," based on feelings of belonging to national societies. Moreover, as the above snapshot of everyday life in Little Bangladesh reveals, Islam and Muslim-ness are very much embedded components of national identities, such as "Bangladeshi" and "Pakistani," and how they are lived out by social actors in day-to-day life.

International migration adds further complication, as migrants become members—and in many cases, citizens—of the receiving state while simultaneously remaining citizens of the sending state. This issue of immigrants having multiple citizenships raises questions about their supposed "dual loyalties" (i.e., competing or conflicting political allegiances between states). For Muslim immigrants, the question of whether their true allegiance lies with the receiving country or with their Islamic homeland is a recurring political debate in many Western countries, surfacing especially in moments of national security crises. However, immigrants themselves can find that their homeland and hostland political identities are at odds with one another. For example, many immigrants from the so-called Muslim world, such as Middle Easterners and South Asians, become citizens in Western countries, the very societies that had once colonized them and that still share less-than-friendly foreign relations with their homelands.

The following section unpacks the dialectic tension between "transnational Islam"[26] and the territorial constraints presented by state borders. Rather than diminishing the role of Islam as a unifying force for Muslims or underestimating the state's ability to control this transnational phenomenon, the aim of the following discussion is to highlight the many ways in which both these dialectical forces shape immigrants' actions, identities, and networks with coreligionists located *beyond* the homeland and hostland.

### MUSLIMS INTERCONNECTED

Transnational Islam refers to the movements and ties of Muslims across borders and the worldwide diffusion of Islamic knowledge and ideas through various forms of media.[27] Analytically, it includes three dimensions: "demographic movements, transnational religious institutions, and the field of Islamic reference and debate."[28] These tangible and virtual connections expand beyond the borders of one country, engaging Muslims from different corners of the world. The Salman Rushdie affair, the wars in Afghanistan and Iraq, the genocide of Bosnian Muslims, the Israel-Palestine conflict, the torture of Muslim inmates in Guantanamo Bay by the CIA and U.S. military personnel, and the Syrian refugee crisis are but a handful of issues that have engaged the attention of Muslims from around the world.

Even within the borders of a country, sociopolitical contexts concerning Muslims are shaped by events rooted "elsewhere." On the one hand, many Muslims believe that their hostlands view them in light of conflicts "elsewhere." As will be shown, in the United States, the government's Middle East policies (such as those pertaining to the War on Terror and the Syrian refugee crisis) and the media's representation of Islam have prompted many South Asian Muslim Americans to evaluate their collective status in U.S. society, because they interpret these elements as indicators of America's negative attitude toward all Muslims. On the other hand, many Muslims themselves identify with coreligionists located in "elsewhere" places. For instance, the Islamic Society of North America (ISNA), the largest institutional coalition of Muslims in America and Canada, regularly sends funds to Muslim countries throughout the world.

However, such transnational or global connections are not *post*-national.[29] Although issues of migrant networks, human rights, religious debates, identity formation, immigrant incorporation, and claims-making may take transnational forms,[30] they do little to diminish the importance of the state. For example, all claims-making based on something as universal as human rights nonetheless takes place within the legal and political jurisdiction of the state and is thus subject to its control. To give a contemporary example, the migrant children being separated from their parents on the U.S.-Mexico border have the same set of universal human rights as those of American citizens. However, whether those rights are respected depends on the U.S. state or, more specifically, the immigration policies of the government at the time. This is because in the eyes of the state, at least to some extent, the rights of its citizens supersede the human rights of foreign nationals. As such, "place," as defined in terms of territorial borders, still matters for immigrants. This is a reason migration scholars continue to focus on states and place, studying how immigrants change the places from which they come and to which they go, and how simultaneously those places change the immigrants themselves.

Indeed, borders continue to have lasting importance in shaping the very nature and practice of religion and religious identities. For example, Islam in some Western countries is strongly cosmopolitan based on the nature of those societies.[31] Similarly, the French *laïcité* laws impose the state's structural power in controlling if and how people can practice their religion depending on whether they are located in public or private spaces within the state.[32] And travel restrictions, such as the "Muslim ban" enacted by President Trump in 2017, can control whether one—regardless of religiosity—can even enter another country, based on the demographic makeup of the sending country. Even after migrants are successful in crossing the border, how they are received in the host state has far-reaching consequences for their religious identities and adaptation to the new society. For example, negative reception has been associated with higher religiosity among Muslim immigrants as a form of reactive identity.[33] Moreover, societal tensions in the sending state continue to define immigrants' collective identities, as immigrants map many aspects of their homeland society onto the hostland.[34]

Muslim immigrants are thus legally, politically, and socially bound by the borders and circumstances of at least two states—the one from which they come and the one in which they live. And yet, despite these formidable constraints, Muslims continue to maintain ties across societal and state borders. Moreover, just because immigrants have come from societies "there" and settled down "here" does not mean these two places are the only ones relevant to the immigrants' sense of self. International migration, for instance, is an inherent component of Islam, as it constitutes one of its five pillars—the *Hajj* or pilgrimage. Believers who are physically and financially able are obligated to perform *Hajj* to Mecca at least once in their lifetime. In 2018, 2.4 million pilgrims performed the *Hajj*, with more than 1.7 million of them coming from outside Saudi Arabia.[35] Pakistan, India, and Bangladesh are consistently among the top ten countries that send pilgrims to Mecca each year.[36] To give another example of the interconnectedness of Muslims worldwide, transnational Islamic organizations and nongovernmental organizations, such as the International Islamic Relief Organization and the British Islamic Relief, are important global actors in the humanitarian and development aid sectors. And using various sites on the internet (such as Islamicity.com), Muslims from anywhere in the world can engage in theological debates with a global Muslim community, participate in virtual lectures, and directly ask eminent Islamic scholars from various countries about everyday religious practices. Through these sites, Muslims also share *Halal* recipes, learn the Arabic language and Islamic history, find the daily prayer schedule, donate *Zakat* or the annual alms to the poor, and even issue and learn about *fatwas* or Islamic rulings.[37] The blogosphere and social media have become particularly instrumental for organizing social movements and gaining a transnational audience, with some notable examples being the Arab Spring in 2011 and Israel's involvement in the Gaza Strip unrest in 2014.[38]

But how and to what extent these ties can be maintained are controlled by the politics of state borders. The Saudi government, for example, enforces *Hajj* quotas, which it uses as leverage in its geopolitical relations with various countries.[39] The governments of other predominantly Muslim countries, like Egypt, Turkey, Pakistan, Indonesia, Nigeria, and Malaysia, also play key roles in regulating the annual pilgrimage. In fact, every prominent Muslim state has a *Hajj* policy and a powerful bureaucratic body to manipulate the *Hajj* for political and economic gains.[40] Consequently, not every believer who is willing and able can perform *Hajj*; rather, that ability depends, to a considerable extent, on inter-state relations at the global level. Moreover, transnational Muslim organizations are often viewed as political actors or "front organizations for global militant networks" in contentious places like Palestine, Sudan, and Afghanistan.[41] As such, they are subjected to suspicion, scrutiny, and control based on anti-terrorism policies. The U.S. Department of Justice, for example, has shut down many Muslim organizations based on allegations that these organizations were funding terrorist activities abroad.[42] Even the seemingly borderless ties on the internet are constrained by territorialization. For instance, through policies such as the USA PATRIOT Act, governments can wiretap and monitor the internet. Since 9/11, U.S. sources have monitored websites that are linked to Islamist groups and that contain elements of cyberplanning. The FBI also investigates Islamic militant activities online to locate command centers and fundraising infrastructures.[43]

Thus, rather than being deterritorialized, Muslim immigrants are *re-territorialized* in a space that is dialectically both global and transnational on the one hand and constrained by state borders on the other. Although devoted to studying the complexities that produce and arise from the flow of people across borders, the scholarship on international migration has largely undertheorized this dialectical tension between the interconnectedness of societies and state boundaries.

## THE GEOPOLITICS OF MAKING IMMIGRANT IDENTITIES

The foundational frameworks in migration studies—assimilation, pan-ethnicity, transnationalism, and diaspora—have either focused exclusively on contexts *within* the homeland or hostland, or they have been limited to studying the dyadic ties *between* the societies of origin and destination. Assimilation perspectives analyze how hostland contexts shape immigrants' homeland identities over time, as immigrants become, in many ways and over generations, similar to the hostland's native population. The panethnicity scholarship focuses on how immigrant groups with overlapping ethnic characteristics mobilize to collectively respond to adverse hostland contexts. The transnationalism approach expands the focus beyond the hostland but only to study the dyadic ties between the sending and receiving societies. And diasporic frameworks draw attention to the various interconnections that link members of a dispersed population both to a common homeland and to each other, but they largely leave out the hostland context. None of these frameworks thus situates immigrants' identity-making at the global geopolitical level where *various* places—not just the sending and receiving countries—interact with one another. However, by locating immigrant identity-making at the crux of global geopolitics, the multicentered relational framework reveals how immigrants, as vectors of globalization, are indeed tied to their homelands, hostlands, and beyond, thus allowing for a more accurate and comprehensive on-the-ground picture of immigrant identity formation.

The multicentered relational framework extends the assimilation model by introducing the concept of "exogenous shocks" (i.e., events that occur outside the receiving state's territory but that are nonetheless relevant to its sociopolitics and geopolitical interests; see chapter 2). The standard approach of the assimilation scholarship has been to focus on the opportunities and obstacles that emerge for immigrants to integrate into the mainstream society as they interact with other immigrant and native groups in the hostland.[44] However, by focusing exclusively on how contexts *within* the receiving country shape immigrants' identities, the assimilation perspective largely overlooks the fact that, because of globalization, contexts of the receiving society do not always remain neatly bound within the hostland's territory. Rather, based on global political dynamics, contexts within the hostland often spill over because of domino effects emanating from *outside* its borders. The multicentered relational framework allows one to trace how these exogenous shocks influence the global geopolitical order, which encompasses hostland sociopolitics and, in turn, shape immigrants' identities.

Theories of panethnicity analyze immigrant groups' internal diversity in more depth than assimilation perspectives.[45] Yet, the paradigm is still limited to the hostland, with scholars focusing on the organizational and institutional determinants of panethnic formation within the receiving country.

Consequently, this perspective has been unable to explain why panethnicity has solidified for some groups (such as Latinos and Asian Americans) but not others. According to existing models of panethnic group formation, the post-9/11 Muslim backlash in the United States and the response of Muslim leaders to that discourse should have led to the crystallization of a panethnic category encompassing the two largest Muslim American immigrant groups—South Asians and Middle Easterners, but they did not. Using the multicentered relational framework, I show that, contrary to burgeoning hostland-centric explanations, the answer to the puzzle of Muslim panethnic formation (or the lack thereof) lies not solely within the receiving country but is tied to ongoing global politics that spill across and beyond its borders (chapters 2 and 3). On the one hand, some South Asian organizations remain strictly secular and distance themselves from activities that could categorize them as "Muslim" in attempts to evade the U.S. state's punitive measures since 9/11. Many, thus, are reluctant to adopt or donate to causes with connections to the Middle East, a region closely associated with Islam. On the other hand, various ethnic/national Muslim groups—including South Asians and Middle Easterners—coalesce around anticolonial and human rights platforms focused on places in the Middle East, such as Palestine and Turkey. In both cases, the enabling and disabling of panethnic coalitions are connected to global political contexts stemming from *beyond* the hostland—from "elsewhere"—in this case, the Middle East. Moreover, the role of religion in panethnicity has thus far been largely undertheorized. Using religion as a lens, I show how "elsewhere" geopolitics pushes South Asian Muslims to coalesce with their *desi* coreligionists, and, conversely, deters Hindu and Muslim South Asians, even those who share the same national origin, away from each other.

Transnationalism expands the analytical focus beyond the hostland by capturing how immigrants maintain ties with their homeland over time and thereby create cross-state communities, which span both the sending and receiving societies.[46] However, this dyadic homeland-hostland paradigm does not fully capture geopolitics at the global level, which also involves other places of salience for immigrants' identities. The multicentered relational framework takes the transnationalism framework a step further by showing that immigrants' identities are also pulled toward and shaped by a third place—the "elsewhere." The immigrants may not think of these "else-wheres" as their homes or even wish to someday settle there. Nonetheless, they forge and maintain connections with these places based on a sense of membership and solidarity (chapter 5), or, alternatively, they find that their allegiances and loyalties to their hostlands are questioned because of others associating them with "elsewheres" (chapters 4 and 6).

Of the foundational migration frameworks, the diaspora framework perhaps provides the most sustained attention to global dynamics by studying the diverse links that members of an immigrant group share with a common homeland and with one another, even while being settled in multiple hostlands. However, still bound within a homeland-hostland dyad, it overlooks the various ways in which globalization and geopolitics bind immigrants to places that are neither their center of dispersion nor a place they perceive as being part of their diasporic community. Immigrants may not identify *with* any particular state outside the hostland, but because of the global geopolitical order, they may still be identified *by* events going on in that very place, thus making that foreign place salient to their identities, regardless of the absence of co-ethnics living there. Instead of focusing on just one center, the multicentered relational framework seeks to understand immigrant identity formation by examining the impact of *multiple types* of centers on shaping immigrants' collective experiences. Although I borrow the term "center" from the diaspora framework, I do not use it to refer to only the sending society or the point of dispersion. Instead, I refer to "centers" as places of salience for *identity categories* rather than for a seemingly bounded *group*. Immigrants, like all social actors, have multiple and various strands of identity. Each of these identities has multiple dimensions. And each of these dimensions has places—real or imagined—that are important in sustaining and shaping particular experiences of the members of that identity category. As such, rather than immigrants having one center based on ethnicity, they have multiple centers based on their various intersecting identities—such as identities revolving around religion, gender, sexuality, and political affiliation—all of which are important for one's sense of self. For example, as I will show, Bangladesh is the center of the collective *ethno-national* identity for Bangladeshi immigrants in America. And yet, Bangladeshis are also predominantly Muslim and members of the *Ummah*. As members of this *religious* community, Bangladeshi immigrants subscribe to contexts in the Middle East that sustain their "Muslim" identity—not because of their co-ethnics living there but based on a sense of religious spiritual attachment. At the same time, an exogenous shock such as the ISIS attacks in Paris suddenly makes France an "elsewhere" center for Bangladeshis—again, not because of other Bangladeshis living there or because of a particular sense of attachment to French Muslims but because of the political dimension of the Bangladeshi participants' Muslim identity, which leads others in America to associate them with that event. As such, rather than their collective experience being shaped by just one center—their point of dispersion, Bangladesh—their sense of identity is shaped by multiple centers, because of their intersecting identities and global geopolitics. How multiple centers interact with one another at the global level and how those interactions shape immigrants' sense of self—both in terms of self-identification and identification by others—are the main questions posed in this book.

## METHODS

Informed by the extended case method of theory building[47] and relational ethnography,[48] I began research for this book with an analysis of existing scholarship on immigrant identity formation to extend how we can better examine this process. My goal was to address the conceptual and methodological restrictions implicit in the concept of "immigrant" itself. An immigrant, as defined by Merriam-Webster, is a person who comes to a country to take up permanent residence. Yet, just because an immigrant has come from "there" to "here" does not mean that those two societies are the only ones that are relevant to their identities. Immigrants' multiple identities, such as those based on gender, religion, and sexuality, intersect with their ethnic/national ones, placing them on a web of interconnecting sociopolitical contexts that transcend homeland-hostland borders. Focusing on one bounded place, such as the immigrants' homeland or hostland, restricts analysis of how these other but nonetheless relevant contexts shape their intersectional identities.

To overcome this limitation, my key object of analysis is the "Muslim" identity category, with its multiple dimensions and negotiated boundaries, its connections to the different places, peoples, histories, and conflicts that sustain it, and the ways in which it is used to organize relationships between perceived members and others. Thus, I focus on a relational social "field" rather than on a fixed "place."[49] I pay particular attention to two distinct but often overlapping dimensions of Muslim identity—the spiritual (by which I mean beliefs and practices based on faith) and the political (by which I mean power struggles involving people and institutions).

The case of South Asian Muslim Americans tells us how foreign places beyond the sending and receiving countries shape an immigrant's sense of self, worldview, and everyday interactions. Although not located in the contentious Middle East, the South Asian homelands have experienced direct conflict with the West, as the British Empire colonized the Indian subcontinent for two centuries. This past has led to several religious-political conflicts, wars, and partitions in the Indian subcontinent, most prominently the 1947 Partition of Bengal between Hindu-majority India and Muslim-majority Pakistan. The Partition caused a refugee crisis, mass resettlements, and genocides on both sides of the border. Then, again in 1971, despite their religious commonality, the two wings of Pakistan along the eastern and western borders of India broke into war, with East Pakistan gaining independence as Bangladesh. These historic conflicts, which are just some remnants of South Asia's colonized past, still deeply inform the "Bangladeshi," "Pakistani," and "Indian" national identities and color the relationships among these countries.

Even in the postcolonial period, relationships between South Asia and the West have not been smooth. The United States' relationship with Pakistan has been particularly turbulent because of Pakistan's proximity to Afghanistan and the connections between its security apparatus and Islamic terrorist organizations, such as the Taliban and Al Qaeda. This relationship reached a notably low point in 2011 when Osama bin Laden was found to have been hiding in one of the most militarily fortified cities in Pakistan. And in 2018, tensions between Pakistan and the United States again escalated, with President Trump calling Pakistan a "safe haven" for terrorists in Afghanistan and freezing almost $1.2 billion of America's security aid to the country.[50] The effects of this rocky but strategically important relationship between these two "frenemy" countries on the global stage can be felt on the ground—immigrants from Pakistan, regardless of their religiosity or sect, are often stereotyped as terrorists in the United States.[51]

However, religious and political life in South Asia has been shaped not only by this region's interactions with the West but also by interactions with the Middle East. Despite having some unique characteristics of its own, Islam in South Asia has been deeply influenced by Wahhabi teachings and influxes of money stemming from Saudi Arabia. Moreover, the South Asian general public is largely informed of Western interventions in many parts of the Muslim world, such as in Palestine, Iran, Iraq, Afghanistan, and Pakistan. Thus, extending the traditional dyadic framework, the case of South Asian Muslim Americans offers a third center of focus—the "elsewhere"—namely Europe and the Middle East.

The findings of this book are based on data collected from California, a state that, in 2016, an estimated 10,205 Bangladeshis, 666,480 Indians, and 54,928 Pakistanis called home. Of these, 4,735 Bangladeshis, 88,505 Indians, and 9,760 Pakistanis were living in Los Angeles.[52] I conducted sixty in-depth interviews with South Asian Muslims across California and collected participant observations at various sites in Los Angeles. I participated in various South Asian cultural hubs, such as language schools, student organizations, ethnic restaurants, and homeland charity associations, volunteering whenever possible as an organizer, language teacher, and peer mentor. I also attended birthday parties, weddings, bridal showers, *Eid* celebrations, family get-togethers, and casual hangouts in homes, college dorms, restaurants, shopping malls, and movie theaters. My observations from these sites revealed the interactive aspects of identity work, such as how respondents present themselves in different contexts, and how events at the global level trickle down to shape their everyday interactions. Moreover, I used these settings to create rapport with the participants, enabling me to later ask for referrals to conduct interviews. At times, my Bangladeshi Muslim background and my fluency in Bangla, Hindi, and Urdu generally eased my access into these spaces as an insider. Yet, my gender, religiosity, level of education, and the fact that I had come from outside of the Los Angeles *desi* Muslim community, which initially meant I was an unfamiliar face, often put me in the position of being an outsider. These insider-outsider dynamics shaped how participants responded to me over time—a finding in and of itself that I discuss in detail later, both in this section and in chapter 4.

Interviewing allowed me insight into the cognitive dimensions and discursive frames of immigrants' identity-making (i.e., how they viewed and talked about themselves in relation to larger sociopolitical contexts). I used semistructured questions and guided conversations to ask participants about a range of topics geared toward understanding if, when, and how their Muslim identity became salient in their everyday lives.[53] In so doing, I hoped to gain a broad yet detailed view of their daily lives while avoiding taking for granted their "Muslim-ness" as a continuously salient form of self-identification.[54] In their responses, I explored the labels participants used to describe themselves and others, how they used those labels, in what contexts they talked about their different identities, and when their "Muslim" identity seemed to shape—or not—their day-to-day lives. When interviewees lived outside Los Angeles or beyond my driving distance, I conducted interviews over Skype or FaceTime. I also made an effort to meet with them in person whenever they visited Los Angeles for personal reasons. Otherwise, I kept in touch with them through text messages and Facebook. Whereas my initial interviews and field visits were exploratory, my observations developed as time progressed, and I strategically collected data to increase variation within my sample. For example, as my participants overwhelmingly belonged to the dominant Sunni sect of Islam (fifty-seven out of the sixty respondents)—reflecting the religious demography of Muslims in South Asia and the global Muslim community—I actively looked for participants who were Shia.

Although the case-study method allowed me insight into South Asian Muslim Americans' lives, it nonetheless introduced several methodological questions pertaining to the generalizability of those observations. For example, how could I know that what I was observing was not particular to a specific location? Moreover, how could I know to what extent my observations were being influenced by interviewer effects or whether the participants were not just responding to my presence at the field sites?

To overcome these potential drawbacks, I complemented my interview and observation data with content analysis of various sources at the community and national levels, namely (1) Muslim American community newsletters; (2) Muslim American organizational documents; (3) participants' Facebook activities; (4) coverage of Muslim-related events by major national news outlets, such as the *New York Times*, the *Washington Post*, CNN, and

MSNBC; and (5) coverage by alternative news outlets to which many participants subscribed, such as Al Jazeera and BBC. Altogether, I followed the Facebook activities of fifty-eight South Asian Muslim Americans, including interviewees, contacts I made during fieldwork, and contacts in participants' online social networks. These sources were analytically useful for triangulating with my interview data and ethnographic observations for two reasons. First, these sources were removed from interviewer effects as the participants, the Muslim American community, and the larger hostland society were acting on their own, without my presence as an interviewer somehow motivating them to react in certain ways in response to research questions. Second, they provided insight into the relevant sociopolitical contexts across the United States and into the identity-making processes of Muslim Americans from various ethnic backgrounds.

For instance, the organizational documents I analyzed were published by the largest Muslim organization in the United States and Canada—ISNA. The documents included annual reports released at ISNA conventions and the organization's flagship bimonthly magazine, *Islamic Horizons*, which had a readership of over two hundred thousand in 2006, making it the most widely distributed Muslim periodical in English. As organizations have been found to manage and sustain group identities through carefully groomed platforms,[55] the ISNA documents provided insight into Muslim Americans' collective use of identity-making strategies. Moreover, they allowed me to observe whether local strategies were similar to those used by Muslim Americans across ethnicities and geographical locations as opposed to being unique to the South Asian Muslim community in California.[56]

The sixty interviewees included thirty-three Bangladeshis, twenty-two Pakistanis, and five Indians. Forty interviewees were female and twenty male. The educational and professional profile of the participants resembled that of the overall South Asian American population, which is mostly foreign born, speaks English "well" or "very well,"[57] and is highly educated.[58] Most of my interviewees were college students, recent graduates, young professionals, engineers, and business owners, although some were also stay-at-home mothers and restaurant or gas station workers. Reflecting the relative recency of South Asian immigration to the United States (compared to Japanese and Mexican immigration), the participants were first-, 1.5-, and second-generation Americans.

The respondents' immigrant generation determined, to some extent, their reaction to the hyperpoliticized climate that characterized most of the duration of my fieldwork. The anti-Muslim rhetoric during the presidential election season reinforced the perception of most of my participants that the West was largely prejudiced against Muslims. However, whereas the older South Asian respondents grew reluctant to talk about Muslim-related issues during recorded interviews, the younger 1.5 and second generations remained vocal about their opinions as Muslim Americans. Many in this latter group saw asserting one's "Muslim-ness"—whether through organizational participation or social media activities—as resisting Islamophobia in U.S. society.

In terms of religiosity, participants reflected the heterogeneity of the Muslim population and challenged the idea of a Muslim monolith. While some regularly maintained the five mandatory daily prayers and observed dietary and clothing regulations as well as gender norms, their political views could be described as liberal progressive in that they espoused feminist ideals and supported LGBTQ rights. "Others had strict views against homosexuality based on religious belief but were 'symbolic faithfuls'—meaning they used 'religious symbols to express feelings of religiosity and identification . . . while hardly ever participating in religious rituals or thinking a great deal about religious teachings or values.'"[59] And yet other participants prayed every day but consumed alcohol and engaged in premarital sex, both of which are strictly forbidden by Islamic scriptures. Many women wore liberal Western clothing but ate only *Halal* food. Some wore the *hijab* but did not pray regularly, whereas others did not wear the headscarf but prayed five times a day and wore modest clothing that covered their arms and legs. A few self-identified as gay or bisexual but still prayed and read the Quran regularly. However, all participants, even those who did not practice Islam in their everyday lives, claimed to be "culturally"[60] or "politically" Muslim, meaning they wanted social justice for all Muslims, even if they did not directly engage in the cause through organizational activities.

In general, I had more access as an insider to Bangladeshis than to Pakistanis and Indians. Whereas I was welcomed into the homes and private lives of many Bangladeshi participants, most of my interactions with the Pakistani and Indian respondents were in more formal settings, such as cultural organizations, places of business, college campuses, and Skype interviews.

Although I struck up friendships with a few Pakistani interviewees and met them in more informal settings such as restaurants and shopping malls, unlike the Bangladeshis, they did not invite me to their family gatherings. The larger proportion of Bangladeshi participants, however, addresses a dearth of research on Bangladeshi Americans in the international migration and race/ethnicity scholarship, where Bangladeshis often comprise a minority, even in South Asian samples.

The gender composition of my informants reflects, to some extent, the obstacles I encountered during fieldwork because of my position as a young, unmarried woman. I often found South Asian Muslim spaces, even those organized for public or community gatherings, to be gender-segregated. This meant that I had relatively easier access to South Asian women than men. Sometimes, I did not have access to predominantly male spaces at all. For instance, when I began fieldwork, I heard via word-of-mouth that every Friday, Bangladeshi Muslims congregated in a prayer room in Little Bangladesh to offer *Jummah* prayers. When I asked the owner of another ethnic store in Little Bangladesh about the time and location of the prayers, he told me that women were not allowed. Surprised, I asked why, because although gender-segregated, some mosques, even those back home in Bangladesh, typically allow women to pray on the premises. Taken aback and seemingly slightly annoyed at my question, he replied that the space was "too small." He seemed to think it an obvious solution that women should not be accommodated on the premises at all if it meant that fewer men could participate in the prayers. Even at *dawats*, or get-togethers, of friends and family in Bangladeshi households, men and women were segregated, usually sitting at a distance in the same room or in different rooms altogether. As such, I was often in the company of women at these gatherings. Once at a *dawat*, I joined the men as I heard them conversing about politics. However, after some time, a male acquaintance politely but firmly instructed me to go "sit with the women."

Although gender dynamics were much more relaxed among the younger generations, I found that unless I specifically requested my female informants to refer me to their male friends, they often hesitated to do so. When I was able to interview men, I sometimes found their demeanor to be guarded, especially if they were unmarried and close to my age. On one occasion, a young Pakistani college student, when meeting me for an interview, politely refused to shake my hand. As a self-described "observant Muslim," he deemed any physical contact between unmarried men and women to be improper. In some instances, I asked wives or close female relations to be present during the interviews to put the male respondents at ease. And although the demeanor of most males eased over time, I was able to establish deeper and more relaxed relationships with my female informants.

Nonetheless, I had to carefully navigate my marital status even with my female participants. Over the years, I found that my "virtue" as a "good woman" was often put into question in my interactions with both the older first-generation Bangladeshi women in Little Bangladesh and the younger second-generation women. For instance, I once took a Bangladeshi male acquaintance to dine at the ethnic restaurant in Little Bangladesh. As was my routine, I peeked into the kitchen on my way out to thank the cooking ladies. These women were middle-aged, with little formal education. They were almost always dressed in *salwar kamiz*, with their *orna* wrapped tightly around their chests and waists and their hair put up in buns under their hairnets. The kitchen was a sweltering place, and these women, usually two or three of them, worked from early morning until late at night. Whenever I visited the restaurant, I made sure to sneak into the kitchen for a few minutes of conversation, a respite the women seemed to appreciate. On that particular occasion, when I popped into the kitchen, one of the women, without exchanging any pleasantries, asked, "Friend or boyfriend?" Taken aback, it took me a few moments to realize that she was referring to my male friend. I smiled and answered, "Neither." With a teasing laugh, she then asked, "*Oma oma bole ki! Maa-Baba janey?*" (Oh my, oh my, what is she saying! Do your parents know about this?) Wishing not to continue the conversation, I replied that they did know, and after thanking her for the delicious food, I left.

Dating, or "affairs" as it is called within the Bangladeshi community, is looked down upon by some, especially when it comes to women. Women who date men without their parents' express public approval and any plans to marry in the near future are deemed "*kharap*," meaning "bad." Conversely, "*bhalo*," or "good girls," are those who do not date but go through arranged marriages based on "proper"—meaning family-condoned and Islam-sanctioned—processes. The question of whether I was a "*kharap*" or "*bhalo*" woman was a common question I had to face in various forms during my fieldwork. For instance, during a house call in Little Bangladesh, I was asked to stay for lunch. The family I was visiting comprised a young couple and their two-year-old son. While having lunch inside their cramped but lovingly decorated apartment, I was telling them about my classes when the husband remarked that education was very well and all but that "other things" in life were important as well. He said that he believed it is important, especially for a woman, to get married at a young age, so that she can develop her thinking to match her husband's. He lamented that young people were now becoming "*bokhate*" (meaning "spoiled" or "deviant") and that they no longer respected traditional values, as exemplified by how they dated openly. He then paused, waiting for my response. I realized that he was implicitly asking me whether I was one of those so-called spoiled youth. To my relief, the wife, who was a stay-at-home mother, then responded, "*Na, o orokom na. O affair korbe na. O bhalo meye.*" (No, she is not like that. She will not do affairs. She is a good girl.)

Navigating my background and gender-based obstacles during fieldwork, I came to realize how this story of South Asian Muslim Americans is also a deeply personal one. In many ways, this research has stemmed from my own story as a first-generation Muslim immigrant from Bangladesh. A decade ago, I arrived in the United States—Mississippi, specifically. There, the privileges of belonging to the religious majority and to an elite-class minority—privileges that I had enjoyed and taken for granted in Bangladesh—were quickly stripped away. I began working full-time at Burger King and Popeye's, six to seven days a week, where my interactions revealed to me my stigmatized status as a working-class Muslim immigrant of color. When a coworker once threatened to report me to immigration law enforcement, his words reinforced my insecurity as a foreigner. But his next words made me realize that my differences from him, and from most others in America, went deeper than skin color and accent. "Are you gonna bomb this place?" he asked.

The years since then have not washed away my experiences of otherness. Rather, with each onslaught of Islamist terror—whether in the United States or abroad—and the subsequent uptick of anti-Muslim sentiment, I, like so many other Muslim Americans, am reminded of Muslim immigrants' perpetual status as outsiders. For instance, in 2015, I was recuperating from a particularly grueling quarter of graduate school at my parents' house in Mississippi when Islamist extremists struck the Paris offices of *Charlie Hebdo*, a satirical French magazine, killing seventeen people. My parents were glued to their televisions watching live coverage of the developments. Although the attacks had occurred far away in France—an "elsewhere" place—they feared an Islamophobic backlash in the tiny, predominantly white, conservative college town in Mississippi where they lived. They called the handful of Bangladeshi Muslims they knew in the area. They, too, my parents learned, were scared. One of them, a Bangladeshi *hijabi* woman, decided to stay home rather than go to the local library where she usually went to study for her medical-license exam. Later that same year, when ISIS struck Paris, I saw the same kind of fear in the South Asian Muslim communities that I was studying in Los Angeles, despite the city's cosmopolitan milieu posing a sharp contrast to that of Mississippi. These similarities among Muslim Americans' reactions to events in faraway foreign lands sparked my interest, leading me to explore just how it is that global geopolitics become salient, shaping immigrants' day-to-day lives.

## ROAD MAP OF THE BOOK

The rest of this book is divided into six chapters, each offering a different analysis of how "elsewhere" combines with homeland and hostland contexts to shape immigrants' identities. Chapter 2 sets the intellectual context for the book by unpacking how the multicentered relational framework reveals the ways in which different dimensions of an identity category connect immigrants to multiple and varied places. I show, however, that not all places in the world are the same, nor do they all become "elsewheres." Rather, different places have varying levels of salience for immigrant identities. In that vein, I show how a faraway foreign place comes to have salience for immigrants based on its location in global geopolitics and based on the way its influence is manifested in immigrants' day-to-day interactions and worldviews. To make these arguments, I pull examples from both immigration history and contemporary world politics. I conclude the chapter by highlighting how the multicentered relational framework extends the assimilation, panethnicity, transnationalism, and diasporic perspectives.

Chapter 3 begins to empirically trace the different dimensions of the immigrants' global ties, starting with those ties rooted in their homelands.

Looking through a multicentered relational lens, I analyze the religious-political dynamics within and between the South Asian sending countries, on the one hand, and those between the homelands and "elsewhere" on the other. I argue that the struggle for nation-building in the South Asian homelands is not insulated within those societies but is instead shaped by their interactions with "elsewheres," such as the Middle East. These struggles are sometimes mirrored among the immigrant communities, while at other times homeland cleavages lose relevance over time. Yet other homeland boundaries gain life anew as they take on new, globally-informed meanings for immigrants based on hostland sociopolitics and "elsewhere' dynamics.

Chapter 4 shifts the analytical focus from the homeland to the hostland, where South Asians become categorized as members of a hypervisible Muslim monolith. It traces how the participants, in reaction to their hyper-visibility as national security threats, self-police their public interactions, striving to appear as "good Muslims." At both individual and organizational levels, participants strategically render some aspects of themselves visible and others invisible to the public, in efforts to resist any negative stereotypes imposed upon them.

Chapter 5 continues the story by locating Muslim Americans on the global stage. It traces how participants are politically oriented toward particular places in the "elsewhere" Middle East and how they engage in Muslim-related politics in those places through U.S. politics. Many of the participants interpret their collective position as a hypervisible group in America, using examples of "elsewhere" places where Muslims are also a stigmatized minority. These "elsewhere" examples, combined with their homeland's colonized past under British imperial rule, the post-9/11 U.S. context, and ongoing tensions with the Middle East, reinforce these immigrants' worldview that the West at large is biased against the Muslim world.

However, based on the reactions of both the participants and the larger U.S. society to six ISIS attacks that occurred during my fieldwork—two in Europe (Paris and Brussels), two in the Middle East (Beirut and Istanbul), and two in the United States (San Bernardino and Orlando)—chapter 6 shows that when it comes to participants being identified as Muslims by others in America, conflicts in "elsewhere" Europe are more salient than those in the Middle East. Speaking directly to the findings of chapter 5, chapter 6 shows that different parts of the world have varying levels of salience in regard to how the immigrants are understood by others. These variations are influenced by the media, global political dynamics, U.S. discourse surrounding Muslims, and the prevailing imaginary of the West and the Muslim world.

Chapter 7 concludes the book by discussing the limitations, generalizability, and future directions of the multicentered relational framework. In putting Muslims and immigrants on the center stage of globalization, this chapter drives home this book's key finding that, contrary to dyadic explanations, how immigrants self-identify and are identified by others are both tied to places beyond the homeland and hostland—to places I call "elsewheres."

# 2 | BEYOND HERE AND THERE

*The Multicentered Relational Framework*

IN 2014, WHEN ISIS was already an all-too-familiar name in the global public's vocabulary, another Islamist terrorist group in Nigeria, called Boko Haram, caught America's attention. Although active since 2002, the American presses (such as the *New York Times* and the *Washington Post*) began reporting on Boko Haram much later, starting in 2009. But at the time, Boko Haram had generated neither public nor much political interest. To most Americans, Boko Haram was still largely unknown, and Nigeria was just another foreign place of little immediate relevance to the United States. However, all this changed in 2014 when news broke that Boko Haram had kidnapped 276 Nigerian schoolgirls. The story, along with Boko Haram's Islamist ideology and ties to ISIS, finally grasped America's political attention. This was in large part because of Michelle Obama, who was the U.S. First Lady at the time, and her publicization of a campaign to bring back the captured schoolgirls.[1] On her official Twitter account, which had over 7 million followers, Mrs. Obama posted a somber picture of herself inside the White House holding a handwritten placard reading #BringBackOurGirls. Although the hashtag campaign was launched much earlier by Nigeria's former education minister Obiageli Ezekwesili, Michelle Obama's tweet became viral, sparking not just support but also criticism of the Obama administration for not showing the same concern for human lives involved in U.S. drone strikes in many Muslim countries.[2] Pictures of men and women holding signs with new hashtags like #WeCantBringBackOurDead and #BringBackYourDrones proliferated the Internet. The controversy surrounding Mrs. Obama's efforts as well as news of Boko Haram's increasing terrorist activities in Nigeria also received a lot of publicity from mainstream American media and cable news outlets, informing an audience beyond social media users. This surge of public interest, which peaked in May 2014, the month Michelle Obama became involved, was reflected in a sharp uptick of U.S. Google searches for "Boko Haram."[3] These reactions reflect how contexts in Nigeria, a foreign land previously of little relevance, gained widespread salience in America's national political dynamics and foreign policy concerns at the time.

To Zinat, a Bangladeshi *hijabi* college student, Boko Haram gave Islam and Muslims "a bad name," thereby shaping how Muslims as a whole were perceived in America. I interviewed Zinat in October 2015, just a month before the ISIS attacks in Paris. She had chosen to meet me at her college campus, where we decided to sit on one of the many wooden benches that lined a walkway running through the premises. It was a busy spot, with streams of students purposefully walking to and from classes, club meetings, or other appointments. Taking advantage of this steady supply of potential recruits, some students were standing on the sides of the walkway to promote their clubs and organizational events with flyers and catchphrases like "Do you want to help save the environment?" Others were holding bake sales, loudly advertising their offers with slogans like "Porto's[4] for five dollars!" A bald black man in trousers and a button-down shirt, with the sleeves rolled up to his elbows, was trying to stop passers-by for a few minutes to evangelize about his church.

It was late afternoon when Zinat met me after her class. The weather a little breezy that day, she was wearing a denim jacket over a long grey dress. Her *hijab* was in one of her usual colors—black. I knew Zinat prior to the interview, as we had both attended cultural events organized by the Bangladeshi Students Association. Soft-spoken and friendly, Zinat was a familiar face and generally well-liked in the Bangladeshi student community. She also seemed to be popular among non-Bangladeshis. During the course of the interview, for instance, some people who knew her came to say hello as they were passing by our bench. I noticed that all those who stopped to chat were women. A couple of them were Arab and *hijabi*. Another was a mutual Pakistani American friend who, although Muslim, did not wear a headscarf. Another woman, who wore ripped jeans with a crop top and bomber jacket, appeared to be East Asian. Zinat greeted them all with a cheerful smile and a hug. She introduced me to one of the *hijabi* women, explaining that they knew each other from the Muslim Students Association.

In the interview I asked Zinat about her family, how she had come to America, and how she had come to wear the *hijab*. I learned that she came to the United States with her family through the Diversity Visa (DV) lottery program when she was less than a year old. Initially, she had some misgivings about wearing the headscarf, because some students back in high school had called her a terrorist the first time she tried on a *hijab* publicly. But right before entering college she began wearing the *hijab* regularly. Our interview became more conversational when I asked Zinat how she felt after this exchange in high school. She expressed her frustration about an array of relevant topics, like Islamist terrorism and Islam's portrayal in American media, especially in light of the *Charlie Hebdo* shooting in January that same year.

> It upsets me and it angers me because I know that Islam doesn't teach us to kill in the name of God. So, the fact that people [terrorists] are taking something [Islam] that is so beautiful and tainting it with their own thoughts . . . it's frustrating to all the people [Muslims] who are good. People [at large] are only seeing the horrific things they [the terrorists] are doing. And those actions are what are blasted on the media. So, people hear about it, and the word "Islam" and the word "terror" are put together. So, they [the terrorists] are adding on to it. If you don't want people to think bad of Islam, then don't do something bad in the name of Islam. So, it's frustrating to the good Muslims who don't get recognition. We [good Muslims] try to show what Islam is really about but that's not shown [in the media]. What's shown is what people are doing wrong in the name of Islam.

When asked how she thought the actions of terrorists, in the name of Islam, affected her as a Muslim in America, she immediately exclaimed, "Oh yeah! . . . I believe it was somewhere in Africa. I can't remember the actual country. Boko Haram. ISIS . . . Nigeria, yeah, that's right. So, what are they doing? None of what they are preaching is what Islam really teaches. I don't get the logic behind it. They want to convert everyone? What is it that they want to do? If they actually look into the faith, what they are doing is wrong. What they just end up doing is to give Islam and people [Muslims] who are good a bad name."

## EXOGENOUS SHOCKS, ANYWHERE, AND ELSEWHERE

The story of Boko Haram exemplifies how a place becomes an "elsewhere" (i.e., a foreign place that suddenly becomes salient for an immigrant group's sense of self). For the most part, despite West Africa having a sizeable Muslim population, with Muslims comprising roughly half of the population in Nigeria, the South Asian Muslims in this book neither knew nor cared much about the countries in that region. By and large, these distant places were "anywheres" (i.e., simply irrelevant to how the participants went about their daily lives). Most were unaware of Nigeria's relationship with their country of origin or the United States. However, Nigeria *became* relevant to participants' sense of self when their hostland's attention was drawn to Boko Haram, its actions within Nigerian territory, and even more, its connections to globalized Islamist terror networks via its affiliation with ISIS. Zinat, for instance, did not know the specifics of Nigeria's location in the world, its shape on the map, the name of its capital city, or its demographic profile. However, based on what she had learned from American news headlines and social media trends, she knew that Boko Haram was located inside that country and understood that what Boko Haram was doing in Nigeria may affect her "here" in America. Thus, an irrelevant "anywhere," such as Nigeria in this case, can become relevant as an "elsewhere" if events in that place draw the hostland's political and media attention in ways that make the immigrant group's already stigmatized identity, in this case "Muslim," even more suspect.

Boko Haram's kidnapping is an example of what I call an "exogenous shock." In economics, the term refers to an unpredictable event that has originated from outside an economic model. And although that event cannot be explained by that model, it nonetheless affects the overall system, either positively or negatively. Exogenous shock, as conceptualized in this book, follows a similar principle: it is an unexpected event that has originated from a foreign place *outside* a state's borders but has still impacted the society *within* the state by disrupting the larger international order.

I argue that exogenous shocks link ongoing contexts in faraway foreign places to immigrants in their hostlands. By itself, a place located beyond the homeland and hostland does not carry salience for immigrant identities. However, these foreign places could become relevant to the immigrants based on global political dynamics, geographical location, or ongoing sociopolitical contexts within those places. I call these foreign—but potentially "elsewhere" places—"anywheres." When an exogenous shock takes place "anywhere" in the world, it initiates a domino effect, impacting the host society and thus transforming that foreign land where the shock originated into an "elsewhere." Nigeria, then, became an "elsewhere" in relation to its impact on the overall U.S. society and to the Muslim immigrants within that society.

In other words, when "anywhere" becomes salient either to the immigrants' homeland-rooted identities (such as ethnicity), to the hostland society, or to the relationship between the sending and receiving countries, it becomes an "elsewhere" for immigrants. Consequently, "elsewhere" is a site that is meaningful not only for immigrants but also for the people around them, which is why the "elsewhere" place affects how immigrants understand their location in both global and hostland social hierarchies. In a nutshell, an "anywhere" place is an "elsewhere" if (1) contexts in the "anywhere" place become relevant to the immigrants' sense of membership to an identity category through exogenous shocks and if (2) those contexts shape how others in the hostland might perceive the immigrants (see figure 2.1).

Exogenous shocks played a role in how Hindu, Sikh, and Muslim immigrants were perceived in the United States. At the turn of the twentieth century, South Asian immigration to California was overwhelmingly by Punjabi Sikhs; this group constituted 85–90 percent of the Asian Indian immigrants to the United States.[5] Muslims comprised the second largest group, followed by a small percentage of Hindus. Yet, all these groups were lumped together as "Hindoos"—a derogatory name for Hindus—both legally, in the census, and in the broader social perception. At the time, religious distinctions among South Asians were not considered relevant to the social

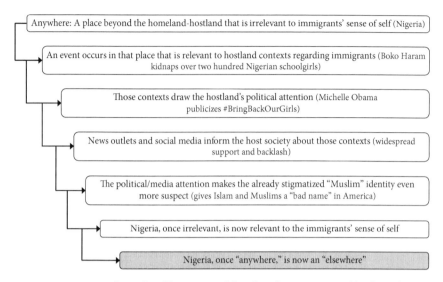

FIGURE 2.1. How "anywhere" becomes an "elsewhere." *Source*: Created by the author.

frames of officials, who did not consult the handful of South Asians about their categorization preferences.[6] Moreover, although Islamophobia was present, it was not particularly strong. Rather, the social and political order was largely defined by race, "Hindoos" being the only example of racialized religious category. However, the political discourse on South Asian immigrants centered mainly on their presumed incapability to assimilate, on subversive anticolonialism, and on the economic threat they seemingly posed to white workers.[7]

Anti-Muslim sentiments took a virulent turn with the eruption of a series of geopolitical events in the Middle East, namely the 1967 Arab-Israeli war, the 1970s oil embargo, 1970s terrorism by Palestinian groups that affected Western countries, and the Iranian Revolution.[8] Muslim immigrants who came to the United States in 1965 and after were affected by these events even though many of them were not from the Middle East. In this context, while South Asians were still grouped together and categorized as potential threats, the nature of the grouping shifted. In this new climate, the political salience of religion arguably took center stage in U.S. public discourse, with the previously lumped together Hindoos now being associated with Islam because of their "Muslim-looking" physical features. South Asians became categorically exposed to America's rising Islamophobia, with Sikhs and Hindus being stereotyped along with Muslims as potential Islamic terrorists. Prior to these exogenous shocks, Muslim-related geopolitics did not matter much to how South Asian immigrants were perceived in America. Since then, however, these discourses have become extremely relevant for both how others view South Asians and how South Asians view themselves. For example, Sikhs and Hindus are often victims of misdirected Islamophobic violence. Conversely, taking stock of the ongoing Islamophobic climate, some segments of the Hindu American population also distance themselves from their Muslim co-ethnics.

### THE MULTICENTERED RELATIONAL FRAMEWORK

The multicentered relational framework allows one to trace how different dimensions of an identity category can connect individuals who self-identify or who are seen to identify as a member of that category to multiple and varied places. A place, as conceptualized in this framework, can have distinct territorial borders, such as the United States. Alternatively, a place can be an imagined, abstract idea of a region that defies geographical borders, such as "the West," which also includes countries like New Zealand or Australia that clearly lie in the Eastern hemisphere. "The Muslim world," denoting a sphere similarly abstracted from geographic space, is a concept generally used to distinguish Muslim societies from non-Muslim ones. Yet the boundaries of the "Muslim world" are becoming increasingly complicated as an ever-larger proportion of Muslims lives and practices Islam in the predominantly Christian societies of the West.

Expanding the homeland-hostland dyad, this multicentered relational framework encompasses three main variations of a place: the sending country; the receiving country; and places that are neither but (1) are of geopolitical importance to the hostland and (2) are salient in the immigrants' worldviews and identification processes. "Elsewhere" is this third place, and it is composed of political events ongoing *within* its territory that are of geopolitical interest to the hostland; international relations *between* it and the hostland; and international relations between the hostland and homeland in relation to the geopolitical events ongoing "elsewhere." The immigrants and their identity categories are located at the intersection of these homeland, hostland, and "elsewhere" places.

In the case of South Asian Muslim Americans, the three centers intersect because of the immigrants' crosscutting memberships in homeland-oriented national collectivities, the U.S. host society, and a global religious community. On the one hand, the immigrants are identified by others in the hostland based on their perceived or real connections to "elsewhere" events. On the other hand, the immigrants themselves identify with peoples, places, and contexts "elsewhere." As such, their sense of belonging and their identification by others often do not remain neatly bound within the territories of either a sending or receiving state; rather, they are pulled toward different centers because of interconnecting sociopolitical contexts. When immigrants identify or are identified by others as members of the "Muslim" category, they are exposed to the effects of the relevant relationship dynamics among the three centers (see figure 2.2).

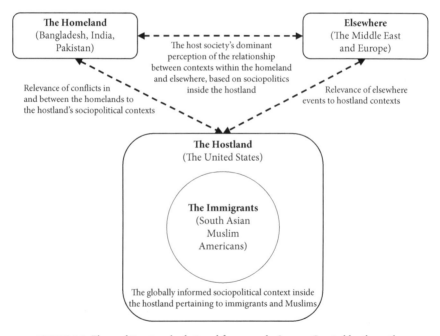

**FIGURE 2.2.** The multicentered relational framework. *Source*: Created by the author.

Thus, this framework locates immigrants' identities on a global scale rather than on a "single social field" composed of two societies, namely the sending and receiving countries.[9] By doing so, the framework seeks to capture if, when, and how the relationships between which centers become salient for the immigrants' worldviews and interactions. In some cases, the relationship between the homeland and "elsewhere" could become salient to the immigrants. At other times, the links between the hostland and "elsewhere" could be more salient. And in many situations, "elsewhere" may not be relevant to the immigrants' sense of self at all.

In fact, the everyday lives of the South Asian Muslim Americans in this book are preoccupied with concerns that are quite mundane. Historic and ongoing global politics are, at most times, not at the forefront of their minds as they go about their busy daily routines. Rather, these individuals are worried about how to "get by" or "get ahead" in life,[10] such as by doing well in classes or at work, by making and maintaining relationships, by raising children, and by balancing the monthly budget. However, with advanced technology and social media—notably 24/7 news channels, real-time notifications sent through smartphone apps, and Facebook trends—these immigrants also attend to national and global news on issues they find interesting. Their access to news often comes through alerts they have set on their smartphones based on their specific interests in world affairs. They also receive notifications of breaking news concerning hostland affairs, such as terror attacks and national emergencies. In either scenario, global and national political discourses are filtered down to the everyday level at a mere touch of a screen, informing not only the immigrants but also other members of the society. Moreover, many of these immigrants gauge public reactions to online news articles by reading through the comments sections that follow. These filtered news sources and public opinions arguably come to shape and reinforce people's interpretations of the world around them.

By providing the analytical space to theorize about whether and how identities are shaped by different places, the multicentered relational framework recognizes that because of the cross-cutting nature of global political contexts and the transnational characteristic of international migrants themselves, what goes on in foreign lands at the other side of the world can still affect what goes on "here" in the hostland.

## THE EFFECTS OF EXOGENOUS SHOCKS

A distinguishing feature of the multicentered relational framework is that it can reveal how different kinds of exogenous shocks come to influence immigrants' worldviews and interactions, which in turn shape their experiences as members of an identity category. But how does an external event that has occurred somewhere faraway in the world become salient in the first place? Analytically, exogenous shocks can become relevant to the hostland, and thereby the immigrants within it, in various overlapping ways. They can become relevant based on the nature of their impact on the global political order, which encompasses the receiving state. They can also be relevant if the shock occurred in a place that was already of geopolitical interest to the host country. Relatedly, the shocks can become relevant to the hostland based on the presence of immigrants from those external places who now live inside the receiving state's territory. From this third viewpoint, disruptions in the international order highlight the immigrants' "foreignness" as they are linked to an external threat; given that the immigrants are located inside the hostland's territory, those external threats are seen as internal. As such, the immigrants are put under heightened suspicion as "outsiders," highlighting their "otherness" or difference from the hostland's native population.

Exogenous shocks can vary based on the nature of the event itself (e.g., religious-political) and on the nature of the impact produced (i.e., positive or negative). Using past and contemporary examples, the following sections describe different types of exogenous shocks based on these two kinds of variations.

Although the book will mainly focus on exogenous shocks that are religious-political in nature, such as Islamist terrorist attacks, exogenous shocks can also come in other forms, such as global epidemics. Some examples are the outbreak of the Zika virus from 2015 to 2016 and of Ebola from 2014 to 2016. The Zika epidemic originated in South America, and Ebola in Africa. Both produced shockwaves in the international order, as exemplified by restraints imposed on cross-border travel between these places of origin and the United States. Moreover, in reaction to the Zika epidemic, the Centers for Disease Control and Prevention (CDC) strongly advised travelers, especially pregnant women, not to travel to countries identified as places of risk—the long list of countries included Bangladesh, India, and

Pakistan. These shockwaves also penetrated U.S. territorial borders, affecting the society within.

That impact can be observed not just in the Zika and Ebola outbreaks in various parts of the United States, but also in how the American public responded to the events. Broadly, the U.S. public reacted to the epidemics with xenophobia and a nativist backlash against immigrants, who were viewed as virus carriers endangering American society. For instance, because the 2014 Zika epidemic originated in South America, many segments of the American public blamed Latino communities for its outbreak, regardless of which South American country the immigrants came from or whether they had arrived in the United States prior to the outbreak. The Ebola scare triggered a similar backlash, but this time against immigrant groups from Africa.[11]

These examples of the hostland's reaction to exogenous shocks reveal the cleavages that run through society. For example, the U.S. society's response to the Zika and Ebola epidemics highlighted not only the boundary between immigrants and natives but also the ideological faultline that exists between conservatives and liberals. The issue of immigration has long been a battlefront in American politics. Those leaning on the left generally advocate for immigrants' rights by highlighting what America stands to gain because of immigration.[12] Conversely, conservatives generally advocate for stricter borders in fear of national security threats and the potential job losses native workers will suffer because of immigrants. Exogenous shocks such as global epidemics add more fuel to this debate as right-wing politicians and commentators use these events as further evidence of the dangers that come with including foreigners into the country. To give one example, in an op-ed piece published in 2016 in the *Washington Times*, a conservative news outlet, Tammy Bruce, a radio host, author, and political commentator, drew parallels between Islamist terrorism, crimes, and global epidemics, attributing all three to the influx of immigrants and refugees into the United States. She wrote, "The uncontrolled and chaotic violation this nation brought to us by President Obama's immigration and refugee schemes pose a number of threats to the homeland as insidious and deadly as the Islamic jihadi." Among these "threats," she listed new and previously eradicated viruses: "In addition to the word 'jihad,'" she continued, "we now must re-introduce into our lexicon the words measles, polio, diphtheria, tuberculosis, malaria, scabies, dengue, and now 'Zika.'"[13]

This depiction of immigrants as foreigners transporting external health threats into the United States is prevalent even at the national political level. For example, in a letter to the CDC in 2014, then–Georgia congressman Phil Gingrey, a professionally trained medical specialist in obstetrics and gynecology, blamed "illegal immigrants," who allegedly came without basic vaccinations, for contaminating the American public with "deadly diseases," such as swine flu, dengue fever, the Ebola virus, tuberculosis, chicken pox, and measles.[14]

The United States, in fact, has a long historical precedent in immigrant scaremongering in the face of global epidemics. Time and again immigrants have been associated with diseases, and as such have been perceived to threaten and contaminate the health of the United States. In the 1800s, Irish immigrants were blamed for bringing cholera to the United States, Italians for bringing polio, and Jews for bringing tuberculosis.[15] In the 1900s, a similar lashing was allotted to Chinese immigrants for spreading bubonic plague in San Francisco.[16] Then in the 1980s, when the influx of Haitian refugees coincided with the AIDS epidemic, Haitians and Africans were blamed for the disease, along with "sexually deviant" groups, ethnic minorities, and intravenous drug abusers.[17] Moreover, in 1983, the CDC categorically added Haitians as "recognized vectors" of HIV, and later, in 1990, banned them from donating blood in the United States.[18] Today it is undocumented immigrants who are perceived as the carriers of numerous diseases.

Exogenous shocks can have both positive and negative impacts on how the hostland views immigrants and how the immigrants view themselves. A negative effect highlights the boundary that separates immigrants from natives in a way that paints immigrants as suspicious outsiders. By contrast, a positive effect points to the present or potential similarities between immigrants and natives. This is not to say, however, that positive exogenous shocks can diminish or erase altogether the boundary between immigrants and natives. Rather, the positive effects create opportunities for immigrants to position themselves more advantageously in the hostland than their current status does.

U.S. immigration history offers several examples of exogenous shocks emanating from foreign lands that led to positive and negative effects on particular immigrant groups. These examples also show that "elsewhere" effects are hardly new. Consider, for example, the anti-Catholicism directed against Catholic immigrants in the United States during the nineteenth and early twentieth centuries. Many Americans viewed Catholics as agents of the Vatican who would subvert democracy if allowed into the United States. As such, Irish immigrants, who were Catholic, faced nativist backlash based on activities in "elsewhere" Rome.[19] These anti-Catholic and anti-Irish sentiments manifested in caricatures and political discourses. Some of these depictions showed a monstrous hand, symbolizing Rome, reaching out to steal America's elections, and the Papacy infiltrating American public schools using Catholic propaganda to corrupt America's youth. In that same vein, a now infamous cartoon, "The American River Ganges" by Thomas Nast, published in *Harper's Weekly* in 1871, showed Roman Catholic clergy members as crocodiles attacking U.S. children and schools.[20] These anti-Catholic sentiments also led to outbreaks of violence, such as the burning of Catholic churches in 1844 and the Ku Klux Klan adding anti-Catholicism to their white supremacy manifesto in the early twentieth century. In this context, it was usual for respectable politicians to wonder aloud about Irish immigrants' alleged dual loyalty (i.e., whether, as Catholics, they could be loyal to both their hostland—the mostly Protestant United States—and the Pope).[21] Anti-Catholic prejudice also restricted Irish immigrants from job opportunities. Stores and businesses, for instance, held signs reading "No Irish Need Apply" when recruiting employees.

Similarly, during the First Red Scare, immigrants from Eastern and Southern Europe in the United States were affected by the Bolshevik Revolution—an exogenous shock that emanated from Russia—even though they were not Russian. In 1917, the Bolshevik Revolution swept across Russia. With the First World War winding down, anticommunism began to permeate American society, with the movement reaching its peak in the period from 1919 to 1920. Many Americans feared that communism, socialism, and anarchism would spread across the United States and undercut the country's democratic values. Further exacerbating these fears was mass immigration of Southern and Eastern Europeans at a time when the country was already struggling with declining employment rates and labor unrest after World War I. Moreover, members of the two U.S. communist parties and other politically radical organizations at the time were overwhelmingly of Eastern and Southern European descent.[22] In this climate, even though the incoming European immigrants were not from Russia—in this case, an "elsewhere"—they faced ferocious backlash as their host society perceived them to be communists determined to overthrow the U.S. government and spark a revolution on American soil.

The case of Chinese Americans in the context of World War II offers an example of when exogenous shocks produced positive effects. For decades prior to World War II, Chinese Americans were vilified in the United States; however, the Second World War, particularly Japan's attack on Pearl Harbor, changed U.S. perception of the Chinese, who it now saw as a crucial strategic ally against Japan. In light of China joining the Allies during the war, immigrants from that country were seen in a positive light, translating to the United States lifting restrictions from Chinese immigration and naturalization in 1943.

In more contemporary times, an event that many South Asian participants believed had a largely positive impact on the Muslim community in the United States was Malala Yousafzai's acceptance of the Nobel Peace Prize. The world's media reported on each phase of Malala's story—from her early activism in Pakistan, to the Taliban's attempt to kill her when she was just a schoolgirl, to her subsequent recovery in Britain, and then to her global campaign for education. In a context where Muslims are often associated with Islamist terrorism, Malala's story is a rare example in which a Muslim generated widespread positive response not just in the West but also across the world. This is particularly notable in the U.S. context, where the media largely portrays Islam as directly opposed to Western Christian ideologies.[23] As such, many Muslim Americans, regardless of ethnicity or nationality, believe that Malala's story has cast a positive light on their religious group, highlighting that they share with non-Muslim Americans the secular values of education, equality, and empowerment. These views were reflected on Facebook, where many South Asian Muslim Americans shared posts about Malala whenever she appeared in the news or on talk shows. Unlike instances where participants distanced themselves from their "Muslim-ness" in public spaces, many South Asian Muslims generally associated themselves with Malala in their posts and comments, expressing their sense of pride as fellow Muslims. These posts usually received hundreds of "likes" from South Asians, Muslims, and non-*desis* alike. One such post by Binti, a Bangladeshi American, read, "I've watched 'He Named Me Malala' at least 5 times and the more I watch it, the prouder I become to be a Muslim female and even more grateful for the right to my education." Asma, another Bangladeshi American, posted her college graduation photo on Facebook with a quote from Malala about education being the most powerful weapon, presumably against both Islamist extremism and anti-Muslim bigotry.

Yet, sometimes, knowing whether the effects of an exogenous shock are positive or negative may not be as simple. The murder of Vincent Chin and the subsequent galvanization of the Asian American panethnic movement provides such an example. Vincent Chin, a twenty-seven-year-old Chinese American, was murdered in 1982 by white assailants who miscategorized him as Japanese. This incident occurred during intense economic competition between the United States and Japan (the "elsewhere"), as the U.S. auto industry faced rising unemployment rates in the 1980s recession. The growing presence of Japanese auto manufacturers in the United States aggravated an already tense situation. In this context, Chin, who was celebrating his bachelor party in Detroit, encountered two white autoworkers, Ronald Ebens and Michael Nitz. Witnesses said the two men directed racial slurs, such as "chink," "jap," and "nip," toward Chin. But most notably linking Chin's murder to the economic competition with Japan, Ebens allegedly said to Chin, "It's because of you little motherfuckers that we're out of work."[24] The interactions led to a fight, in which Ebens repeatedly struck Chin in the head with a baseball bat. Chin succumbed to his injuries and died four days later. Ebens, however, never spent a day in jail. His defense argued that the statements Ebens was accused of making towards Chen were made up. Then three years after the murder, a mostly white federal court jury issued Ebens a verdict of not guilty. Chin's murder and Ebens' nonguilty verdict shook not just Chinese Americans but also Asians across ethnic lines. Asian Americans' collective outrage at the U.S. justice system's refusal to recognize

Chin's murder as an event of racism against Asians served as a wake-up call for the community to begin advocating for change by forming multiethnic and multiracial alliances.

From a multicentered relational perspective, on the one hand, the combination of the economic threat from "elsewhere" Japan and the recession in the United States proved to have a negative effect. The exogenous shock amplified the existing racism against Asians in the United States. Chin's murder exacerbated racial tensions, reiterating the boundary between Asians—and by extension, immigrants—and the predominantly white native society. On the other hand, the murder of Vincent Chin also served as the catalyst for Asian American panethnicity to crystalize, paving the way for various ethnic and immigrant communities to coalesce and collectively mobilize against racialization. An "elsewhere" perspective situates the events above, along with similar "made in America" situations, in a global perspective, ultimately revealing how globalization influences immigrant identity formation.

### DIFFERENT KINDS OF ELSEWHERE

An "elsewhere" can be salient to an immigrant in different ways, based on which dimension of identity the place highlights. This book examines two kinds of "elsewheres" in the Middle East that are salient for the South Asian immigrants' self-identification as Muslims: one kind is salient to the spiritual or faith-based dimension, as in the case of Saudi Arabia; the other kind impacts the politics surrounding Muslims, regardless of the immigrants' religiosity, as in the case of Palestine. The significance of both these places stems from the notion of the *Ummah*, a global ideological collective of Muslims, and from the role of the Middle East as the religious and political center of that imagined community.

The term "*Ummah*" has multiple meanings in the Quran, ranging from "followers of a prophet; a divine plan of salvation; a religious group; a small group within a larger community of believers; misguided people; and an order of being."[25] Colloquially, the *Ummah* is understood as an imagined global community of Muslims. Based on this idea, the *Ummah*'s instrumental use lies in its ability to subsume and override various forms of differences, such as those based on ethnicity. From a sociological perspective, the notion of *Ummah* has been successful in transforming disparate Arab tribes into a more cohesive Arab community. Over time, as Islam spread to other parts of the globe, the idea of the *Ummah* also succeeded in generating a sense of unity and membership among believers throughout the Muslim world. However, this "Muslim world" is composed not only of the followers of Islam but also the places, histories, and contexts important for those believers' religious or spiritual membership. It is this aspect of interconnectedness that makes the concept of *Ummah* pertinent to globalization and, by extension, to the purpose of this book. Because by subscribing to the idea of a global religious community, South Asian Muslim immigrants become connected both to fellow Muslims and to Muslim-related contexts rooted "elsewhere," both in the past and in the present.

However, this *Ummatic* sense of community itself is meaningful only in relation to "outsiders" (i.e., non-Muslims). In other words, if everyone in the world were Muslim, there would be no need for a community exclusively for those who follow Islam. As such, on the one hand, the idea of the *Ummah* has a unifying effect, in that it can unite Muslims from diverse backgrounds and walks of life under a shared banner. On the other hand, it differentiates between insiders/believers and outsiders/nonbelievers. Although narratives of "God's chosen people" and "us as opposed to them" are not unique to Islam but are attributes of many other world religions (such as Catholicism and Judaism), the fluidity and vagueness of the *Ummah*'s meaning allow religious and political ideologues to manipulate the term for conducting and justifying state affairs against a religious-political "other."

For example, organizations such as *Jamaat-i-Islami* and the Muslim Brotherhood propagate that "the West" has historically undermined "the *Ummah*," thereby "the Muslim World," through military invasions in the Middle East.[26] In this politicized use of the term *Ummah*, the Middle East, a region where the countries tend to be predominantly Islamic, represents the larger "Muslim world"—an imagined mass of peoples and places from all over the world, perceived to be internally homogenous because of their religious association to Islam. "The West," then, is its opposing counterpart—an imagined homogenous mass of nonbelievers and non-Islamic states. Religion and politics are thus intertwined, so much so that these conflated meanings have become widely accepted and are seldom questioned in everyday life, both in "the Muslim world" and "the West," allowing leaders on both sides to use these narratives to further their geopolitical interests.

This view of "the West" versus "the Muslim world" has become particularly entrenched because of years of conflict between the Middle East and European colonial powers and, later, between the Middle East and the United States. It gained further momentum based on clash of civilizations discourses, the rise of Islamic radicalism and terrorism, the protracted U.S.-led wars in Afghanistan and Iraq, and U.S. involvement in conflicts in Syria, Iran, and Yemen. As such, the *Ummah*—both as an imagined global community based on Islamic faith and as a transborder political entity composed of organizations, networks, and institutions—has a common religious and geopolitical center, the Middle East. Although South Asian Muslim Americans seldom use the term "*Ummah*" in their everyday lives, the idea of a global religious membership is latent in the ways they feel connected to Muslims and Muslim-related contexts in different parts of the world. As will be shown, many of these immigrants use the dichotomy of "the West" against "the Middle East" as an interpretative lens to make sense of the world and explain various conditions in their lives. For them, just as the Middle East stands as a proxy for "the Muslim world," the United States often represents "the West."

To some extent, the significance of the Middle East is entrenched in the religion of Islam itself. The Middle East is the home of the three holiest sites in Islam—Mecca, Medina, and Jerusalem. Mecca and Medina are located in Saudi Arabia, the birthplace of Islam and Prophet Muhammad. The kingdom is also the location of the holy house of *Ka'aba*. Five times from dawn until after sunset, Muslims around the world are obligated to turn toward the *Ka'aba* and offer *salat* (prayers) to Allah. Moreover, one of Islam's five pillars mandates that all able-bodied Muslims travel to Mecca and Medina to perform *Hajj* (pilgrimage) at least once in a lifetime. With regard to Jerusalem, the simple matter of where it is located on the map remains at the core of one of the world's most enduring geopolitical conflicts—that between Israel and Palestine. Contestations about territorial control of this holy site not only reflect political instability within the region but also create spillover effects across borders, thereby involving U.S. politics. An example of this cross-border spillover is the unfolding violence in Gaza in response to President Trump moving the U.S. embassy to Jerusalem in 2018, thereby recognizing the city as Israeli territory, in contradiction to the long-held U.S. and United Nations positions that it be the capital of both Israel and Palestine.

On the ground, Saudi Arabia's authority over the Muslim world translates to a hierarchy of religiosity that ranks believers based on their nationality. For instance, among the different Muslim nationals that South Asian Muslim immigrants encounter after migration to America, they perceive Arab immigrants, specifically those from Saudi Arabia, to be the most knowledgeable.[27] In contrast, many South Asian Muslims perceive Islam in their homelands to have become diluted by local cultural elements, with only Arabs having preserved the authenticity of Islamic practices.[28] As such, Saudis are ranked at the top of this hierarchy. Indeed, during my visits to Little Bangladesh, I found that if dates for *Eid* varied between the homeland and the United States, many Bangladeshis celebrated the festival the day the Arabs observed it, viewing the Saudi lunar calendar as the most Islamically "authentic." Similarly, native Arabic speakers were held in high regard even within the larger South Asian Muslim community, because they were believed to know the Quran, which is written in Arabic, most accurately. As such, instead of using their homelands' typical pronunciation of Islamic terms and phrases, some South Asian Muslims adopt an Arabic accent to invoke their knowledge in Islam. For instance, the Urdu and Bangla words for the Islamic ablution rituals are "*wazu*" and "*oju*." However, despite being fluent in their homeland languages, many young Pakistanis and Bangladeshis say "*wudu*," as pronounced by their Arab peers. Similarly, the holy month of fasting, typically pronounced "*ramzan*" and "*romjan*" in Urdu and Bangla, is often pronounced "*ramadan*"; the noon prayer, "*zuhr*" (Urdu) or "*johor*" (Bangla), as "*duhr*" (Arabic); and the call to prayer, "*azaan*" (Urdu) or "*aajaan*" (Bangla), as "*adhan*" (Arabic). When I asked a young Pakistani woman, who was fluent in Urdu, why she pronounced the name of the afternoon prayer with an Arabic inflection ("*A'sr*" instead of "*Aasr*"), she replied, "Because that's the proper way to say it." Within the South Asian Muslim community, these "proper" pronunciations implied an authoritative knowledge over Islam that, in turn, brought respect and social status from Muslim co-ethnics. And in settings with a population of diverse Muslim nationals that included Arabs, such pronunciations gave the *desi* speakers the image of well-versed Muslims on equal footing with their Arab-speaking coreligionists.

However, although Saudi Arabia is generally revered by Muslims because of its centrality in the Islamic faith, there is also a sense of dis-identification from this "elsewhere" among some of the younger U.S.-college-educated participants, because of the country's role in global politics. Specifically, these participants, who are considered more "woke" and actively engaged in U.S. politics than their parents, criticized the Saudi leadership—which regards itself as the custodians of the Muslim world—for its failure to bring peace to Muslims globally. For example, Daliah identified herself as a "Bangali Muslim woman" and a "woman of color," often doing so vocally in the many *desi*, Muslim, and Bangladeshi cultural organizations she actively participated in during college. When I first met her through the Bangladeshi Students Association, she was a senior, on her way to becoming an engineer after graduation. I soon learned that she was also an active member of the Palestinian-rights campus organization where she often proudly represented Bangalis in support of Palestine. A self-proclaimed feminist with progressive liberal views, Daliah was a vocal supporter of Bernie Sanders during the 2016 Democratic primaries. She frequently shared her political views and concerns for various social justice causes on Facebook. Although she did not wear the *hijab*, she wore modest clothing, prayed regularly, read the Quran, and kept up to date with news concerning Muslims, both in the United States and abroad. At the same time, however, she openly dated her long-term boyfriend, a Bangladeshi Muslim, and had previously dated white Americans. As a second-generation Bangladeshi, she spoke Bangla with a heavy American accent. And conversations with her were usually peppered with Arabic words, which she was careful to pronounce with Arabic inflections.

One day, Daliah and I were driving to interview a Bangladeshi family about their experiences during the 1971 Bangladeshi War of Independence. The interview was for the Bangladeshi student organization's community outreach project. It was a long drive to the family's residence. Although Daliah's parents lived nearby that family, she had offered to pick me up from my place, close to campus. She was driving, and I was in the passenger seat. I took the opportunity to ask her about the Bangladeshi community in the area. Dahlia described the community to be "inward-looking" as she believed it to only focus on issues that concerned Muslims. She also viewed Bangladeshis to be often "closed-minded," especially when it came to race relations. Particularly, she believed there needed be a campaign to eradicate anti-blackness from the *desi* or South Asian community at large. She then asked me what I made of the Bangali community thus far. I told her I found that many Bangladeshis, despite identifying as Muslims, tend to think of themselves as not having the same level of Islamic knowledge and prestige as Arabs, especially Saudis. She then responded,

> Oh, I don't think that. I hate Saudi Arabia. Their treatment of women and the Shia minority is terrible. And look what they are doing for Palestinians. Nothing. I don't think they are better Muslims or that they are the leaders of the Muslim world. All they care about is oil and money.

While this response offers an example of why some politically active Muslims dis-identify with Saudi Arabia, it also reflects the symbolic value many of them give to Palestine in evaluating world politics, as the majority of the participants did. Indeed, in many of the participants' worldviews, the Israel-Palestine conflict arguably stood as the most potent symbol of the West's continuing anti-Muslim attitude at the global level. As will be discussed extensively in chapter 5, to the first-generation immigrants, Palestine was a reminder of the consequences of Western intervention in various parts of the Muslim world, including in their homelands, where they were under British colonization for over two centuries. Many in the second generation, on the other hand, felt obligated to support and, in some cases, participate in Palestinian rights organizations, based on a sense of *Ummatic* solidarity. Moreover, many of these young college-going South Asian Muslims drew parallels between their own experiences as members of a stigmatized religious minority in the United States and those of Palestinians in Israel. Even in mainstream U.S. politics, participants of both immigrant generations evaluated politicians based on their stance toward Palestine, among other issues. For instance, during the 2016 Democratic primaries, most participants favored Bernie Sanders over Hillary Clinton because they viewed Sanders as being more open and sympathetic toward Palestine than Clinton, whose Middle East policy they saw to be too pro-Israeli and thus biased against Muslim interests.

There are also different kinds of "elsewheres" based on where an exogenous shock originated and how salient that place is for the larger host society and the immigrants' place in it. ISIS attacks that took place in Europe and the Middle East produced different levels of impact on the South Asian Muslim community and U.S. society at large. Overall, the ISIS attacks in Europe had a higher level of salience than those in the Middle East. In contrast to the European attacks, which produced intense and widespread reactions in U.S. society, those in the Middle East were largely overlooked, despite being of similar scale and conducted by the same terrorist organization. Whereas the attacks in the West were largely seen in America as being close to home, those in the Middle East were viewed as "Muslims killing Muslims" in a faraway foreign land. This contrast suggests that the level of salience of an "elsewhere" place depends, to some extent, on both its geographic position on the world map and its location in the prevailing public imaginary. Moreover, the varying levels of salience of different "elsewhere" places reflect the hierarchy that exists in the global distribution of power and the geopolitical dynamics among different regions of the world. Whereas the world stays tuned to what goes on in the developed core countries, such as the United States and countries in Europe, far less attention is given to the internal dynamics of the developing countries in the periphery.

Building on these variations, the multicentered relational framework examines immigrant identity formation based on the different kinds of relationships between its centers—the relationship between the homeland and "elsewhere," that between the hostland and the homeland, and that between the hostland and "elsewhere."

## THE DIFFERENT FACETS OF THE MULTICENTERED RELATIONAL FRAMEWORK

Although immigrants have myriad global ties that transcend their societies of origin and destination, their identities are not somehow always connected to ongoing dynamic in faraway foreign lands. In fact, as tempting as it was as a researcher to note only those instances when "elsewhere" appeared relevant, I found many occasions when those places did not matter much to South Asian Muslims. Yet, although global politics may not always be salient in how immigrants see themselves, immigrants nonetheless stand exposed to hostland contexts by virtue of being both physically present in the receiving state and embedded in its sociopolitics. These hostland dynamics, at times, associate immigrants to "elsewhere" conflicts, shaping how these people are viewed by others around them.

My observations from informal get-togethers of friends and family in Bangladeshi households, called *dawats*, help to illustrate this point. *Dawats* were an important way for Bangladeshi immigrant families to socialize. As a fellow co-ethnic, I was invited to many of these gatherings in different Bangladeshi communities in Los Angeles. These *dawats* gave me insight into what Bangladeshi Muslims talked about when they were at home among themselves. In general, *dawats* are intimate affairs, as they mark a family's willingness to include the invited guest into their private, personal lives, showing the guest where they live, introducing the person to family members, sharing their home-cooked food, and exchanging news about one another's health. At the same time, *dawats* produce opportunities to expand one's *deshi* connections, cajole people into divulging about certain affairs, and even bring up sensitive topics like children's marriage prospects in a delicate way. With these aims, *dawats* serve similar purposes here as they did back in the homeland. But for immigrants, many who remain "strangers in a strange land" long after arriving in the hostland, *dawats* are opportunities to meet people from back home and create a support network. They provide immigrants with some respite from the pressures of work and what seems like an endless process of settling into the host society. This explains why *dawats* are predominantly a first-generation affair, with families, usually married couples with children, inviting guests from the same ethnic/national group.[29]

A prominent topic of conversation at many of these gatherings, especially among the first generation, dealt with clashes between the major political parties back home rather than with global political affairs. However, this is not to say that "elsewhere"-related issues never came up. For instance, at a *dawat* that took place soon after the 2013 Boston Marathon bombings, I overheard some guests exchanging news of their friends and family in Boston. Trisha had a female acquaintance there who wore the *hijab*. One of the guests, a woman, asked if she was okay, implicitly referring to the Muslim backlash that followed the event. Trisha's husband replied, with some degree of nonchalance, that the woman was okay but that she had been shoved from behind in the streets and called derogatory names. "But," he added, "it was nothing much—she didn't get injured."[30]

Homeland charity organizations provide another, clearer example of homeland-hostland connections being influenced by "elsewhere" effects, albeit in a more formal setting than *dawats*. I had come across HELP,[31] a charity run by first-generation Bangladeshis, when volunteering as a teacher at a Bangla language school. Many of the families at the school were involved with HELP, which collected donations for development in Bangladeshi rural areas. Throughout the year, HELP periodically sent newsletters to its members reporting on its projects. Jamal, a father of one of the students at the language school, was a board member. He and some other Bangladeshi engineers in Los Angeles managed the organization. According to him, HELP sends almost $45,000 every year to Bangladeshi rural areas. Its biggest event of the year was the charity ball, held at a community center in an affluent location in Rancho Cucamonga. Membership to the organization and its annual balls was by invitation only, sent from the board members through email. Jamal had sent me mine. I had to pay $45 for the ticket and make a donation of $50 or upwards to attend the ball. At the event, the board members gave a presentation of HELP's history and mission. At one point, one of the board members described how they rigorously screened potential projects to ensure they had no connection to religious causes. He said, "We Bangladeshis have to remember that this is a post-9/11 world and that we are Muslims [and that] Bangladesh is an Islamic country."[32] He said that they vetted each project to carefully trace where the donation money went and how it was spent, because as a predominantly Muslim group sending money to an Islamic country, they feared they could be under surveillance in the United States. Their fear and suspicion were not without cause given that Bangladesh had, in fact, been one of the twenty-six Muslim-majority sending countries in the U.S. government's "special registration" program, which had been set up to enhance national security after 9/11.

Trisha's conversation at the *dawat* and the board member's speech in the homeland charity both highlight the consequences of lumping South Asians with other "Muslim-looking" groups like Arabs and Middle Easterners in America. Intra-group differences are conflated in this hostland context, with "normal" homeland divides (such as party politics) going unnoticed by the American population. Rather, conflicts associated with the Middle East—a region that has gained political salience in the West because of a long series of exogenous shocks—gain a notoriety that other homeland conflicts, even if they generate violence, do not. For example, in July 2016, a group of domestic terrorists inspired by ISIS killed twenty-two people at a bakery in Dhaka, Bangladesh's capital. Most of the victims were foreigners. The story was covered extensively in the mainstream U.S. news media. Many political commentators interpreted the event as indicative of ISIS expanding its influence to Muslim-majority countries beyond the Middle East,[33] giving the impression that Bangladesh, too, is a dangerous Muslim country like those in that "elsewhere" place. Many Bangladeshi Americans, especially those who belonged to the first generation and strongly identified with the homeland, paid close attention to how Bangladesh was portrayed in the news coverage. In addition to having concerns for their homeland and loved ones left behind, they were worried that, because of the terrorist attack and the subsequent depiction of Bangladesh in the U.S. media, the Bangladeshi national identity would become closely associated with "Muslim," turning them into suspect terrorists in the eyes of the American public.

Conversely, while many South Asian Muslim Americans *themselves* appear to feel a sense of solidarity with Muslims worldwide, including those in the "elsewhere" Middle East, this sense of belonging at times exists in tension with their more particularistic homeland identities, such as "Bangladeshi," "Pakistani," and "Indian." The boundaries differentiating these national identities have gained salience over the years because of the 1947 partition of Bengal, the 1971 war between East and West Pakistan that liberated Bangladesh, and ongoing conflicts over issues such as undocumented immigration from Bangladesh to India and the Kashmir conflict between India and Pakistan.

Each of these nationalistic identities is deeply intertwined with religion, which has historically been the source of conflict both *between* Muslims and non-Muslims as well as *within* the Muslim community. The historic rivalry between the predominantly Hindu India and the Muslim-majority Pakistan is a prominent example of religion continuing to fuel tensions between Muslims and non-Muslims in South Asia. Frequent outbreaks of communal violence between Hindu nationalists and the Muslim minority in India offer another example of conflict unfolding within the same country as part of its nation-building project. In contrast, the Bangladesh-Pakistan war, the

Sunni-Shia sectarian divide in Pakistan, and the ideological clashes between secularists and Islamists in Bangladesh illustrate how religion and politics inform cleavages among Muslims.

These religious-political contestations, however, hardly remain contained within the borders of the homeland. Rather, they travel to the United States, either through the flow of information or via the immigrants themselves, when they come here and build their communities. For South Asian Muslim Americans, some of these homeland cleavages make their Muslim identity salient (such as when Indian Muslims hear about Hindu nationalists persecuting the Muslim minority back home), while others highlight their national identities (such as when tensions escalate between India and Pakistan over the seventy-year dispute regarding the status of divided Kashmir).

Yet, homeland cleavages have less relevance in the hostland, where they have little impact on immigrants' everyday lives. Rather, the sociopolitical environment inside the hostland has more immediate impact. In the case of South Asian Muslims, whose homelands are not in direct geopolitical conflict with the hostland but who are still often conflated with other immigrant groups from supposedly hostile countries, banding together on a united platform against a common adverse situation is more constructive than reiterating homeland cleavages. This hostland context allows for new, diasporic ethnic identities, which are both pan-national and pan-religious, such as "*desi*."

For example, most of the 1.5- and second-generation participants often referred to themselves and their peers as "*desi*," which means "of *des*" or "from the homeland." In this context, *des*, or the homeland, refers to a homogenous common place of origin comprising all three South Asian countries and located far away on the other side of the world, where the culture is different than that in America. Nonetheless, *des* has an enduring but somewhat symbolic presence in life here in the United States, differentiating all *desis* from other groups in the hostland. When used, the *desi* label conflates the historic homeland cleavages and nationalistic differences. This was made clear when tensions between India and Pakistan heightened in 2015 over the Kashmir conflict. In response to this news from home, the Pakistani and Indian student organizations on a college campus I observed put together a publicity event to demonstrate "*desi*" solidarity. The organizations were composed mostly of the 1.5 and second generations. Although each ethnic group had its own campus association, these students' friendships spanned across national lines. Reflecting how social media acts as a conduit to channel certain kinds of homeland and "elsewhere" news to immigrants, the students learned about the rising tensions through Facebook, where a hashtag campaign launched in India called #ProfileForPeace had gone viral among South Asian users.[34] As part of the campaign, many Indian and Pakistani users had posted pictures of themselves, holding placards with peaceful slogans, on Facebook and Instagram. The Pakistani and Indian student organizations materialized this virtual campaign on their campus by creating a large cutout of an Instagram frame and taking pictures of their members holding each other's national flags. Some held up signs with messages advocating for friendly relations between their homelands, highlighting commonalities in the two cultures, such as their love for *biryani* and cricket. These pictures, which the students then posted on social media, received hundreds of "likes" from their *desi* friends.

Things changed in 2016, however, when the Kashmir conflict again escalated. Some of the same students who had advocated for peace between their homelands in the publicity event this time became embroiled in a long and heated argument on Facebook about what role each homeland played in perpetuating the violence. Alam, a first-generation Pakistani, for instance, disparaged India as a "deceitful" and "war-mongering" state. His comments incited passionate defense from his Indian friends on Facebook, even though many of them were involved in the Pakistani Students Association and had close Pakistani American friends. A range of topics that reflected the historic India-Pakistan rivalry peppered the hundreds of back-and-forth comments these students posted on Facebook—topics surrounding the partition, each country's economy, violations of ceasefires, India's use of rubber bullets versus Pakistan's use of live ammunition in Kashmir, Pakistan's ties to Islamist terrorist groups, and so on. Students from both sides posted links to various sources, such as the *New York Times* and Wikipedia, to support their views. However, when their argument regressed to name-calling—"nationalist" being a particularly stinging label for both sides—mutual friends stepped in, reminding students about their friendships and the fruitlessness of this never-ending debate.

These activities highlight ways that homeland tensions can unintentionally cause cleavages among those same groups that hostland realities can bring together. On the one hand, spikes in homeland tensions that trended on social media tended to capture the attention, imagination, and passion of young South Asian Americans, suppressing in these moments a sense of panethnic *desi* solidarity. On the other hand, the reality of living so far away from their homeland in a country that cares little about sifting through the granular distinctions within their ethnic groups encourages these same people to band together as *desis*. I saw this again with particular force when attending a Pakistani student cultural event. Every year, Pakistani student organizations from several universities in California organized this event. Claiming to showcase elements of Pakistani culture, the event was arguably one of the highlights of the year for the *desi* student community on these campuses. The Pakistani organizations from each campus took turns hosting the event. The host campus's ticket office distributed tickets to students for free but charged a nominal fee for general admission. Students from each organization performed dances, songs, and plays. Given the more or less friendly competition among the participating campuses, these performances were serious business and, for the students, a matter of pride, as they sought to represent their own universities to the larger *desi* community. As such, the students devoted hours to rehearsals, either before, between, or after classes, and gossip within the South Asian campus community often centered on how the performances were shaping up. The event was advertised widely on Facebook, and organizers encouraged people to bring their families. There was, however, a somewhat strict "*desi* clothes only" dress code.

Several Pakistani and Bangladeshi students I knew from my fieldwork regularly performed at these events. Given the buzz among many of my respondents, some of whom I knew closely through the Bangladeshi Students Association, I decided to attend.

I had expected the event to be an intimate gathering of *desi* folks, as was the case in some of the other South Asian events I had attended. That presumption swiftly evaporated, however, as soon as I arrived. There was a long line at the entrance that went down two flights of stairs. Attendants were to show their tickets and check in at tables organized into alphabetic groups. I had shown up an hour early but was still clearly late, because I was

separated from the check-in desk by a full flight of stairs with a long stream
of waiting guests, all dressed in what seemed to be their *desi* best. Even
though I, too, was wearing one of my better *salwar kamizes*, I felt under-
dressed as I looked at some of the gorgeous dresses and jewelry the other
women were wearing, indicating the fairly well-off socioeconomic status of
the attendees. I recalled to my mother, after returning from the event, that it
could have been a Bollywood social for celebrities. What also struck me was
that the guests were of different age groups. I had expected a campus event
with mostly students attending. But some had looked old enough to be the
students' parents, aunts, and uncles. Others accompanied smaller children,
from toddlers to middle-schoolers.

I entered the ballroom with only a few minutes left until the scheduled
opening, but I needed not to have worried as the program started thirty
minutes late. I was not surprised, however, as I had learned that "*desi* people
run on *desi* time," a common joke that meant that South Asians are always
late. The ballroom was exquisitely decorated. There were round tables neatly
placed across the floor. At the front of the banquet hall was a huge stage with
a dark backdrop. At the back stood a line of tables laden with dinner boxes
of *biryani* and *kebab*, to be served after the performances. There was also a
donation box for attendees who wished to send money for relief efforts in
Pakistan. Each of the round tables was decorated with small candles, flow-
ers, and glitter. The seating at several tables was already full. The number of
attendees looked to be close to two hundred, perhaps more. I sat at a table
where I spotted a few familiar faces from my campus fieldwork. Looking
around, I recognized quite a few students—many of them Pakistani but not
all; several attendees were Indian and Bangladeshi.

The event began with the Pakistani national anthem. Then after a short
introduction, the president of the host Pakistani student organization opened
the stage for the performances. To my amusement, most of the performances
used popular Hindi songs from Indian movies. Although there were some
songs that were originally performed by Pakistani musicians working in
Bollywood, those, too, were in Hindi rather than Urdu, the state language
of Pakistan. In between the performances, an official from the Pakistani
embassy and a representative from a Pakistani nonprofit organization gave
short speeches about the importance of young Pakistanis becoming engaged

both in the diasporic community in America and in relief efforts back home. Although the speeches and student introductions were mostly in English, interspersed throughout were Urdu phrases, references to Islam, and insider jokes about Pakistani culture and tradition.

My biggest surprise at the event, however, came toward the end, when performers, some Bangladeshi, dashed onto the stage carrying a large Pakistani flag and cheering, *"Pakistan Zindabaad!"* (Long Live Pakistan). Given the bloody history of the 1947 India-Pakistan partition and the 1971 war between Pakistan and Bangladesh—events that continue to define nationhood in these countries—this juxtaposition of Bangladeshis joyfully waving a Pakistani flag and cheering "Long Live Pakistan!" after dancing to Indian Bollywood music would likely have been impossible and largely condemned as unpatriotic in all three South Asian homelands. In the multiethnic United States, far from these immigrants' homelands, however, this kind of panethnic solidarity is not only conceivable but perhaps even desired. For many South Asians in America, too, particularly those of the first generation, for whom memories of homeland cleavages tend to still be fresh, participating in such a seemingly effortless show of panethnic *desi*-ness would likely be very difficult. Nonetheless, while the first-generation participants of the study found it difficult to sweep aside a long history of homeland conflicts and rarely had friends outside their national group, they still wanted their children to make *desi* friends and encouraged them to partake in panethnic cultural events. And indeed, I found these cultural events to be important avenues for South Asian youth to make *desi* and co-ethnic friends with whom they kept in contact even after graduation. In a few cases, participation in these cultural associations even led to students finding their future spouses.

Notably, in both the above examples, "elsewhere" appears to be mostly irrelevant for the immigrants' sense of self. Rather, priority is given to homeland commonalities and hostland dynamics. Indeed, the *desi* identity tends to largely overlook the religious-political divides within and between the three immigrant groups, for the sake of achieving a sense of panethnic unity. Yet, in other instances, homeland-oriented identities (such as *desi*, Bangladeshi, Pakistani, and Indian) can accentuate South Asians' religious differences from one another based on "elsewhere" dynamics. As cleavages from back home spill over borders, whether through social media or through immigrants themselves, they are no longer influenced only by the goings-on within the homeland. Instead, these cleavages gain global dimensions because of sociopolitics in the hostland and contexts happening "elsewhere." For example, Hindu nationalists, currently the political party in power in India, perceive the country's Muslim minority as Pakistani loyalists who have been coddled under the opposition party's more secular-oriented governance; therefore, every election year, the way Muslims will be treated is a charged topic that makes its way to each party's narrative. Sikh-Muslim relations are also fraught because of Sikh persecution by Muslim Mughal emperors from the sixteenth to early eighteenth centuries. In this context, the turmoil in the Middle East and the Islamist terror attacks in various parts of the world have compounded anti-Muslim sentiments in many segments of the Hindu and Sikh populations, both at home and abroad. Conversely, although panethnic *desi* platforms diminish, to some extent, the "Muslim-ness" of Indian Muslim Americans, the persecuted status of their coreligionists back home makes their Muslim identity particularly salient for their sense of selves. Both their direct experiences with co-ethnics in the diaspora and their memories of the homeland, passed down in their families, are colored by these immigrants' minority Muslim status. In effect, whether intentionally or not, the Indian Muslim participants tended to have more Pakistani and Muslim friends than Hindu Indian ones. Whereas these respondents often felt excluded by their Hindu conationals based on religious identity, they felt welcomed among Muslims and Pakistanis because of it. Some Indian Muslims I knew in the Los Angeles *desi* community even married Pakistanis based on their common religious identity (more on this theme in chapter 3).

The immigrants' premigration biases stemming from homeland cleavages combined with dynamics in the hostland and "elsewhere" can also influence their orientations to the receiving society's political divides. For example, although more than half of the Indian American diaspora generally supported the Democratic Party,[35] Hindu nationalists had conversely embraced right-wing American politics because of its anti-Muslim platform.[36] Hindu nationalists both in India and the United States supported Donald Trump during the 2016 presidential election because they viewed his anti-Muslim platform to be advantageous for their nationalist politics against both the Muslim minority in India and their regional rival Pakistan.[37] They rallied support for Trump using ISIS imagery to stoke Islamophobic fears among Hindu Indians.[38] And a group called Hindus for Trump, composed of Hindu nationalists in India and the United States, ardently supported Trump's proposals for a "Muslim ban" and a "Mexican wall" because these echoed their own similar intentions. Hindu nationalists have long accused Pakistan of sponsoring Islamist terrorism and have wanted to build a wall along the India-Bangladesh border to keep Muslims from entering India.[39] In the words of Kushal Pal, an engineering consultant and Hindu nationalist, in an interview with the Australian Broadcasting Corporation, "Many Muslim countries engage in acts of terrorism which is harmful for India. . . . India is suffering from terrorism and Trump is against the terrorism therefore he is favourable for India."[40]

However, as noted earlier, racial lumping in the United States overlooks all these historic rivalries and divisions, and in the face of perceived threat from a "Muslim other," renders the intra-ethnic differences trivial. Once in America, Hindus and Sikhs, in fact, are often mistaken for Muslims, the very people whom segments of these religious groups despise. Regardless of their views, they become associated with Muslim-related conflicts stemming from "elsewhere," and the examples of Srinivas Kuchibhotla and Alok Madasani in chapter 1 highlight just how dire the consequences of that lumping can be. In this context, the Middle East, which arguably should be an "anywhere," becomes an "elsewhere" for these "Muslim-looking" non-Muslims. While in some instances, these shared hostland experiences with Muslims can lead to a sense of panethnic *desi* solidarity, they can also deepen the intranational religious divides in the diaspora. Hindu Indian Americans, for instance, deploy various strategies to distance themselves from their Muslim co-ethnics by overemphasizing their non-Muslim identity using anti-Muslim platforms.[41] The Hindus for Trump movement had similar motivations but tended to both suppress and encourage different panethnic solidarities. On one side, Hindu nationalists' support for Trump and his anti-Muslim platforms highlights Hindus' differences from their Muslim counterparts, thereby suppressing *desi* solidarity. Conversely, the Hindu nationalists' support for a right-wing, anti-Muslim agenda reinforced the Indian Muslim participants' outsider status in their own homelands. This sense of being othered by their Hindu conationals highlights, instead, the similarities the participants share with Muslims from other nationalities in America, thereby encouraging a Muslim panethnicity.

Sifat, a second-generation Pakistani immigrant, exemplifies the third dimension of the multicentered relational framework—that between the *hostland* and "elsewhere"—and how it can influence immigrant identities rooted in the homeland. At the time of the interview, Sifat was studying to be a dentist. Having graduated from college a few years before, she was still in touch with her close friends, several of whom were Pakistani Americans themselves. She had met them through the Pakistani and Muslim student associations. Like the majority of my female participants, Sifat did not wear the *hijab*, opting instead for "modest" clothing—full sleeves and trousers. She was, however, one of the few Muslim women who revealed to me that they had previously dated non-Muslims—in her case, a white Christian. She had planned to convert him for marriage, but the relationship did not work out. At the time of the interview, she was single and looking to settle down. While she did not much care about her partner's ethnicity, she prioritized marrying a Muslim man.

Although I met Sifat for the first time over Skype, I found her to be open and friendly, at times even outspoken about her feminist and liberal political views. Despite our being virtual strangers, she shared with me her frustrations about her uncle's belief that Muslim men should have four wives—a common belief, according to her, among many older Pakistani men. In her view, being Pakistani meant having to confront many such sexist notions based on misinterpretations of Islam, which she believed colored every aspect of her homeland's national identity. Nonetheless, she identified herself as a proud Pakistani and took offense when her homeland was negatively portrayed in the media. She found it particularly frustrating when she believed that her homeland and her identity as a Pakistani were associated with the Middle East, violence, and Islamist terrorism. In her words,

> In the past, my dad, when he was still a student [at a college in the United States], he was considered an Arab and was sort of given that form of discrimination or racism. True to this day as well, a lot of people don't

really know what "Pakistani" is. They will ask you, "Are you Arab? Are you Middle Eastern? Wait, are you Indian? Are you Asian?" They don't know. Still, back then, it wasn't too much. People would say, "Pakistani," and they would be like, "Oh, where is that?" They wouldn't really know much about it. The label "Pakistani" in recent times has come to be associated with the Middle East, Muslim, and terrorists. Nowadays, people have the little bit of knowledge and education that they have about this particular part of the world through the news, the American media. . . . So I recently visited Pakistan a couple of months ago, and some of my friends were, "Oh, were you safe? You were able to walk around? There were no gun shootings, no bombings?" And I was like, "Oh, there is nothing like that going on over there. I walked the streets normally in my jeans and my shirt. I didn't have to cover up. I don't know what you guys think happens there." And those friends were like, "We always see in the media that there are always bombings over there, schools are being blown up, people are being blown up, they are taking foreigners and kidnap them." And I was like, "No—that is just what the media is feeding you. When you go to Pakistan, the major cities, you will see that they are pretty modern. Their sense of fashion, the technology there, education. We have some of the best schools in Pakistan." So here, you can see that the little bit of education that they do have about this small country is from the media, and that's sort of how, nowadays, you would experience being seen as Pakistani.

Naser, a first-generation Pakistani immigrant, offered another example of this experience. He is the only respondent to have come to the United States from the Middle East. Although born in the United States to Pakistani parents, Naser lived in Saudi Arabia until he was eighteen years old. The family had initially moved to Dubai when he was three because of his parents' work. When he was six, Naser and his family moved to Saudi Arabia where his father worked as a high-ranking finance officer in a steel conglomerate and his mother as a professor at a renowned university. Growing up in Saudi Arabia, Naser went to an American co-ed high school and visited the United States three or four times to see his relatives in Texas and the East Coast. After graduation, Naser followed the footsteps of his older brother and applied to American colleges. Having received admission, he moved to the United States, where he planned to settle after graduating as an accountant. Growing up in the Middle East, Naser spoke fluent Urdu and Arabic. As a practicing Muslim, he prayed five times a day, ate only *halal* food, and was fairly active in the Muslim Students Association. I met Naser for the first time at his college campus and later at a hike organized by the Muslim Students Association. In my interactions with him, he came across as thoughtful and shy, but with a witty sense of humor, often cracking self-deprecating jokes in Urdu. He was also informed about U.S. and world politics, often posting on Facebook his take on ongoing news events regarding Muslims. Before his graduation, to the surprise of many in the campus *desi* community, he became engaged to a fellow college student, a Bangladeshi Muslim, whom he had met through the Muslim and Pakistani student associations.

In his interview, Naser described how his Pakistani identity, combined with his Saudi background, colored many of his interactions in America, beginning with his arrival at the airport.

> When I landed at the airport, the expected, you know, racial profiling: "Please step aside," and this and that. They [the TSA officers] asked ridiculous questions. The last visit I made [to the United States] was in 2010. And that's all it said on my passport. That I landed. They looked at my passport and they were like, "What were you doing for three years? Where are you going? Why did you come here?" I was like, "I don't live here. I am just here to study. I was in Saudi Arabia." They asked, "Why were you in Saudi Arabia? What were you there for?" This and that, you know.

In regard to engaging in student organizations on campus, he said,

> When I came here, my parents told me to stay away from politics. Also, I heard a lot of stories about how becoming political is not really the best thing to do. Especially as a college student, especially if you get stopped at the airport all the time. If you are, you know, if you come from Saudi Arabia or are from Pakistan.

On his life outside of campus, Naser said,

So there was this white guy I lived with after coming here. He is studying political science. He has known me for seven months, right? And then one day, and he is dead serious when he asks me, "Hey you wouldn't join ISIS, would you?" I was like, I don't know what to say to someone like this.

Together, Sifat and Naser's stories illustrate how the nature of relations between the immigrants' hostland (the United States) and "elsewhere" (the Middle East) can shape their homeland identity—in their case, Pakistani. By itself, Pakistan as a place appears to mean little to the larger American society, with few people seeming to know its location on the world map. It is largely seen as a foreign place, far from the United States. Similarly, "Pakistani"—by itself an ambiguous label—simply refers to a category that is different from "American." As these examples show, however, Pakistan has meaning when placed in relation to the Middle East and its contentious relationship with the United States, particularly in the context of Islamist terrorism and violence. At the global level, Pakistan has been a key ally for the United States' War on Terror in the Middle East, despite various instances of conflict between the two nations. As an Islamic country riddled with sectarian violence but possessing nuclear capabilities, Pakistan continues to be of strategic importance to the United States in maintaining its influence in the Muslim world. Moreover, Pakistan's continuing struggles with various Islamist groups, such as the Taliban, Al Qaeda, and Lashkar-e-Taiba, have often spilled over beyond its borders, affecting not just its neighboring countries but also those in the West. In this context, the label "Pakistani" has come to have the same set of connotations as "Arab," "Middle Eastern," and "Islamic terrorist," shaping how many Pakistani Americans, like Sifat and Naser, are viewed by segments of the U.S. society.

## A NEW DIASPORIC MODEL

What distinguishes the multicentered relational framework from the foundational paradigms in migration studies is the analytical space it provides to trace the effects of exogenous shocks (i.e., events that originate from beyond immigrants' sending and receiving countries but still disrupt the global geopolitical order). Specifically, this new framework differs from the assimilation perspective, in that it shows how exogenous shocks can shape immigrants' identification by others in the hostland. Whereas the assimilation perspective highlights the processes, resources, and obstacles through which immigrants become similar to the hostland's native population over time, the multicentered relational framework shows how ongoing conflicts beyond the societies of origin and destination come to highlight immigrants' "otherness" from the mainstream host society. Indeed, U.S. immigration history shows that exogenous shocks from "elsewhere" have long shaped how the United States has viewed various immigrant groups. And because of globalization, it is not illogical to expect that exogenous shocks will affect immigrants in the future, whether through religious-political conflicts or global epidemics.

However, "elsewhere" may have a more immediate impact on immigrant lives in the hostland today than in times past. Smartphones and 24/7 breaking-news cycles are connecting faraway, seemingly disparate societies more quickly, easily, and cheaply than before, creating pathways for "elsewhere" events to converge with the sociopolitics of the sending and receiving societies almost immediately after those events occur. While this interconnectedness of societies has both expanded and diversified people's worldviews, it has also led to the entrenchment of old divides, at times in newer iterations and with more globally informed meanings. The multicentered relational framework is attuned to these effects of globalization on immigrants' lives and allows scholars to examine just how these connections are made, filtered down, given meaning, and understood by both immigrants and those around them. By showing how "elsewhere" contexts can both bring migrants and stay-at-homes together and also separate and divide them, the multicentered relational framework extends the homeland-hostland paradigm in the transnational perspective. While transnationalism extends the hostland-only focus in assimilation by introducing the immigrants' homeland ties, the multicentered relational framework goes a step further, showing the convergence of not two, but three, types of societies through immigrants—the societies of origin and destination and those societies beyond, or "elsewhere."

The multicentered relational framework is also analytically distinct from the diasporic model in that it shows that immigrants may not always be connected to peoples and places based on a sense of diasporic affinity with co-ethnics or on allegiance to a common homeland. Rather, immigrants are connected to multiple and varied places based on global geopolitics. Moreover, diasporic frameworks are still bound within a dyadic homeland-hostland paradigm in which an ethnic migrant group originating from a common homeland—"there"—is settled in multiple host societies or "here." In contrast, a multicentered relational framework argues that immigrants have various, multidimensional identities, each of which could be influenced by events taking place "elsewhere." The next chapter uses this new paradigm to examine how homeland-"elsewhere" connections shape immigrant identities.

# 3 | GLOBAL DIMENSIONS OF HOMELAND TIES

**MIGRATION STUDIES TRACE** how immigrants traverse boundaries to get to new societies, change their surroundings, and, in the process, become changed themselves. In this approach, the homeland seems to matter only when the immigrants are present in it or when they transform their sending society by remitting resources from the hostland.[1] It is as if the homeland stays static and isolated without the immigrants' presence, its contexts neatly bound within its nation-state borders. That is, of course, not the case. Immigrants' homelands are not cut off from the rest of the world once the immigrants have left; rather, homelands continue to change and interact with other countries in numerous ways as part of the global geopolitical tapestry. Indeed, as immigrants make return visits to their homelands, they find that as they themselves have changed while living abroad,[2] so, too, have the people, places, and societies they left behind.[3]

This analytical blind spot, which renders homelands as cohesive and unchanged, limits scholars from observing how geopolitics links the contexts of the sending society with not just the hostland but also beyond. For instance, the South Asian homelands and their ties with the hostland United States do not exist in a geopolitical vacuum. Located on the banks of the Indian Ocean, with China and Russia in the north and Afghanistan and Iran in the northwest, India, Pakistan, and Bangladesh occupy a strategic position in

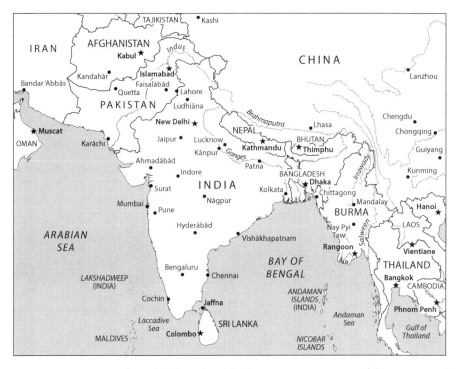

MAP 3.1. Map of Bangladesh, India, and Pakistan. *Source*: Courtesy of the University of Texas Libraries, University of Texas at Austin.

world politics. While it has its unique, autonomous dynamics, South Asia is also part of the larger geopolitical multiverse in which it is located, one that also includes the Middle East, and North, Central, and East Asia (see map 3.1). Its security and stability are directly linked with that of its surrounding regional giants—namely, China, Iran, Saudi Arabia, and Russia—explaining why global powers frequently jostle for influence in South Asia. Regardless of the presence or absence of those who were born citizens of the area, the South Asian homelands continue to maintain relationships with these various countries, many of which are or could become "elsewheres" for the immigrants in America. As will be shown, the nature of each country's relationship with certain "elsewheres" has historically influenced dynamics *within* and *between* Bangladesh, India, and Pakistan, with these homeland–"elsewhere" connections continuing to inform these country's nation-building projects. However, these ongoing struggles for nationhood are not limited to the homeland territories; they are also transported to the receiving societies, often through the immigrants themselves, who mirror these struggles within their ethnic communities and enclaves in the host society.[4] As such, this chapter will show how once they are "here," the immigrants' homeland-rooted identities gain new, global dimensions based on the hostland's interactions with "elsewhere."

## HOW ELSEWHERE HISTORICALLY INFORMED RELIGIOUS AND POLITICAL LIFE IN SOUTH ASIA

During their colonization of the Indian subcontinent for over two centuries, British administrators categorized their subjects based on religious affiliation—a system that differed from precolonial classifications.[5] They viewed Muslims and Hindus as "two separate communities with distinct political interests" and strategically developed different education, electorate, and civil-service policies for each group.[6] These divide-and-rule policies added political salience to the religious differences already existing between Muslims and Hindus.[7] As such, religion became a fundamental factor in constructing each group's nationalist ideas even as the entire subcontinent fought for independence from the British. Hindu-Muslim tensions heightened, imploding in the 1947 Partition of Bengal along religious lines as carved by the withdrawing British forces. India was predominantly Hindu, and West Pakistan and East Pakistan (now Bangladesh) comprised one Muslim state, although they were geographically separated, being located on either side of India. The Partition pitted these newly formed states against each other, instigating large-scale massacres and forced migrations of both Hindus and Muslims: Hindus fled from Pakistan to India, and Muslims from India to Pakistan. Memories of these atrocities fueled by religion remain in Indian, Pakistani, and Bangladeshi national consciousness to this day.[8]

After the partition, despite their common religious affiliation, East and West Pakistan considered themselves culturally, economically, politically, and ethnically different from one another. Culturally, East Pakistan aligned more with neighboring India than with West Pakistan located over 2,000 kilometers away. For instance, people in East Pakistan and the West Bengal region of India spoke predominantly in Bangla and shared similar tastes in food, fashion, literature, and music. However, the balance of power between

East and West Pakistan was in favor of the latter, leading East Pakistan to resist and claim economic and political emancipation. War ensued, during which time West Pakistan launched what East Pakistan claims was a systematic genocide against them. Ironically, West Pakistan justified the genocide of East Pakistanis on religious grounds, as they claimed to be saving the country's Islamic ideals from India's Hindu influence.[9] Then in 1971, after nine months of war, East Pakistanis gained their independence. Bangladesh was created, proclaiming to be an independent state based on democratic, secular ideals.

Despite sharing this legacy of British colonization, India, Pakistan, and Bangladesh continue to experience religion as a defining element in politics. In India, Narendra Modi, a Hindu nationalist, was re-elected as prime minister in a landslide victory in the 2019 national elections. In Pakistan, religion has a firm grip on social and political life as well, and the country struggles with sectarian conflicts and Islamist militancy. In Bangladesh, too, Islamism, specifically homegrown extremist groups with links to global terrorist networks, has steadily gained hold over politics and society.

In terms of inter-state relations, India and Pakistan are locked in a bitter military, political, and cultural rivalry. Only 14 percent of Pakistanis view India in a positive light, whereas only 14 percent of Indians view Pakistan favorably.[10] Frequent outbreaks of violence, such as in the 2008 Mumbai attacks by Pakistani Islamist militants,[11] amplify the historic hostility between the two nations. Both countries also repeatedly clash over the control of Kashmir, the effects of which reach immigrant communities. The birth of Bangladesh in 1971 also stands as a bitter moment in India-Pakistan relations. During the war, India provided military assistance to Bangladeshi liberation forces for its own geopolitical interest. The secession of Bangladesh from Pakistan meant that India's historic regional rival was dealt a significant blow, and India would no longer have to be concerned about Pakistan's presence on both sides of its border. Since the war ended, however, Bangladesh and India have often clashed. In addition to religious hostilities between the two countries, issues such as undocumented Bangladeshi immigrants in India and India's obstruction of shared water resources flowing into Bangladesh have produced anti-Indian sentiment among many sections of the Bangladeshi population. Bangladesh-Pakistan relations have not been smooth either. Only 13 percent of Bangladeshis view Pakistan favorably, reflecting the continuing significance of the 1971 war in Bangladeshi national consciousness.[12] Conversely, Pakistan has not forgotten the bitter episode of Bangladesh's secession. Adding further tension is the fact that Bangladesh and Pakistan differ widely on the number of Bangladeshi deaths in the 1971 war. Whereas Bangladesh argues 3 million people were killed in the hands of the Pakistani army, Pakistan chalks down the number from 50,000 to 100,000.[13]

Influence stemming from another "elsewhere"—the Middle East— complicates the religious and political landscape of these homelands even further. Cross-border connections between South Asia and the "elsewhere" Middle East go back centuries,[14] facilitated by the back-and-forth travel of tradesmen, conquerors, scholars, artisans, and, in more recent times, migrant laborers. These forms of exchange have transformed both regions. For the Middle East, a sizeable portion of its migrant labor—a vital resource for its rapid infrastructural development—comes from India, Pakistan, and Bangladesh.[15] And for South Asia, the effects of its connections with the Middle East penetrate not only its economy but also other areas of life, notably religion. Bangladesh, for example, sends almost half of its stock of 7.7 million migrant workers to the Middle East, in return receiving over $14 billion in remittances.[16] This huge migrant force, upon their return, brings with them a diversified body of religious knowledge, which they then transfuse into their social surroundings through interactions with friends, neighbors, and others.[17] For instance, many Bangladeshi migrant laborers returning from Saudi Arabia view themselves as "agents of religious change," bringing Islamic practices in Bangladesh in line with the observations they made while abroad in "the land of Allah."[18]

Regionally, as well, influence from Arab countries has transformed South Asia's Islamic infrastructure. Historically, the Indian subcontinent has had many Muslim rulers, most notably the Mughals, but they were often isolated from the rest of the Muslim world and had to wage war with other Muslim sultans in the region.[19] Moreover, because the number of Muslims in the subcontinent came second to that of Hindus, the Muslim sultans were reliant on the loyalty of a vast body of non-Muslim subjects. Among the general population, there was a lot of cultural mixing between Hindus and Muslims, with Hindus often visiting the graves of Sufi masters and Muslims leaving offerings at Hindu temples.[20] In this context, the Muslim rulers mostly maintained religious tolerance over the region's multireligious population while also cultivating a new form of religious culture based on Arab and Persian traditions.[21] As such, the Islam that evolved in South Asia syncretized elements from Hinduism and local cultural beliefs, such as the visiting of shrines and the graves of holy men, the incorporation of music into worship, and the meditative practices influenced by yoga, which were not sanctioned in mainstream interpretations of Islam.

However, with Saudi Arabia's global export of Wahhabism,[22] influence of this puritanical strand of Islam began to grow over Islam in South Asia, particularly through vast donations made by the Saudi government, individuals, charities, and organizations to the region's mosques and *madrassas* (Islamic schools).[23] In 2017, for instance, Saudi Arabia reportedly agreed to donate almost $1 billion to Bangladesh for the construction of 560 mosques—one in every town—and one permanent campus for the Islamic Arabic University in Dhaka, the country's capital.[24] These numbers are important because, in addition to teaching a fundamentalist version of Islam, Wahhabi-funded mosques and *madrassas* are used for financing *jihadi* networks in South Asia, such as Al Qaeda, the Taliban, and Lashkar-e-Taiba.[25] Students inculcated in these mosques and *madrassas* organized into the powerful fundamentalist organization in Bangladesh called Hefazat-e-Islam, which acts as an Islamist pressure group in Bangladeshi politics.[26] The Bangladeshi government, wishing not to butt heads with the country's increasingly powerful Islamist influence, generally chooses to peacefully negotiate with Hefazat leaders. For example, in 2017, the Ministry of Education, in an effort to accommodate the demands of Islamist hard-liners, acquiesced to Hefazat's demand to remove stories and poems from textbooks written by and Hindu and perceived atheist writers.[27]

"Elsewhere" influence in South Asia's religious infrastructure has been especially consequential for Pakistan, which is struggling with the increasingly challenging problem of Islamist militancy. Among the three homelands, Pakistan has had particularly close ties with Saudi Arabia based on both their common geopolitical goals and religious ideologies.[28] Saudi Arabia claims to be the custodian of Islam and Islam's holiest sites. And Pakistan is the only country in the world that was created as a state exclusively for Muslims (unlike Bangladesh, which, although a predominantly Muslim country, was founded upon secular ideals). Geopolitically, Saudi Arabia has vested interests in Pakistan, which shares borders with Iran, Saudi Arabia's long-time nemesis in both religious and political affairs. Saudi Arabia sees Sunni-majority Pakistan as its key ally in countering the Shia-majority Iran's growing influence in South Asia.[29] As such, Saudi Arabia supported Pakistan's turn toward Islamization, and, perhaps most notably, financed its nuclear weapons, making Pakistan the only Muslim country to possess them.

The South Asian immigrants in this book came to the United States from this national and regional context. Once here, in America's post-9/11 terror-panic climate, these immigrants, already "strangers in a strange land," come under further scrutiny when exogenous shocks bring their homeland's Middle East connections into sharp focus. Next, I unpack just how each homeland's "elsewhere" interactions come to shape its emigrants' sense of selves in the hostland.

## ELSEWHERE-HOMELAND DYNAMICS REACHING ACROSS BORDERS
### Pakistan

The 9/11 terror attacks were an exogenous shock for Pakistan, one that also left a lasting impact on Pakistan-U.S. relations. The relationship between the two countries generally rests on strategic mutual dependence. Pakistan relies heavily on U.S. foreign aid for its domestic development, and America needs Pakistan as an ally given the latter's geographical location along Afghanistan's southern border. After 9/11, the Pakistani army supported the United States in its War on Terror and fought the Taliban and Al Qaeda in the Afghanistan-Pakistan corridor. However, Pakistan's alliance with the United States came at a hefty price for Pakistan's own domestic and regional interests. The Pakistani army's opposition to Al Qaeda meant open conflict with Pakistan's Islamist political power base, which it needed in order to use militant *jihadi* groups for managing Afghanistan and the Kashmir conflict with India. Further, Pakistan's Islamist militant groups were becoming increasingly difficult to control with Saudi Arabia and other Gulf countries providing them support. In recent years, Al Qaeda, still entrenched in Afghanistan and Pakistan despite having suffered heavy blows since 2001, has been working closely with the Taliban, unifying Pakistan's myriad militant groups under a "global *Jihad*."[30]

These connections between Pakistan's internal dynamics and global Islamist terrorism have affected Pakistan's national image on a global scale, and in so doing have affected the lives of its emigrants abroad. Indeed, Pakistan's national image over the years has become intricately tied to its history of Islamist politics and militancy, to its ethnic and sectarian conflicts, and to its role in global geopolitics, particularly those involving the United States in the context of the War on Terror.[31] Many Americans view Pakistan as a "safe haven" for terrorists. In January 2018, President Trump accused Pakistan of being exactly that and froze the U.S. foreign aid that Pakistan vitally needed.[32] But the event that brought Pakistan's connections to Islamist groups into perhaps the sharpest focus in the American mind-set was when U.S. Navy SEALs found Osama bin Laden hiding in one of Pakistan's most fortified cities. The event made world news but also led the two countries to point fingers of blame at each other. Whereas America accused Pakistan of knowing about bin Laden's presence in their country and intentionally hiding that information from them, Pakistan denied these accusations, instead blaming the United States for violating Pakistan's sovereignty. This distrust also permeated into public opinion in both countries: as a result, 74 percent of Pakistanis viewed the United States as an enemy[33] and more than half of the population disapproved of the United States entering Pakistani territory to kill bin Laden.[34] Meanwhile, just 10 percent of Americans believed that the United States could trust Pakistan.[35]

The Pakistani Americans I observed shared many of their compatriots' views of America. Inside a crowded coffee shop I interviewed Atif, a college student, who spoke to me at length about his experiences immigrating from Pakistan and settling into American society. When the interview flowed into politics, Atif shared his views on American intervention in Muslim countries. Interestingly, whenever a reference to bin Laden came up, Atif would not say his name. Instead, he would nod suggestively, referring to him as "the guy" or "that person." The coffee shop was packed with students and the tables were close to each other, so it was easy to overhear what folks at the surrounding tables were saying. As such, I gathered that Atif did not want to draw attention to himself by uttering bin Laden's name. He said,

> I don't support that part of their [America's] foreign policy, especially
> towards Muslim countries. . . . I don't agree with them [Americans][36]

breaching other countries' sovereignty, especially with the killing of that person [Osama bin Laden]. . . . They [Americans] didn't necessarily have to breach into a city thirty miles away from the capital of the country. That's sort of an act of war, if you think about it.

At an event organized by the Pakistani Students Association in 2015, it was evident that Pakistanis here were in sync with the views back home regarding U.S. foreign policy toward Pakistan. The event was a talk given by a young Pakistani lawyer and activist on sectarian conflicts in Pakistan. It was widely advertised in the campus *desi* community. Although I arrived thirty minutes late, people were still trickling into the huge auditorium. As I made my way to the back of the packed room, I noticed many familiar faces, mostly Pakistani students but also a few Indians and Bangladeshis. There were also older men and women who came from outside the campus. Most of the audience was dressed in *salwar kamiz*[37] and *kurta*,[38] some in green, the color of Pakistan's flag. The presentation had already started, and the audience was listening with rapt attention. Many nodded vigorously while others were wide-eyed at the pictures of violence being projected on the screen. Several hands shot up as soon as the floor was opened for discussion. The audience members, both young and old, expressed unhappiness and anger toward Pakistan's political leadership. One commented that although the War on Terror was a global event, it took place on Pakistani soil, thus impeding the country's development further. Another member of the audience, a young girl in a red and gold *salwar kamiz*, remarked that the war against Al Qaeda allowed the United States to "interfere" with Pakistani politics. A young man in a black *kurta* followed up her comment, saying that this had always been the case, and he gave the example of the time when "the Americans left us to deal with the drug problem after the Afghan war."

Yet, despite this show of collective resentment toward the United States, the views of many Pakistani Americans toward their hostland are not as negative as those of their compatriots back home. For instance, Alam, a college freshman, grew up in a political family in Pakistan. He claimed to have been brought up in close contact with the country's political elites, giving him an insider's view into both the "corruption" and the "sincere attempts to bring development" to his homeland. His family was conservative, and Alam himself was very religious. He prayed five times a day, recited verses from the Quran regularly, and considered Islam to be "a complete guide" and his "moral compass." A proud Pakistani, Alam came to America as an adult with the view that the United States is "anti-Islamic" and that "Americans generally do not like Muslims." His first real exposure to American society, however, was in college, and he was pleasantly surprised to find his campus to be "very inclusive of diversity" because he had not been "discriminated for being Muslim." "If they hear I am Pakistani or I am Muslim," he said, "they become curious—in a good way. Like, they want to know more about my culture." What most impressed Alam about America was its "law and order." In his characteristically heavy accent, Alam exclaimed,

> I say America is more Islamic than Pakistan! . . . You can say you are an Islamic country and that most people are Muslim. But you have to establish order [in the way] it is [prescribed] in Islam to be really Islamic. In America, there is law and order—look at the nature, everywhere it is beautiful, and I see Allah's grace in this country. Like, even if a big name does crime, he will go to jail. The level of corruption in the government is very low than Pakistan. I feel like this is the kind of order with justice and equality that is in Islam.

This is what happens when many immigrants, like Alam, arrive from foreign lands to make new lives. Immigrants do not always echo only the opinions of their co-ethnics back home; rather, they become a conduit through which the two societies of origin and reception meet. Regardless of the assumptions that immigrants bring from their countries of origin regarding the hostland, their first real exposure to the hostland happens only after they enmesh themselves in their new surroundings. Now far from the confines of their homelands' dominant perceptions of the hostland, the immigrants begin to evaluate their new environment for themselves. And as they do, they often find many of their preconceived notions about the hostland inaccurate. Conversely, they also change how many in the hostland view the sending countries (such as when Alam informs his peers about Pakistan). Through this process of societal contact, the immigrants' (and the natives') worldviews both expand and diversify. In the process, immigrants both transform and are transformed, as they become more similar to the people in their new society and more different from the people they have left behind.

"Elsewhere" dynamics complicate this process of societal interconnection by adding another layer: the global dimension of a sending country's national image. For example, a question that Alisha, a second-generation Pakistani and healthcare assistant, regularly encounters from patients is where she is "originally from"—her *hijab* and ethnic facial features are a giveaway of her "foreign-ness" and "Muslim-ness," despite her milky-pale complexion. In one such instance, after she replied that she was originally from Pakistan, a patient asked, "So, do you practice Sharia law?" Alisha replied that she tries to lead an Islamic lifestyle. The patient then asked, "Do you drive?" Alisha laughed and said that it is in Saudi Arabia, not Pakistan, where women are not allowed to drive.[39] She further explained that it is Saudi law, not Sharia law,[40] that restricts women from getting behind the wheel. "The Quran doesn't mention cars," she had quipped. While Alisha had shared this story with me in easy laughter, not all instances she remembered were as light-hearted. For example, another patient once said to her, "I don't know if you mind, but what do you think of ISIS?" This was a question that multiple Pakistani respondents reported to have heard at one time or another. Another recurring question that many Pakistani respondents heard from their American friends was about whether they were safe during their trips to Pakistan.

Although usually asked with friendly concern or open curiosity, these questions reveal an underlying assumption about Pakistan's global image in American society: that Pakistan is a "Muslim" place just like Saudi Arabia and other ISIS-controlled territories in the Middle East, all of them seemingly backward and dangerous places that practice the Sharia law. This conflation of Pakistan with other "dangerous" Muslim countries puts Pakistanis in a collectively precarious position, where they are expected to answer for violence in Muslim countries that are not their homeland.

Many of the respondents viewed the media as partly responsible for perpetuating a violent image of Pakistan to Americans through its selective coverage of their homeland's sectarian and Islamist conflicts. This media-filtered global national image also influenced how some young Pakistanis who grew up in America viewed their ancestral homeland. Anwar, for instance, was born in Pakistan, but came to the United States with his family when he was around five years old. He claimed to be proud of his Pakistani American identity, which he maintained by speaking Urdu fluently and flying home to his parents' homes in

Karachi and Lahore every two to three years. Yet, he said he sometimes caught himself having "biased views" of Pakistan, biases he felt he had internalized while growing up watching American media. He recalled one incident during his visit to Lahore that particularly made him realize his biases:

> I remember seeing a white, blonde British woman in Pakistan. I was horrified for her—because of the fear that was ingrained in me—and I was like, "Oh, my God, what are you doing?" I was actually sitting by her in a movie theater, and I was like, "Can I ask you a question?" And she was like, "Yeah." And I was like, "I am from the U.S. I am a college student. I hope it's not a weird question to ask you, but do you feel unsafe here?" And she was like, "I have been living here for the last nine years." I had to then check my understanding of reality, because that wasn't the answer I was expecting. I was expecting her to say something like, "I am a hostage—save me!" Hahaha! And I would be like, "Okay, let's get you back." I realized then that that's not how the whole country is. Yes, there is terrorism. Yes, the government is corrupt. But the people of Pakistan are some of the best people in the world. And that the violence is contained only within a certain region.

Whereas to Sunni Pakistanis, like Anwar, violence in Pakistan generally meant Islamist militancy in the border areas, to Shias, a minority severely persecuted in Pakistan,[41] violence was found anywhere in the country. As Nargis, a Shia Pakistani American, described it, "Your male relatives can go to the mosque on a Friday and not come back because it was blown up in a bomb or someone attacked the people praying inside." Although rooted in a centuries-old schism in Islam, tensions and proxy wars between Saudi Arabia, the Sunni global power, and its Shia rival Iran have added more potency to Pakistan's sectarian conflict. Even in America, where Sunnis and Shias face the same kind of Islamophobic hostility, Pakistan's history of Shia persecution has led the second-generation Shia Pakistani respondents to view their ancestral homeland and their "Muslim" identity differently from their Sunni peers.[42] These immigrants grew up listening to stories of persecution from their relatives here and back home, from their Imams at the Shia mosques, and from news online. These stories and recurring outbreaks of violence back home shaped their worldviews of Shias' collective position in homeland politics, global dynamics, and the *Ummah*.

These variations in homeland experiences sometimes led the Shia and Sunni Pakistani participants to have different "elsewheres." Whereas Saudi Arabia stood as a prominent "elsewhere" for Sunnis, foreign places with predominantly Shia populations (such as Iran) or places with ongoing conflicts involving Shias (such as Malaysia) were salient as "elsewheres" for the Shia respondents. For example, Rashed, a first-generation Shia Pakistani immigrant, said,

> Shias are very critical of Muslims for the fact that, collectively, they talk about the oppression they are facing in America for being Muslims, but they don't address the oppression that they themselves impose on Shias in the lands that they call Muslim countries, you know? . . . In Malaysia it is *illegal* to be a Shia. In Saudi Arabia, they are putting a teenager to death because he criticized the government's inactions to provide for Shias who are the minority community. . . . We [Shias] have faced the oppression historically. Wherever Shias were the minority, they were mostly the subject of oppression. . . . It opens your eyes to the world.

During my fieldwork, I did not once hear my Sunni participants mention either Malaysia or Iran. And when they did mention Saudi Arabia, its salience had little to do with the country's treatment of its Shia citizens. But for Rashed, Nargis, and Arifa, Malaysia and Saudi Arabia were prominent examples of places that represented Shia's collective victimhood in the global *Ummah*. With regard to Iran, all three Shia respondents compared their homeland experiences as minorities to those of Iranian Americans. Arifa, for example, believed that, whereas Shia Pakistanis in America were more attached to their sectarian identity, Iranians were more attached to their Iranian identities. "In Iran, them [Iranian Americans] being Shia is not under attack," Arifa said. "So, they don't feel like they have to preserve and maintain that cultural relevance [of being Shia]."

### Bangladesh

Bangladeshis living in the United States face a unique challenge when it comes to grappling with their homeland's global national image. Henry Kissinger infamously labeled Bangladesh as an "international basket case"[43]—an image that Bangladeshi Americans have not only been unsuccessful in shaking off, but one that has gained more import over the years in light of related news that made world headlines. A casual online search for recent news on Bangladesh in the major American newspapers generated headlines on the 2013 collapse of the Rana Plaza garment factory, the 2016 ISIS attacks in Dhaka, the never-ending traffic jams in Dhaka's streets, and the dismal conditions of the country's Rohingya refugee camps. Simultaneously, Bangladeshi Americans are often rendered invisible in U.S. society, seldom recognized because they are typically lumped together with co-ethnics from their homeland's more powerful neighbors, India and Pakistan.[44]

In this context, Bangladeshi Americans cherish the few symbols of national pride that are globally recognized, such as the 2006 Nobel Peace Laureate, Dr. Muhammad Yunus, and his microfinance organization Grameen Bank. However, these symbols are not immune from Bangladesh's often-turbulent party politics,[45] a regular topic of conversation when Bangladeshis (particularly those of the first generation) get together. In fact, this was the theme of a conversation I overheard some men having at a Bangladeshi *dawat*. The food was yet to be served, and guests were chatting in the living room. Although I had to sit with the women, according to the gender norms, I tried to listen to the men, who were seated at the opposite end of the room. They appeared to be talking about Bangladeshi politics based on the snippets of conversation I overheard: words and phrases like "Hasina" (the Bangladeshi prime minister's name) and *"Arey na na ki boltesen? Ekdom corrupt"* (No, no, what are you saying? Fully corrupt.) made their way to my corner of the room. At one point, their conversation grew louder and more heated. One of them appeared agitated and said, *"Bangladesh er pokkheyi shombhob. Grameen Bank—koi eita ke aro government protection dibey, pura prithibir kachhe amra eita ke niye gorbo kore bolte pari. Nah! Eita ke ekke barey boshay dilo! Hasina eita ke niye pochayei chharlo!"* (It is only possible for Bangladesh. Grameen Bank—the government—should be protecting it. We can tell the world proudly about it. But, no! The government had to completely ruin it! Hasina just had to take Grameen Bank and make it all rotten!)

In July 2016, however, Bangladesh made world news when five young Bangladeshi men, after pledging allegiance to ISIS, killed twenty people at a café in Dhaka's prestigious diplomatic district. Among the victims were three American college students. Mainstream U.S. news outlets extensively covered the attack and interpreted the event as ISIS now shifting its focus to

Muslim countries beyond the Middle East.[46] The effects of the event were felt among the Bangladeshi Americans I was observing. Their almost immediate reaction was to contact loved ones back home to ensure their safety. I, too, received phone calls and messages from other Bangladeshis, checking in to see if my relatives in Dhaka were safe. Some first-generation immigrants took note of how the media was covering the story and its implications on how Bangladesh was being portrayed to the American audience. Some wondered what the repercussions might be with Bangladesh's name now associated with ISIS. A few grew frustrated over CNN's coverage of the story "all day long." To them, the more the media covered the ISIS attack, the more their homeland became associated with Islamist terrorism in the American public mind-set.

At the organizational level, the Bangladesh Unity Federation of Los Angeles (BUFLA), the largest Bangladeshi organization in the city, issued a press release. It condemned violence in the name of Islam and highlighted verses from the Quran that forbade religious coercion and the killing of innocents— the usual strategies that many Muslims are forced to adopt following Islamist terrorist attacks to preempt Islamophobic backlash. Interestingly, in addition to presenting Bangladeshi Americans as peace-loving, BUFLA distanced the diaspora from the homeland, which it described as being in "turmoil":

> Bangladesh Unity Federation of Los Angeles condemns the act of terrorism in Bangladesh and offers out heartfelt condolences to the victims of this horrific tragedy in Dhaka.
>
> We have written too many condolences on this issue alone and frankly are sick of it. I am sure the whole Bangladeshi diaspora is, but there is no denying now that the country is in turmoil. We are all united in our stance that DAESH[47] or whoever claimed the responsibility is not representing us Muslims in any shape or form. Islam is a Religion of Peace, and anyone saying or acting otherwise neither is related to Islam and Muslims, nor speak for the religion of Islam.
>
> If you are Muslim—you cannot terrorize the general population, and if you are a terrorist—you cannot be a Muslim. Islam and Terrorism are mutually exclusive of each other. Here are some of the examples in Quran which specifically forbids killing of innocents and coercing people to become Muslims—as is being done by DAESH in Iraq and Syria.[48]

The ISIS-inspired attack renewed the ambition of Bangladesh's ingrown Islamist militants, triggering pinpoint assassinations of any perceived critics of Islam, a category that included secular bloggers, atheists, Hindus, academics, and homosexuals. These brutal killings, too, made their way to American news outlets. Some Bangladeshi Americans lamented over the direction of Bangladeshi politics, while others felt a sense of resignation, given the country's history of corrupt political regimes. Most of the reactions, however, came from the first generation. On social media, the 1.5 and second generations were largely silent about the attacks—a silence that was quite noticeable, given that this demographic usually commented enthusiastically on these platforms in regard to Muslim-related politics. Their silence did not go unnoticed even by some young Bangladeshi Americans. In a text conversation on the night of the July 2016 attack, Shopna—a *hijabi* second-generation Bangladeshi—said, "I'm very glad that your family members are okay and *Alhamdulillah* mine are too. But I'm feeling very affected by this today. I'm also disappointed because certain people who always post about these things on social media are for some reason silent today."

In December 2017, Bangladeshi Americans again faced unwelcome attention when a Bangladeshi immigrant named Akayed Ullah set off a low-tech bomb in New York City's subway system. He had entered the United States in 2011 through an "extended family chain migration."[49] He had reportedly been radicalizing since 2014 and, in 2017, conducted the attack for ISIS.[50] Although he was the only one injured, the Bangladeshi community in New York feared an Islamophobic backlash.[51] Indeed, soon after the attack, President Trump tweeted about how "chain migration" allowed national security threats like Akayed Ullah to enter the country, using the event to propagate closed borders. Noticeably, Bangladeshi Americans again largely responded with silence on social media. *Why* that has been the case on both occasions is but one piece of a larger puzzle, which I explain later.

### India

Of the three homelands, India is the only country where Muslims are a minority.[52] And yet, this minority is comprised of 180 million Muslims who are at the crux of many political conflicts in India. According to India's common law, a remnant of British colonization, each religious community is to be governed by its own codes of personal law. However, this often pits Hindus and Muslims against each other because of their respective traditions. For example, Hindus believe cows are holy, but Muslims sacrifice cows in the name of Allah on *Eid*. Since Hindu nationalist leader Narendra Modi became prime minister in 2008, this issue of Muslims sacrificing cows has become especially charged as a source of anti-Muslim violence and as seeming justification of Muslims' "unassimilability" in India. Indeed, more than three-quarters of the Indian public perceive Muslims as "extremists" and "outsiders," and as somehow less committed to India as a nation than Hindus.[53] Using the issue of cow sacrifice as an example, a *New York Times* report[54] gave an eye-opening account of the overall condition of the Muslim minority in India. It reported that the punishment for cow slaughter proscribed in many Indian villages had become more severe because of aggressive campaigns run by Prime Minister Modi's party affiliates and foot soldiers. A conviction for this crime, for instance, could lead to anywhere from a five-year prison term to life imprisonment. Even more alarmingly, it reported that Muslims were frequently lynched for receiving an accusation of possessing beef and for ferrying home cattle purchased legitimately from markets outside the villages. In addition to mandating that Indian Muslims give up beef, these campaigns also demanded that they "not date or marry" Hindu women and, instead, "reconvert" to Hinduism, because their ancestors were allegedly Hindus forced to convert to Islam under the rule of medieval Muslim kings.[55] Moreover, Muslims were now required to sing "*Vande Mataram*," India's national anthem, "to prove their loyalty to India." The report continued, saying that Muslim children were required to perform yoga in schools to show respect for India's culture. And as reparation for allegedly demolishing temples to build mosques, affiliates of Modi's party, the Bharatiya Janata Party (BJP), said, "Muslims in modern, democratic India should voluntarily hand over various mosques and shrines to the Hindus."[56]

India's Hindu-Muslim tensions drew a palpable boundary in the South Asian community in Los Angeles. For example, Liana, a second-generation Bangladeshi Muslim, was a college senior about to apply to a psychology graduate program. She wore a *hijab*, in her own words, on an "on-and-off basis." The previous summer she had worked at an Indian restaurant for a few weeks, where she directly encountered the line that separated her from the Indian Hindu customers. She recalled,

> Over the summer I had a job at an Indian restaurant . . . during Ramadan. . . . The owner is Hindu . . . [but] the person who was training me was a Muslim and she didn't have a *hijab* on. . . . After a few days of training, the Muslim worker pulled me to the side and told me, "Do you mind taking your *hijab* off?" I was very confused and asked her why. And she was like, "Oh, because a lot of customers have complained, Hindu customers, that they don't like being served by a Muslim person."

The history of Hindu-Muslim riots in India affected, with particular force, the worldviews of Indian Muslim American families whose relatives were *Mahajirs* (emigrants forced to flee to Pakistan from India after the partition). Although the first-generation Indian Muslims maintained relations with Indian Hindus, their primary relationships remained largely within *Muslim* South Asian communities, comprised mostly of Pakistanis. For these Indian Muslims' children and grandchildren, who were born and raised in the United States, these historical conflicts largely lost their edge. These descendants learned their homeland's history by listening to stories told by their parents or grandparents, interpreting it with a globally informed but U.S.-centric lens. These ways of viewing history differently have sometimes led to intergenerational arguments. Hamid, a second-generation Indian Muslim, for instance, often had debates with his grandfather about his friendships with Hindus. His grandfather would comment sarcastically, *"Ha, ha, ajkaal toh Hindu Musalman sabh bhai bhai hai."* (Yes, yes, today Hindu and Muslim are all brothers.) And, Hamid would retort by asking him where the brotherly love among Muslims had gone, given the many examples of Muslims killing Muslims around the world. Nonetheless, some communal tensions still percolated among the 1.5 and second generations. The handful of Indian Muslim students I observed said that they often felt sidelined or excluded in the predominantly Hindu Indian student organizations because of those groups' Hindu-centric themes. Hamid, for instance, recalled how both the Indian and South Asian student associations at his campus began their cultural events with Hindu rituals like *aarti* and coconut-breaking.[57] Feeling thus symbolically excluded, Muslims, even those who were Indian, rarely attended those events, choosing to instead participate more actively in events organized by the Pakistani and Muslim student associations.

This Hindu-Muslim divide from the homeland gains global dimensions in the hostland based on "elsewhere" dynamics (see figure 3.4). Regardless of their religious background, Indian immigrants bring with them the homeland Hindu-Muslim conflict when they come to America. However, here, the sociopolitical context is much different from that at home. The society here is resolutely more multicultural than in India, with immigrants from all parts of the world calling the United States their home. At the same time, America is at a geopolitical and ideological war with the "the Muslim world." Events such as 9/11 and the War on Terror, and exogenous shocks such as ISIS attacks and the Syrian refugee crisis have greatly impacted how the society here views "outsiders," both those who are Muslims and those who are perceived as such. Moreover, Hindus here are not the dominant majority. Adding insult to injury, rather, they are perceived to be the same as Muslims, causing them to face the same post-9/11 terror-panic climate as their historic rivals from back home.[58]

This lumping together of Hindus and Muslims has obvious racial undertones, as the indicators to determine one's Muslim-ness are too often one's skin color, ethnic physical features, Muslim-sounding name, facial hair, foreign accent, and clothing (e.g., turbans, scarves, and head coverings). In this racialized hostland context, "Muslim" not only connotes a religious identity but also operates as a racial category that homogenizes South Asians with Arabs, Middle Easterners, North Africans, and blacks, all of who fall on a wide spectrum of physical appearances. Notably, the category also includes "Muslim-looking" non-Muslims, such as Hindus, Sikhs, Christians and Jewish Middle Easterners, and agnostics.[59]

Rather than causing Hindus and Muslims to unite against this common hostility, the categorical backlash against Muslims and Muslim-looking groups has added more fuel to the Hindu-Muslim divide. Whereas, to distance themselves from the Muslim terrorist stereotype, South Asian immigrants generally put on an "American identity"—such as displaying American flags, putting patriotic bumper stickers on their cars, shaving off facial hair, and avoiding the *hijab* in risky situations[60]—for Hindu Americans particularly, putting on such an identity entails highlighting their *Hindu*-ness. For instance, many Hindu Indian American organizations overemphasize an anti-Muslim agenda, often justifying and legitimizing militant Hindu nationalism in a way that could appeal to Americans at large.[61]

These impression-management strategies do not solely mirror a homeland divide but are also carefully crafted to create pathways for Hindu Indians to engage in U.S. politics[62]—a reason at the heart of why Hindu nationalists overwhelmingly supported Trump. His inflammatory rhetoric against Muslims overlapped with the anti-Muslim sentiments incited by Narendra Modi in his rise to becoming India's Prime Minister.[63] As such, Hindu nationalists viewed Trump's confrontational approach toward Muslims and Islamist terrorism as beneficial for their nationalist politics against both the Muslim minority in India and in their regional rival Pakistan.[64] In the hostland, Hindu nationalist support served an additional purpose—to collectively and visibly distance Hindus from Muslims.

The example of "Hindus for Trump," a coalition of Hindu nationalists in America, illustrates these dynamics clearly.[65] In October 2016 the Republican Hindu Coalition organized a benefit event in New Jersey called Humanity United against Terror. Staying true to the name, the theme of the event was terror threats. The proceeds were to be donated to the Hindu victims of Islamist terror in Kashmir and Bangladesh.[66] The chief guest was none other than Donald Trump who, in his speech, claimed to be "a big fan of Hindu" and "a big fan of India."[67] Imagery depicting Trump as a Hindu nationalist proliferated in the huge event arena. At various places stood posters in which Trump was photoshopped sitting in a yoga pose on a red-white-and-blue lotus flower. Splashed across the lotus flower was the Sanskrit word *Om* (a sacred sound and spiritual icon in Hinduism) in the colors of the American flag (see figure 3.1).[68] The image was clearly an attempt to combine symbols of "American-ness," such as the red-white-and-blue color scheme and the American flag, with Hindu nationalism, the lotus flower being a religious symbol in Hinduism and the official symbol of the BJP.

Those attending the event were handed fliers that, in sharp contrast to Trump's peaceful and holy depiction on the posters, painted Hillary Clinton and Sonia Gandhi, Trump and Modi's respective opponents in the

**FIGURE 3.1.** Poster from the Hindus for Trump fundraiser. The image was also used as the profile picture for the Hindus for Trump Facebook community page, which was used to campaign for Trump during the 2016 U.S. presidential election. *Source*: Hindus for Trump Facebook Group 2015a.

American and Indian elections, as evil creatures with protruding horns (see figure 3.2).

The highlight of the event was a Bollywood dance performance. The dance began with Bruce Springsteen's song "Born in the USA," with the dancers waving American flags. After a few notes the segment segued to two couples waltzing to a romantic melody as red hearts were projected on the mega screen behind them. Abruptly, their dance came to a halt as a group of dancers dressed as *"Jihadis"* in beige *thobes* (traditional Arab attire) broke onto the stage with lightsaber-like laser weapons, yelling Arabic-sounding words. The background music resembled an *azan*, the Islamic call to prayer. The *"Jihadis"* laughed villainously, pointing their weapons at the two terrified couples. Then suddenly, dancers dressed as Hindu Navy SEALs burst onto the stage to fight off the *"Jihadis"* and save the day. Finally, the performance

**FIGURE 3.2.** Flier from the Hindus for Trump fundraiser. *Source:* Hindus for Trump Facebook Group 2015b.

ended with the "Star-Spangled Banner" playing loudly in the background, as the dancers, some costumed in SWAT vests and others in civilian clothing, stood solemnly, with their hands over their hearts. Behind them on the screen was an image of the American flag waving slowly in the wind.[69] Right on cue, Trump then entered the stage with rapturous cheers from the audience. Replicating the Hindu ritual for starting an important ceremony, he lit a *diya* (candle). In his speech, keeping in tune with the dramatic dance performance, Trump drew parallels between Islamist terror attacks in India and the United States, clearly catering to his Hindu nationalist fanbase.

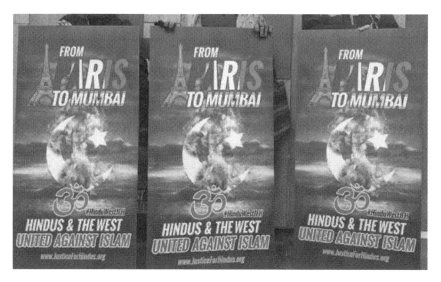

**FIGURE 3.3.** Poster used by protesters at a Justice for Hindus rally. The picture has been modified from the original to protect protesters' anonymity. *Source*: Hindus for Trump blog 2020.

On another occasion, this time at a rally in front of Trump Tower, members of Hindus for Trump staged a peaceful demonstration, asking Trump to "save" Hindus and Hindu refugees in Bangladesh, Pakistan, and India. In that demonstration, members drew attention to Islamist terror attacks "from Paris to Mumbai," holding banners that said in bold letters, "Hindus and the West united against Islam" (see figure 3.3). The intended messages of both the benefit event in New Jersey and the demonstration in New York were similar: (1) Muslims—whether Pakistani, Bangladeshi, or Arab—are potential terrorists who pose a global threat (i.e., "from Paris to Mumbai"); (2) Hindus are non-Muslims; and (3) Unlike Muslims, Hindus are peaceful and loyal citizens of the United States, united with "the West" in its war against Islam. Together, these examples of Hindus for Trump show that the scope of the Hindu-Muslim divide is no longer contained within India. Rather, the perimeters of the conflict have now expanded to include U.S. sociopolitics as well as Muslim-related geopolitics that involve the homeland and "elsewhere," such Europe and the Middle East.

### ELSEWHERE DIMENSIONS OF PANETHNIC
### SOUTH ASIAN IDENTITIES

For many Indian Americans who are Muslim, their Hindu compatriots' support for and eagerness to glorify Donald Trump as a stalwart barricade against Islamist terrorism highlighted their own "outsider" status as Muslims in the United States—and in their own homeland. This sense of "otherness" sometimes meant that Indian Muslim Americans formed communities with Muslims from *other* South Asian nationalities. Indeed, the Indian Muslims I observed came from communities that were predominantly Pakistani or Bangladeshi. This is not to say that they did not have any Indian Hindu friends. On the contrary, the college-going Indian Muslims had several Hindu friends; however, their close-friend circles and the *desi* communities in which their families engaged were predominantly composed of Muslims from South Asian nationalities other than Indian Hindu. Moreover, whereas the younger Indian Muslim Americans were open to marriage across ethnic and racial lines, they strongly preferred to marry other Muslims. Indeed, two of the five Indian Muslims I interviewed married Muslims with Pakistani heritage; another was in a committed long-term relationship with a Bangladeshi. At the organizational level as well, Muslims' marginalized status in India, along with the symbolic exclusion of Muslims in Indian community associations (which tend to be predominantly Hindu) and political support for U.S. Islamophobia from Hindu nationalists, push many Indian Muslim Americans to make panethnic relationships with Muslims from other nationalities in America (figure 3.4).

The subcontinent's colonized past, however, continues to inform South Asian Americans' collective consciousness long after they have arrived in their new country. And this sense of shared homeland experience is prevalent even among those born and raised in the United States. For instance, one of Alisha's (a Pakistani American's) favorite television shows is the BBC period drama *Downton Abbey*. "Why do you like it so much?" I once asked. "It makes me reminisce about the good old days when everything was so quaint and proper, haha!" she replied. Moments later, however, she said, "This is so insidious though. It [the show] gives this wonderful impression about the British Empire—even *I* am reminiscing about the good old days, and my ancestors were being oppressed and colonized [by the British] at the time!"

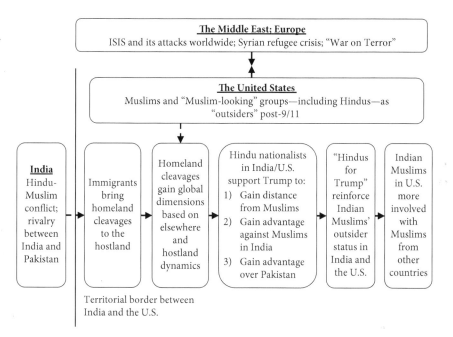

**FIGURE 3.4.** Global dimensions of Hindu-Muslim tensions in the multicentered relational framework. *Source:* Created by the author.

These echoes from the past are at times a source of struggle in the ethnic community as some attempt to draw boundaries between themselves and other (white) Americans. *"Gori mem"* is Hindi for "white lady," an expression used in colonial times by natives of the subcontinent to refer to British officers' female relations. It still carries negative connotations among South Asians. The few male Indian American and Pakistani American interviewees who publicly dated white women told me that *"desi* aunties"—a term that young participants often used for older South Asian women who they viewed as purveyors of community gossip—reproachfully referred to their white girlfriends as *"gori mem."* Even though the girlfriends were American and not British, that the aunties used this expression reflects how many *desis* continue to understand their world using a post-colonial lens. In this view, sometimes "American" and "British" have the same meaning—they both implicitly mean "white outsiders," people who are different from *desis.*

South Asians' shared homeland experience is also a source of solidarity as particularistic national borders lose relevance over time in the face of new, hostland contexts. The identification of South Asian Americans with the secular, diasporic label *"desi"* serves as a prominent example. Prevalent in several South Asian languages, the word *"desi"* describes anyone from *des*, or the homeland. It is a panethnic label, as *des* refers to the Indian subcontinent at large, subsuming its many national and ethnic divisions. In a diverse, multicultural society such as the United States, this term is particularly useful for drawing boundaries between "insiders" (*desis)* and "outsiders" (non-*desis).* However, making such discrete distinctions between "us" and "them" is not always clear or easy, even for those whose *"desi*-ness" is undisputed. This became clear at an open-for-all Bangladeshi campus event when an unfamiliar student arrived as a guest. His ambiguous ethnic features confused the Bangladeshi student organizers about how to interact with him. He had a creamy complexion, somewhere between brown and white. His hair, cropped short, was dark and thin, not like the thick, wavy shock of hair many *desi* guys sported. He was wearing a loose cotton shirt, very similar to a *kurta*. I was standing a few feet away from him with some of the student organizers. One of them asked in a low voice, "Do you think he's *desi*?" Another one, a Pakistani American, replied, "Hard to tell. He looks Asian. He could be Chinese, but he could also be someone from Nepal or India." Later that night, I learned that the student was Chinese but was interested in learning about South Asian cultures, having traveled to India in the past.

Reflecting the larger trend, the panethnic *desi* identity was generally more prevalent among the young South Asian participants, giving them a sense of solidarity as racialized brown Asians with shared cultural backgrounds.[70] Yet, religion remained a significant dividing line that distinguished some *desis* from others. Consider, for example, a campus movie-screening event organized by Bangladeshi students (1.5 and second generations). The movie, a Bangladeshi production, was called *Matir Moyna*, or *The Clay Bird*.[71] It depicted a family grappling with political, religious, and cultural turmoil in a small Bangladeshi village shortly before the outbreak of the 1971 war. The protagonist was a little boy who was sent off to a *madrasah* by his religiously conservative father who supported a unified Pakistan, while the boy's uncle was guerilla freedom fighter. The student organizers had selected this movie because it was one of the few award-winning Bangla movies on the 1971 war that had English subtitles and was easily accessible online. None of them, however, had watched the movie prior to the event. The screening was taking place on a rainy evening, so the turnout was low, with just about ten to twelve attendees, most of them Bangladeshi. Only two of the attendees were Pakistani and one an Indian Muslim. I had come to know all of them from campus cultural events. After the movie, the organizers opened the floor for discussion, which they had requested I moderate, as I had watched the movie many times and was more familiar with Bangladeshi history than they were. After a few moments of silence, a Bangladeshi male student said, "I think it's a good thing we are all Muslim here." I was taken aback; given the plot of the movie and the event's purpose to inform the audience about Bangladesh's War of Independence, I had expected the students to react to the Pakistan-Bangladesh conflict. I asked why he thought so. He replied, "Well, you know. Islam already has a bad rap here with the media and stuff. I just don't think the movie would go over well with folks who aren't Muslim. They are gonna see Islam as violent, and it's [the movie is] just gonna give Muslims a bad name." Some students nodded in agreement.

While I would describe the students at the event as "culturally Muslim,"[72] I would not describe them as religiously very observant. For instance, none of them had excused themselves to go pray when the movie went past the evening prayer time. Yet all of them fasted during *Ramadan* and, save for two of the students, refrained from drinking alcohol. All of them, however, generally followed the often silent but nonetheless forceful Islamic gender norms. When posing for a group photo, for instance, they would leave distance between a girl and a boy, so that neither was physical touching. They jokingly referred to this as the "halal gap." Yet these students also identified as *desi*, often engaging in panethnic cultural activities with a degree of comfort that was absent among first-generation immigrants, for whom particularistic national boundaries were still bright (see chapter 2). Even in the context of the movie screening, the historical conflict between Pakistan and Bangladesh did not seem to matter much to the students. Instead, what was more salient to these students' sense of selves was the globally informed hostland sociopolitics that defined their experiences as *Muslims* in America. Indeed, it was so salient that despite the main conflict in the movie being ethnic/nationalistic, in the context of America's post-9/11 terror-panic climate, students' *desi*-ness and their ethnicity—whether Pakistani, Indian, or Bangladeshi—lost its relevance. The male student did not say that it was a good thing that they were all *desi* here; rather, as in the example of how Indian Muslims coalesce with Muslims from other ethnicities rather than with Hindu conationals, the fact that the attendees were all Muslim is what seemed to give him and the others in the room a sense of understanding, solidarity, and belonging.

Yet Muslims do not always coalesce under a panethnic banner. As in the example from chapter 2 on HELP, the Bangladeshi homeland charity organization, some Muslims strategically create distance from their Middle Eastern coreligionists in fear of drawing negative attention to their Muslim-ness (see also chapter 4). But what conditions push South Asians to forge panethnic coalitions with Muslims from other ethnicities? First, as per the existing scholarship on panethnicity, a common hostile hostland context—in this case, the post-9/11 Islamophobic terror-panic climate—is needed to induce a sense of shared experience and solidarity between South Asian Muslims and co-religionists of other ethnic backgrounds. As I show in chapter 5, many South Asians interpret their lives as Muslims in America by drawing parallels with Muslims living as stigmatized minorities in other countries in the West. Stories of Muslims "in danger" both "here" and "elsewhere" indicate to them a global Muslim plight, which they feel they must respond to by uniting and mobilizing, starting in their local communities. Second, the exogenous shock from "elsewhere" must be seen both by immigrants and others to have an effect on the hostland's sociopolitical climate and to produce an immediate impact on the immigrants' lives here in the hostland. For example, while many were engaged in staying informed about and helping Syrian refugees, they were unaware and virtually silent about Rohingya refugees in South Asia. This selective panethnic solidarity could be partly explained by the fact that Muslim-related politics in the Middle East has a more immediate impact on the hostland than religious politics in South Asia. Third, immigrants need to be exposed to resources that can enable panethnic coalitions to emerge. For South Asians to forge coalitions with Middle Easterners, for instance, they would first need access to information about Muslim-related geopolitics in those places. Whereas panethnic narratives and information that encouraged those platforms were prevalent on U.S. college campuses via various organizations, they were less so in off-campus ethnic enclaves. Although social media and smartphone apps have made the global flow of information technologically easy to access, not all immigrants can afford the time or effort it takes to divert their attention to "elsewhere" geopolitics away from their mundane, but more immediate, day-to-day struggles. The mostly working-class to lower-middle-class immigrants who lived in Little Bangladesh, for instance, were overwhelmingly more concerned about paying the bills and holding on to their hourly-wage jobs at gas stations and grocery marts than about keeping informed of faraway "elsewhere" conflicts. And last, whether immigrants actually engage in panethnic coalitions depends on the generational composition. Whereas the first generation generally preferred to keep within their particularistic national and religious communities, the 1.5 and second generations were more open to building cross-ethnic and interfaith relations. Moreover, the younger immigrants were more vocal than their parents' generation about the need for panethnic Muslim unity as a form of organized resistance against Islamophobia.

## VECTORS OF GLOBALIZATION

Homelands are not geopolitically static or isolated once their people leave for the United States. South Asia has long maintained relationships with the "elsewhere" Middle East, the effects of which have influenced various aspects of society in the immigrants' homelands, including politics and religious life. These interconnections with "elsewhere" have come to affect immigrants by shaping not only their national and Muslim identities but also the ways they are perceived by the larger host society. In addition, the subcontinent's past at the hands of British colonizers is still salient in the worldview of South Asians, including those who have immigrated to the West. The remnants of these countries' colonized past are deeply rooted in their language, politics, religious life, and community-building. South Asian Muslim Americans are aware of the continuing conflicts between the West and the Muslim world.[73] Their perceptions of these geopolitical conflicts shape how these immigrants navigate their Muslim-ness in the hostland, collectively locate themselves at the global level, and bring their worldview into their political engagements. These understandings of homeland-"elsewhere" dynamics are critical to getting a clear picture of the ways in which immigrants function as vectors of globalized ideas and perceptions, a picture that will be covered in the chapters ahead.

# 4 | THE GEOPOLITICS OF BEING "GOOD MUSLIMS" IN AMERICA

**ANWAR WAS ONCE AT A MALL** with his family when his mother unwrapped a piece of candy while strolling by a row of shops. He recalled that she had thrown the wrapper at a trash container but missed, with the wrapper falling close to the container, on the floor. She did not stop to pick it up but walked past. But Anwar's father suddenly stopped on his tracks, turned around, and asked Anwar's mother to pick up the wrapper and put it inside the trash bin. Baffled, Anwar's mother asked him why he was making such a big deal. "Do you realize what you just did?" Anwar's father replied. "No, what did I do?" She answered. "You just dropped trash on the ground," Anwar's father replied. Anwar's mother, now slightly annoyed, asked, "Okay . . . why did you stop us all for that?" The words that Anwar's father spoke next had struck Anwar so much that he remembered them even after several years since. His father had said:

> Remember you [Anwar's mother] are wearing a *hijab*. Everybody around you is looking at you and saying that you are Muslim. And if you litter, they are going to say bad action, headscarf, and they are immediately going to equate those two together. Negative, negative, Muslims are bad. That's how easy it is for people to judge us. So, we have to be role models to show others this is who we are, these are the actions that we do, and this how we behave, and then you [people] be the judge.

Anwar recalled that his mother then walked back a few steps, picked up the candy wrapper, and threw it carefully into the trash bin. This example[1] highlights a central struggle that many South Asian Muslim Americans are compelled to deal with every day. On one hand, as South Asians, they are often stereotyped as model minorities because of their high levels of formal education, success in STEM fields, strong work ethic, and perceived political passivity.[2] On the other hand, in moments of national crisis, they are viewed as security threats because of their real or perceived adherence to Islam. This double-edged racialization categorizes South Asian Muslim immigrants as perpetual outsiders in post-9/11 America—as hypervisible and exposed to constant public scrutiny. It is the reason Anwar's parents felt the need to subvert any negative stereotypes attached to *hijabis*—and, by extension, Muslims—and make themselves visible in what they thought was a positive light. Exogenous shocks emanating from "elsewhere" exacerbate these social pressures on Muslims in the hostland. In a context where Islam is closely associated to violence and terrorism in global discourse, Muslims—especially those who are visibly so, like Anwar's mother—often have to perform the role of "good Samaritans" in public.

Although Muslims have long been viewed as suspicious outsiders or an "Other" based on orientalist notions of Islam and the Middle East,[3] the 9/11 attacks and the subsequent terror-panic climate have amplified the fears, hostility, and suspicion toward Muslims as terrorists.[4] As a result, Muslim immigrants have been the targets of several government-run surveillance programs in the United States. For example, from 2002 to 2011, the National Security Entry-Exit Registration System (NSEERS) enforced foreign nationals from twenty-six Muslim-majority countries to be registered, fingerprinted, and photographed upon U.S. entry followed by annual reports to U.S. immigration agencies. And from 2001 to 2013, the New York Police Department and the CIA maintained a secret surveillance program in conjunction with Muslim communities in New York, which monitored and analyzed everyday life in those communities, going so far as to recruit insiders from the community as informants.[5] Even after many of these post-9/11 surveillance programs ended, the fear of being surveilled did not perish, with President Trump promising to create a database that would register and track all Muslims in the United States. Moreover, the FBI plans not only to continue using undercover informants to detect terrorist plots—a practice that tends to disproportionately target Muslims[6]—but also to expand such operations, to purportedly defend against ISIS.[7]

Even before 9/11, the U.S. media arguably played an influential role in perpetuating the stereotype of Muslims as terrorist threats through its portrayal of Islam and its followers.[8] But since 9/11 the media has particularly served as a key force in creating a cultural shift, in which anti-Muslim fringe organizations have gained more influence in media discourse than mainstream pro-Muslim civil rights organizations.[9] Despite being fewer in number, fringe organizations have been heavily overrepresented in media discourses after 9/11 compared to mainstream civil rights organizations, which have been underrepresented. Consequently, anti-Muslim messages from these previously obscure groups have now become mainstream discourses that shape popular understandings of Islam. For example, although most civil society organizations deployed pro-Muslim discourses after the 9/11 attacks, it was the anti-Muslim fringe organizations that gained visibility in mainstream media through eye-catching public displays of fearmongering and anger.[10] These displays dominated the mass media, providing a sense of legitimacy to these fringe organizations on the one hand and validating Islamist extremists' claims that the United States was biased against Muslims on the other. This kind of institutional amplification of the fear and anger that pervaded many segments of public and political opinion after 9/11 created a "gravitational pull," which shifted mainstream discourses about Islam more toward the views of the anti-Muslim fringe groups.[11]

Even mainstream news organizations such as the *New York Times*, the *Washington Post*, the *Los Angeles Times*, and *USA Today* have been found to cover Islam and Muslim-related news in ways that closely associate Muslims with fear, radicalization, and international terrorism.[12] For instance, research on U.S. media coverage of terrorism revealed a pattern that reiterates the so-called clash between "the West" and "the East" or between "Christian America" and "the Muslim Other."[13] In cases where terrorists are Muslim, media coverage moves from identifying the perpetrator as Muslim to connecting the terrorist with an international terrorist cell, with the attacker's motivation being a holy war against the United States. Contrastingly, where terrorists are non-Muslim, the attacks are covered as isolated incidents, with the perpetrator being humanized as a "mentally unstable" or "troubled" individual whose shocked family members condemn violence.[14] Moreover, a study analyzing the coverage of all terror attacks in the United States from 2011 to 2015 showed that attacks conducted by Muslims received five times more media coverage than those by non-Muslims.[15] Despite Muslims carrying out only 12.4 percent of attacks in the United States, they received 50.4 percent of terror attack media coverage. The South Asian Muslim participants in this book were aware of this contrast in news coverage and viewed it as Western media's "double standard" or "bias" against Muslims.

Overall, the spate of ISIS terrorist attacks across the globe, the contentious national debates surrounding President Trump's "Muslim ban," and the mass media's coverage of Muslim-related conflicts depicting Islam as being directly opposed to Western, Christian ideologies have all added to the hypervisibility of this minority as a "threat" in American society. This context of hypervisibility and increased surveillance of Muslims as potential terrorists has contributed to creating a climate of insecurity, fear, suspicion, and anxiety that organizes Muslim American community life in many ways, such as through self-policing. And for many Muslim Americans, self-policing comes in the form of taking everyday precautions, in apprehension of being perceived as threats, as unwelcome outsiders, or as anti-American. These self-presentation strategies become particularly important when Islamist terrorist attacks do occur and Muslims are held collectively accountable for the violence, even if it is taking place "elsewhere." As such, in these instances, many of my South Asian Muslim participants felt compelled to loudly condemn terrorism and perform a "good Muslim" script, otherwise, they risked being perceived as terrorist sympathizers or accused of enabling terrorism by remaining silent.

This Muslims-are-to-blame mentality is institutionalized through government-run counterterrorism initiatives such as the Countering Violent Extremism (CVE) program, which places the responsibility on Muslims to weed out extremists from their midst. Launched in 2014, CVE purportedly aims to prevent U.S. residents from becoming "radicalized" and to address the root causes of violent extremism by engaging community and religious leaders, law enforcement officials, healthcare professionals, teachers, and social service providers.[16] If anyone from one of these groups identifies "visible" signs of individuals from their community joining extremist groups or becoming terrorists, he or she is to take action by pointing out that suspect to law enforcement authorities.[17] In practice, these programs focus mainly, if not only, on Muslim communities, as evidenced by President Trump reportedly proposing to rename the initiative Countering Islamic Extremism or Countering Radical Islamic Extremism.[18] The government-run undercover surveillance programs, such as CVE, which were put into place almost immediately after 9/11, sowed mistrust within Muslim communities as friends and neighbors suspected one another of being either government infiltrates or extremist sympathizers.[19] By placing Muslims in the position of being their own surveillants, CVE paves the way for further mistrust.

Moreover, if a terrorist attack is perpetrated by a Muslim American, it seemingly justifies blaming Muslims in these communities either for "failing to adequately spy" on their community members or for "enabling" the attack by not reporting relevant information to law enforcement authorities. This is indeed what happened in December 2015 after a self-radicalized couple of Pakistani heritage, Syed Rizwan Farook and Tashfeen Malik, pledged allegiance to ISIS on Facebook and conducted a mass shooting in San Bernardino, California. Trump, then the Republican presidential candidate, falsely accused the couple's family, friends, neighbors, and coworkers of seeing ammunition in the couple's residence and then knowingly neglecting to alert law enforcement authorities of the attack plot. Shifting the blame and burden of responsibility to all Muslims, he claimed "Muslims have to report the problems when they see them."[20] In this overall climate of suspicion and fear, the onus to prove oneself "innocent," "good," or "unthreatening" thus falls upon Muslim individuals.

The interactions of South Asian Muslim Americans illustrate how they present their "Muslim-ness," both among themselves and when interacting with the larger U.S. society. Many participants, in response to the hypervisibility of Muslims in the ongoing geopolitical climate, strive to keep their Muslim-ness away from the public eye. However, if the need to address their religion in public settings arises, they qualify themselves as "good," "moderate" Muslims. Daily presenting themselves as such involves avoiding Muslim-related political conversations and highlighting universal—but apolitical—attributes, like freedom, empowerment, and peacefulness through their behaviors and dialogue with others. *Hijabis*, automatically stigmatized because of their clothing, often overemphasize these values to be perceived as "good" Muslims. Domestic events, such as natural disasters, offer opportunities to enact a "good Muslim" script. But these strategies are double-sided—on the one side, they provide Muslims with some protection in times of heightened Islamophobia, but on the other they silence Muslims and render them politically passive. Islamic organizations also aim to highlight the compatibility of Islam and American values; however, their goal is to insert Muslims into U.S. politics so that Muslims can advocate for their interests here and "elsewhere" as "Muslim *Americans*." Hence, these organizations and Muslim American community leaders strive to "Islamize" parts of American culture, on the one hand, and "Americanize" tenets of Islam, on the other.

### EVERYDAY EXPERIENCES UNDER MUSLIM HYPERVISIBILITY

We moved to Orange County in 2001, two weeks before 9/11 happened. It was a white suburb, but we didn't realize how much white it was until we started school. I remember we went to school, and it was like everyone was white. So, one day [in 2011], my brother's friend had a beard, and they were getting their tires changed. He [the friend] was just pointing at a map and was saying, "This summer we are going to drive from here to all the way to New York." My brother [pointing to places on the map] was like, "Okay, so you are driving here." Two days later, an FBI agent came [to our house]. I was at the door. I was like nine, and I called my mom. And then they [the FBI agent] were asking me, "Oh, where is your brother?" and we were like, "He is in college. What is this about?" And he was like, "Can you please ask him to call me?" It turns out that someone in the neighborhood reported suspicious behavior about my brother potentially planning something dangerous.

At the time Tabassum, a Pakistani American, shared this incident with me, she had just graduated from college and was working as an intern at an environmental organization. It was evening, and we were meeting at a Thai restaurant close to her old college campus. She was wearing a scarf wrapped loosely around her neck over a white, short-sleeved top. Her dark, wavy hair, uncovered, went a little past her shoulders. She had a pale olive complexion, long dark lashes, big brown eyes, a small nose, and thin lips—all of which together made her appearance, in her words, "ethnically ambiguous."[21] She had a relaxed attitude, so the interview, which ended up lasting almost two hours, flowed like a conversation.

Tabassum explained that while she herself was not "Muslim-looking," her brother's and his friend's facial features, especially the friend's beard, gave them a more stereotypical Muslim image. As such, their merely consulting a map was likely perceived by a passerby as their planning a terror attack. Indeed, facial hair is popularly perceived as a mark of deep Islamic religiousness and has become a physical characteristic particularly associated with the stereotypical image of a Muslim man, both in the United States and abroad.[22] Thus, bearded men, regardless of their actual faith, have often been the subjects of suspicion and violence in the United States. One of the first known murder victims after 9/11 was, in fact, a Sikh man named Balbir Singh Sodhi, who was gunned down at a gas station in Arizona because his turban and beard made him look similar to Osama bin Laden.[23] Over a decade after 9/11, Sikh men continue to be harassed because of misdirected Islamophobia, as exemplified by Prabhjot Singh, an accomplished doctor and professor who was attacked in Manhattan. A group of young men had reportedly pulled his beard and kicked him repeatedly after yelling, "Terrorist . . . Osama . . . get him!"[24] Indeed, among the many self-presentation strategies that South Asian men adopted immediately after 9/11 to signal their patriotism and loyalty to the United States was cutting their hair and taking off their turbans.[25] So what I found surprising about Tabassum's story was that it was her brother's friend who had sported a beard—not her brother. This seemed to imply that just being in the company of a bearded man had made Tabassum's brother a subject of public suspicion.

Some participants even feared being perceived as "too Muslim," which generally meant being perceived as deeply devoted to Islam and practicing of the faith either because of their own actions or because of their association with other explicitly devout Muslims. Being thus perceived, they feared, might make them subject to government surveillance. For example, a few years after 9/11, the family of a Bangladeshi college student, Lamia, had relocated to a predominantly white neighborhood from a suburb known to have a large Muslim population. They had lived in the Muslim neighborhood for over a decade, but her parents owned a small business and feared that if they were publicly seen as being close with Muslims, they would draw suspicion. And if they were suspected as terrorists, they would lose customers or, worse, be sent back to Bangladesh. Even over a decade after 9/11, when I interviewed Lamia, she said her parents still declined invitations from friends and old neighbors to attend prayers at their old mosque on *Eid*. Sometimes, her parents refused to even answer phone calls from friends they considered "too religious," an expression that Lamia said meant they regularly attended mosques, wore *hijabs* or other forms of conservative clothing, were highly observant of Islamic practices, and publicly spoke of their faith. I found other participants to fear surveillance as well. Some were reluctant to talk about religious topics over the phone in fear of being wiretapped by the government—a lingering suspicion from the days after 9/11, when the U.S. government had indeed listened in to phone conversations of private citizens under the broad surveillance measures allowed by the USA PATRIOT Act.[26]

This issue of participants choosing to share their Muslim-ness with some but not with others, for fear of being surveilled, was both an important finding and an obstacle in my fieldwork. In general, participants seemed to strategically avoid drawing attention to their Muslim-ness in public or engaging in conversations with strangers or non-Muslims on topics pertaining to Islam. On most occasions, I formally interviewed the participants before spending time with them in more unstructured settings. I used the formal interview sessions not only to introduce myself as a researcher and derive responses but also to create rapport with the participants, which later enabled me to ask for referrals. During interviews, I usually asked participants to walk me through an average day of the week. I hoped their responses would give me insight into what tasks, places, and people they deemed relevant to their daily lives. At that stage, I was still an unfamiliar "outsider" in the field, with only my "Muslim-sounding" Arabic name and physical features indicating my religious and ethnic background.

I noticed that although many of the interviewees described their daily routines in intricate detail, they hardly mentioned observing religious practices. This was the case even for those who wore religious markers (such as the *hijab* and the *Zulfiqar*, a pendant only Shia Muslims wear) and for college students who I knew were active in Muslim student groups on campus. Participants also appeared indifferent to social and political issues that existing surveys found important to Muslim Americans, providing aloof responses like "I don't know" to questions about such issues. Overall, it appeared as if their religious identity was not relevant to their lives at all, even though polls consistently showed that Muslims (71 percent) were second only to white Evangelicals (82 percent) in saying that religion was very important in daily life.[27]

As I became more familiar with respondents, however, I observed that my participants' Muslim identity implicitly shaped many aspects of their daily routines. For instance, in addition sharing their views on mundane topics like dating, weekend plans, concerns about classes, rivalries within their communities, family disputes, and so on, participants also shared how they saw Muslim-related issues that were ongoing not just in the United States but also "elsewhere," in places like Syria and Palestine. In most cases, religion seemed to be a natural or taken-for-granted part of their lives—a way in which they organized their activities and interactions without dispensing much thought. Instead, they appeared to be more actively concerned about course grades, monthly rent, employment, childrearing, marriage, workplace interactions, and so on.

A typical day would begin with one preparing for work—making breakfast, packing a lunch, and dressing appropriately for the day ahead. Students would rush from their dorm rooms to back-to-back classes and study sessions, while professionals would commute to their workplaces. At around noon, some participants preferred to have lunch by themselves or call their families to discuss how their day has been, whereas others would meet up with friends or coworkers. For office workers, the second half of the day resembled the first. For college students, afternoons usually included campus organizational meetings, errands, study sessions, and sometimes dinner with friends before they headed back to their dorms in the late evening. In homes, dinner usually included family time, with the television playing either homeland news channels or South Asian soap operas in the background. In college dorms, dinner usually consisted of homecooked meals, which mothers had prepared and delivered in Tupperware over the weekend and which students then microwaved and enjoyed while watching sports, Netflix, or television shows like *Grey's Anatomy*, *Gossip Girl*, *Friends*, and *Scandal* with roommates.

My ethnographic observations, however, gave me a different view of their routines that brought to light the latent salience of their Muslim identity. For example, as individuals dressed for the day, some consciously selected clothes that would enable them to offer prayers between scheduled events, usually during lunch or between classes. Women wore "modest" clothes, meaning full sleeves, jeans, or long dresses, whereas men wore trousers instead of shorts. Some of the organizational meetings that students attended on campus were Muslim student associations or Palestinian rights organizations. Some students were *zabeeha* and thus ate only *halal* food, making microwaved homecooked dinners the most cost-effective and convenient option. Several college-going participants had known their roommates long before college through their families and community mosques, while others found each other through Muslim student organizations on campus.

Again, many participants claimed to refrain from drinking alcohol because it is *haram*.[28] This posed a problem in their social networking, as drinking is embedded in American culture as a form of casual socialization. Whereas some participants avoided situations involving alcohol altogether, others, like Rashed, an aspiring Pakistani American filmmaker, had to find creative solutions to "fit in" without drawing attention to his religious identity. According to Rashed,

> I would be one of the earlier people to arrive, and I would go to the kitchen, pour myself a glass of coke and just grab on to the glass for the rest of the evening, haha! And then when people ask me if I am drinking, I am like, "Yeah . . . I got a drink!" Because I didn't want to have that conversation like, "Oh you don't drink? How come?" "Religious issues." "Oh, really? Who are you?" "I am Muslim." "Oh. Okay, cool." What does that conversation change? If you learn that I am a Muslim, that doesn't change anything. Only that now, you closed yourself off to me. And I feel like I won't be able to connect to people. So, sometimes I pretend to be hyper, like I am drunk and having fun.

However, while many respondents were initially aloof with their responses regarding Islam, some interviewees conversely *over*emphasized their Muslim identity, or at least specific aspects of it, based on their perception of me as an "insider." For example, Arabic words such as *InshaaAllah* (meaning "if God is willing") or *MashaaAllah* ("God has willed it") would frequently pepper their responses, and they would talk at length about how much their religion mattered to them. Over time, however, as my observations began to extend beyond the formal interview setting, I often found that these same participants, when hanging out with their *desi* or Muslim friends, seldom used as many Arabic words as they had during the interviews. Moreover, when I spent long stretches of time with participants whose interview responses had indicated a high level of religiosity in daily life (e.g., praying five times a day), I often observed the opposite to be true (e.g., prayer time would pass by without the participants' notice).

Usually, participants who overemphasized their religious identity with me were those I had not met before the scheduled interview. Due to my use of snowball sampling, these interviewees and I would have a mutual friend put us in touch for an hour-long interview. I usually requested that the mutual friend provide only general information about me to the potential interviewee; specifically, that I was a scholar studying Muslim American community life. Before the interview, my only interaction with the participant would be by text, to schedule a time and place. And during the interview, I almost never shared my own religious or political views, so as not to prime the participants' responses. However, although I did not wear a *hijab* and wore regular Western clothing, my brown skin, accented English, and facial features always led my new interviewees to correctly identify me as *desi* and Muslim. The specificity of whether I was a Muslim from Bangladesh or Pakistan, however, came up later over the course of the interview.

My insider status also colored the way interviewees interpreted my questions. For instance, some respondents presumed I was referring to Islamophobia even when I had asked them general, open-ended questions about their religious experiences. On the other hand, their interpretation could also be an indication as to how much Islamophobia had come to characterize the Muslim American experience, particularly in the polarized sociopolitical climate in the period from 2015 to 2017.[29] Indeed, the theme of Islamophobia would often predominate the interviews. Sometimes, the participants would ask me if *I* ever felt stigmatized as a Muslim. I always answered their questions but only after the interview was over.

If I had relied on their interview responses as my only source of data, I likely would have found their Muslim identity, or the stigma attached to it, to affect *every* aspect of their lives. Yet my everyday observations showed that these people also led regular lives, preoccupied with mundane concerns such as managing the monthly budget, getting promoted at work, marrying off their children, applying to graduate school, and maintaining relationships. Direct, firsthand experiences of Islamophobic encounters were few and far between, although news of hate crimes and anti-Muslim sentiments "here," "there," and "elsewhere" informed the participants' worldviews, which they, in turn, used to make sense of their collective experience as Muslims.

### "GOOD MUSLIMS" ARE "MODERATES"

Adeena, a Bangladeshi woman, had been living in Los Angeles for almost thirty years. She wore a *burqa* (an outer garment covering her from top of her head to the ground) whenever she stepped out of the house. I interviewed her daughter, Farhana, who was a junior in college at the time. Neither Farhana nor her two teenage sisters wore the *hijab*. Although she and her sisters often urged Adeena to wear bright colors, Adeena always opted for mute, neutral colors like white, black, and brown to blend in with the crowd as much as possible. However, in one incident, which occurred soon after the 2015 ISIS attacks in San Bernardino, Adeena had donned her usual black *burqa* to go shopping before suddenly taking it off. Farhana recalled that Adeena then brought out a pink *hijab*. To Farhana's surprise, Adeena explained, "If I wear black, people stare at me longer. They notice me more." According to Farhana, Adeena thought that black was too closely associated with stereotypical images of "oppressed," "conservative" Muslim women in the Middle East. In contrast, Adeena found pink to present a friendlier, more open image.

Performing a "good Muslim" script, as Adeena and Anwar's parents had done, is a common strategy for Muslim Americans to collectively enact in moments of national crisis. Domestic events, such as natural disasters and domestic political contentions, usually gain widespread coverage in mainstream American media and dominate the news cycle. As such, these events provide opportunities to project a positive image of Muslims as peace-loving fellow Americans. In the aftermath of Hurricane Harvey, for instance, hundreds of Muslims in Texas made themselves visible as good Samaritans as they concertedly provided relief, turned mosques into shelters, and raised thousands of dollars for victims through Islamic organizations and youth groups.[30] Some volunteers wore T-shirts displaying the names of their mosques and Islamic organizations. These pictures were posted on social media along with links to fundraisers and hashtags like #HumanityFirst and #WeAreOneNation. The major national and global newspapers and cable news outlets covered these Muslim Americans' widespread relief efforts. One headline, from *HuffPost*, read "Muslims Opening Their Doors to Flood Victims: 'We Feel and Suffer the Same,'"[31] and another, in the *Los Angeles Times*, read, "Muslim Volunteers Spend *Eid* Helping Houston Hurricane Recovery."[32] Many Facebook users shared these news articles, adding visibility to Muslim Americans' relief efforts and reaching those who primarily received their news from social media.[33]

Another example of Muslim Americans concertedly putting forward a positive, peaceful image of Islam came in July 2018, when a particularly heated political conflict was unfolding around President Trump's "zero tolerance immigration policy." This policy separated children from their parents who crossed the U.S.-Mexico border without proper documents, causing outrage among politicians in both the Democratic and Republican parties and among many segments of the American public.[34] In the midst of this emotionally charged national debate, the Muslim community in Tampa Bay, Florida made news by offering to host all 2,300 migrant children in federal custody.[35] In a press conference, Ahmed Bedier, the spokesperson of the Islamic Society of the Tampa Bay Area, highlighted Islam's emphasis on family unification, saying,

> Our religious faith calls upon us to protect the young, to protect children, and emphasizes the importance of keeping families connected. In fact, there is a strong tradition in our faith that the Prophet Muhammad (peace be upon him) had once said, "There's a grave punishment for the person that separates a child from their mother. . . . And we have hundreds of Muslim families that are prepared to host these children in their

homes at their own cost with the goal that they will be continued to be taken care of and hosted until they can be reunified with their parents and next of kin."[36]

However, on an *everyday* basis, just how does one perform a "good Muslim" script? And what challenges and advantages does one encounter in enacting that performance? I found that the South Asian Muslim participants at times relegated their Muslim-ness to the private sphere; however, they did not forsake their Muslim identity altogether. Rather, if there was a need to address their religion in public, they qualified themselves as a "moderate" or "good" kind of Muslim. In contrast to the lone "Muslim" label, which most of my informants believed to connote "terrorist" in the larger political discourse about Islam in the West, the "*moderate* Muslim" category indicated the positive values of peace and hard work shared by all Americans.

Today, "moderate" is a contentious word, carrying both religious and political meaning. Scholars, media personalities, bloggers, and political commentators from both liberal and conservative sides use it to interpret Muslims in relation to Muslims' views of Western democratic values and Islamic terrorism. However, "moderate" can mean "devout" to some and "liberal" to others, leading to endless debate over who "moderate Muslims" are as opposed to "radicals" and "extremists."[37] For example, while the West largely views Wahhabis as "extremists," Saudis generally deem Wahhabism "moderate."[38] These labels become all the more powerful because of the consequences they carry. A call for a more "liberal" interpretation of Islam can be seen as "radical" and result in punitive measures, as it has in Saudi Arabia.[39] Conversely, women choosing to cover themselves based on notions of freedom and empowerment can be viewed as "extremist," as has been the case in France with regard to the *niqab* (a religious covering showing only the eyes) and the *Burkini* (a modesty swimsuit covering all but the face, hands, and feet).[40] A few even use "moderate" as a derogative term. For example, while American political commentators perceive the Muslim Brotherhood as being composed of "radical Islamists," based on its hostile view of the United States, Jihadists condemn it as "moderate" for rejecting global *jihad* and embracing democracy.[41] Some argue that there is no such thing as a moderate Muslim because there is a moral vacancy within the religion itself.[42] Still others argue that the word "moderate" is meaningless to describe ordinary followers of a peaceful religion.[43]

Thus, "moderate" is a label that is inextricably linked to the global phenomenon of Islamic terrorism and has come to be popularly understood as a category that stands in contrast to "radical" and "extremist." In simpler terms, "moderate Muslims" generally refers to those who adhere to secular ideals such as democracy and freedom, gender equality, separation between mosque and state, just governance, and the vehement denunciation of violence.[44] In contrast, "extremists" or "radicals" are understood as those Muslims who believe in an "Islamic state" and condone violence as a means to establish it.

According to these discourses, the participants were all "moderate" Muslims. They were in favor of democracy as practiced in the United States because they viewed it to be in accordance to the *Shura*, or the egalitarian political system in the Quran. Although critical of the United States' foreign policy in regard to Muslim countries, they did not view the United States' political system to be contradictory to the Islamic values of freedom, social justice, and equality. Instead, they viewed American democracy as an example of just governance in compliance with Islamic ideals. Further, all participants vehemently rejected violence in the name of Islam. And, more important, the participants used the term "moderate" to describe themselves in ways that fell in line with the general discourse surrounding the label. For example, Nazia, an Indian American college student, described herself as a "practicing" Muslim, by which she meant that she prayed five times a day, fasted during Ramadan, wore modest clothing, and never dated or drank alcohol, although she did not wear or plan to wear the *hijab*. When I asked her about her religious upbringing, she replied,

> I would say it was kind of moderate. They [her parents] are not very conservative in the sense that I have to sit at home, or they never followed the very strict rules, I guess. I don't know how to describe this. They are not liberal in the sense that they don't drink, and they don't let me drink. They have been very open-minded, especially after moving here [ten years before]. They have been more open to differing ideas. For example, different social issues. They are okay with me having a different point of view on certain things. More like open with the idea of me being

independent . . . But, dating? No, that's not okay . . . But religion was the central part of our family life. With just following rituals and practices to big festivals. So, it was a big part. It is still a central part of my life. I feel like I am closer to it [in college] because I am more independent to think about it the way I feel comfortable. Whereas, at home it was a lot of influence from my family. The way that I thought about it, it gave me a way to connect with it on my own.

Although Nazia used the word "moderate," she did so in relation to her own interpretations of "conservative" and "liberal." Her parents were "moderate" because they were "not very conservative," a label she gauged in light of their attitude toward gender roles and their implementation of Islamic rules in the household. Yet, at the same time, she did not think her parents were "liberal," as they strictly followed some Islamic regulations, like the restriction of alcohol and dating. Despite coming "closer" to religion on her own in college, Nazia went on to say later in her interview that her religiosity tended to align with her parents', meaning that she too fell within her understanding of a "moderate" Muslim.

However, the label "moderate" is not an accurate description or indicator of the participants' religiosity. Although participants overwhelmingly described themselves as "moderate," their religiosity reflected the heterogeneity of the Muslim population and challenged the idea of a Muslim monolith. Just in the United States, for instance, Muslims are highly diverse in terms of ethnic, religious, and sectarian affiliations. The Muslim American population is largely made up of immigrants and their children from across the world. Of the U.S. Muslim population, 55 percent is Sunni, 16 percent is Shia, and 14 percent identify as "just Muslim."[45] Another 65 percent say that religion is very important in their lives, and 42 percent claim to pray five times a day; many others say that religion is less important and that they are inconsistent in performing the daily prayers. A common thread that seems to tie these diverse individuals together is their concern about religious extremism; however, Muslims may be more concerned about extremism in the name of Islam than non-Muslims, with most U.S. Muslims saying that violence against civilians cannot be justified in the pursuit of religious, political, or social causes.[46] The South Asian Muslim participants' heterogeneity (which

I described in chapter 1) reflected this vibrant yet complex diversity and added nuance to these numeric descriptions. However, their Muslim-ness, and the discourses surrounding Islam, seemed to tie these diverse individuals together with a common thread, as almost all participants, even those who no longer practiced or spiritually identified with the religion, claimed to want social justice for all Muslims.

In general, the participants colloquially used the label "moderate" to mean "not extremist" or "not terrorist." In other words, the participants and the broader American public seemed to understand "moderate" Muslims as the "good" kind of Muslims—nonviolent and peace-loving. This became clear in my interview with Tahira, a Bangladeshi American engineering major. Tahira described herself as "moderate" to distinguish herself from Islamist terrorists, who she viewed as reinforcing Islamophobic stereotypes.

> When I see those things on the news, I definitely feel angry. It's making people who think Islam is a violent religion . . . it helps their case. It shows them like, "Oh, look, they blew this up. How can you say this is a peaceful religion?" We are trying so hard to convince people that Muslims are not terrorists. There is a small minority who are . . . who does violent things. But our religion doesn't teach us to do that. When those kinds of things happen, I get angry at the people who view our religion as violent but angrier at the people who actually did it. If you [referring to the terrorists] are Muslim, why don't you understand that our religion doesn't teach these things? So why are you making people view it like that!

When I probed her to define who she meant by "we," she responded, "Like normal, moderate Muslims."

Striving to be seen as good, moderate Muslims, however, comes with a price. Mahmood Mamdani points to the slippery slope in using categories like "moderate" and "extremist." He argues that doing so shifts the cultural discourse from talking about terrorists and civilians to differentiating between "good Muslims" and "bad Muslims." Such talk further entrenches the perceived link between Islam and terrorism in that it presumes terrorism as an "essential" characteristic of Muslims—those who have rejected this violent inclination and embraced secularism are the "good Muslims"; whereas, the terrorists or the "bad Muslims" are expressing Muslims' so-called characteristic tendency to inflict violence upon "the West."[47] This binary also implies that "good" or "moderate" Muslims who are rejecting terrorism are not being their "authentic" selves, and so should always be watched, in case they give in to their "essentially" violent character.

In my interview with Amir, a Pakistani American college senior, he addressed this burden that categorization places upon Muslims not only to distinguish themselves from "bad Muslims" but also to stress the similarities they share with other (i.e., non-Muslim) civilians. For example, when I asked Amir whether he would describe himself as a "moderate" Muslim, he appeared offended. He asked, "Uhh, what do you mean by that? Who is a moderate Muslim?" I replied, "I don't know. I am not sure. What do you think?" He shook his head slightly and said,

> See, I think that word [moderate] is problematic. It's like saying there are good Muslims and then there are bad Muslims and we have to be like, "Oh no, we are the good ones. We are just like you [non-Muslim Americans]! We believe the same things you guys do!" It's as if the burden is on us to show them that we are not like the terrorists you see on TV blowing up things.

But *how* do the participants make themselves visible as "moderates"? I found that they tend to remain largely silent about their religion and political views in face-to-face public interactions, underlining their preference to keep indications of their Muslim-ness inside the private sphere and within social media, a virtual platform on which they can regulate privacy settings. Indeed, a nationwide poll conducted in 2019 by the Institute of Social Policy and Understanding (ISPU) supports my findings, showing that while Muslims profess religious devotion more privately, they are less assertive of their religion in public.[48] I argue that the reason this is so is because, in the ongoing sociopolitical climate, expressing political opinions or critiquing the U.S. media and foreign policies as being biased against Muslims could not only reinforce their perceived "otherness" but also expose them to anti-Muslim backlash. Therefore, Muslim-related politics, especially issues that tend to generate an emotional response from the public, are usually discussed in intimate, informal places where "Muslim" is the "normal, default, taken-for-granted" and "unmarked" category.[49]

For example, I was talking with Faizah, a Bangladeshi American college student, at her campus one day, when I learned that she was going to go watch a movie with some of her friends. I asked if I knew them, as she had introduced me to some of her friends earlier. She replied, "No, I don't think so. They're my white friends." By "white," I took her to mean "non-Muslim" and "non-*desi*"—common descriptions that some South Asian college students colloquially used to distinguish between their friend groups. Indeed, I later learned that this "white" group of friends included not only Caucasians but Latinos as well.[50] I asked what movie she was planning to watch. She replied, "*Pitch Perfect 2*." I laughed, saying I would not have thought her to like "sugary teen movies." Smiling, Faizah replied, "Of course! I am not gonna go watch *American Sniper* with them!" When I asked why not, she said, "It's too political. I don't ever talk about politics when I am with them." *American Sniper* was a biographical movie that had come out the year before about the American marksman in the Iraq War who had the highest number of kills in U.S. military history. Faizah, however, used the title to refer to all political movies concerning wars in the Middle East, a place that is a hotbed of geopolitics between "the West" and "the Muslim world." Movies such as this might trigger discussions about Islam or Muslims and put Faizah on the spot, a situation I understood she wanted to avoid with her non-Muslim friends. Contrastingly, a movie like *Pitch Perfect 2* was from an apolitical, "safe" genre that would highlight Faizah's commonalities with her friends, such as their similar taste in and consumption of American pop culture. To be fair, most people engage in various forms of relationship management with friends with whom they disagree or are likely to disagree. But in Faizah's situation, as with the other South Asian respondents, a point of possible disagreement or tension is her affiliation with Islam.

Indeed, politics was a topic that respondents more commonly discussed in the private sphere than in public spaces. For example, in addition to homeland politics, the 2016 U.S. presidential election cycle was a topic of conversation at *dawats* in many South Asian Muslim homes, indicating that the participants, at least to some extent, were staying informed about mainstream U.S. politics. Moreover, many participants stayed informed about Muslim-related issues not only in America but also in other parts the world, particularly the

Middle East. Deeming mainstream American news channels, such as CNN, MSNBC, and Fox, to be biased against Muslims, many of the respondents subscribed to Al Jazeera and the BBC. This was one reason many participants knew about the 2015 ISIS bombings in Beirut even though the attacks were not widely covered in American mainstream news outlets. Many 1.5- and second-generation immigrants also subscribed to the newsfeeds of Islamic civil rights organizations on social media, where groups like the Council for American Islamic Relations (CAIR) posted their take on Muslim-related events. These younger participants also sometimes shared Muslim-related news trends with their parents who were not on social media. For example, Farhana, when she was just a few years old, came to the United States from Bangladesh with her parents and two older sisters. Her immediate and most of her extended family lived in the same neighborhood in California. Most of her close friends, whom she had met in college through her Islamic studies class, were Muslim and *desi*. Farhana also considered herself a practicing Muslim. In her interview, Farhana said that she did not watch the news but that she read articles that trended on social media. It was on Facebook, for instance, that she had come to know about the three Bangladeshi British Muslims who, on their way to join ISIS in Syria, were captured by law enforcement authorities.[51] When she went home for the weekend, she shared the story with her mother, Adeena, and her two sisters. It prompted them to have a conversation about how ISIS can lure young Muslims to join their *jihad* using Facebook. Adeena, who was not on social media, was particularly worried about her daughters and warned them against speaking to strangers, especially on social media, about their religion.

When political topics did come up in discussions outside participants' religious-ethnic communities, many of them opted to listen quietly in order to gauge others' views of Muslim-related issues, even if the conversation was not directly about Muslims. For instance, on one particular college campus, I witnessed a group study session during student government elections, during which two members from opposing student political parties brought up the ongoing debate surrounding Palestinian and Israeli rights, a contentious topic that had created divisions in the campus community. The three Muslim students who were there did not contribute to the discussion, although I knew from my earlier conversations with them that they were well informed about the ongoing debate and had already decided to vote for the party supporting Palestinian rights.

However, this strategy to appear "moderate" by remaining distant from political issues in public can potentially render Muslims politically passive. The advice that many South Asian parents ingrained in their children emphasized hard work, education, and professional success, all of which they believed was possible if their children kept their heads down and stayed away from politics. For instance, South Asian Muslim parents usually instructed their children to "never get in fights" and "just walk away" if they were to encounter Islamophobic interactions. Moreover, when sending off their children to college, one of the common pieces of advice that parents gave was not to engage in political organizations but to instead focus on education and building a stable career, preferably in a STEM field. The mind-set of these parents was that their children could enter politics when they were "ready," meaning they could risk stepping into the political maelstrom when they had the safety net of professional success, recognition, and social status. Some parents especially forbade their children from becoming involved with political student organizations regarding the Palestinian-Israeli conflict. Parents worried that being too vocal about this politically charged issue in public would draw attention to their children's Muslim-ness and even depict them as politically subversive or "radical" Muslims, thereby hurting their career prospects.[52]

In her interview, Faizah described the instructions she had received from her parents before going off to college. To provide some context to the interview excerpt below, Faizah is referring to an incident colloquially called the "Irvine 11," in which ten Muslim students at the University of California, Irvine were found guilty and sentenced to three years of informal probation for disrupting a speech by Israel's ambassador, Michael Oren, on campus.[53] The incident had sparked debates about free speech and highlighted the fault line between Muslim and Jewish groups on many college campuses in the United States.[54] Whereas the Jewish campus community reportedly lauded the verdict, Muslim student groups, several civil rights organizations, and non-Muslim Americans overwhelmingly criticized the decision to take this nonviolent student protest to court and then to issue the students a verdict of guilty.[55]

Faizah, who previously described her family as "moderate," confessed that her parents had told her "not to get involved in the MSA [Muslim Students Association] and not to be too close to *hijabis* and people who are very, very religious by our standards." Asked to elaborate, she went on to explain her parents' reasoning:

> Because, especially in college I guess, people can have very extreme views. My parents didn't want my faith to get in the way of my education. It hasn't, but I guess there is a possibility that it could have. Especially like in campuses where the Muslims are really active, and they make themselves very, very known when they act politically. So, for example, when the Irvine 11 happened, the Muslims made it a point to be known. And that wasn't the most positive thing. My parents were aware of these events, and they were like, "You know, if that's what the MSA is like, then try to distance yourself from it—you don't want to be involved in that." I think they would have been very upset if they knew that I was involved in divestment [against Israel], to be honest, because that gets a lot of negative attention from different groups and makes you known politically. You make enemies even being involved with Muslims or the MSA in that sense. So, my parents didn't want that.

The parents of Hamza Siddiqui, a leader of University of California, Irvine's Muslim student union at the time, had concerns similar to those of Faizah's parents. According to an article in the *New York Times* about the incident, his parents had "warned him to keep quiet and not involve himself too closely with the student group," because they worried that he could get suspended and "jeopardize his prospects for law school."[56]

Overall, for many Muslim Americans, the Irvine 11 incident arguably sent yet another signal of their collective otherness in U.S. society. For instance, according to the *Los Angeles Times*, Shakeel Syed, the executive director of the Islamic Shura Council of Southern California, said this in regard to the guilty verdict: "Absolutely unbelievable. I believe the heart of America has died today. This is clearly an indication that Muslims are permanent foreigners, at least in Orange County."[57] And echoing Faizah's quote above, the verdict also sent a warning to the majority of Muslim Americans who, unlike the Irvine 11, were not typically vocal about Muslim-related politics in the United States.

Nonetheless, describing oneself as "moderate" has instrumental value, especially in times of extreme Islamophobic tensions. Muslim Americans, then, must either explicitly differentiate between themselves and Islamist extremists or risk being perceived as potential terrorists themselves.[58] However, to convincingly make their case in such moments of crisis, Muslim Americans have to carve out their visibility as "moderates" and do so incrementally over time, as the above examples show. Moreover, even on an everyday basis, being publicly perceived as "moderate" carries the benefit of being accepted (at least conditionally) by peers and coworkers.

The question of who is or what constitutes a "good Muslim" also appeared in Muslim settings. But here, it was one's devotion to Islam that indicated whether one was a "good" Muslim. Because of their explicitly visible marker of faith, the *hijabi* women were particularly viewed as representatives of Islam, even when they were among Muslims. They were held to higher standards and were expected to follow the Islamic rules and regulations more stringently than those without the headscarf. Although Bushra, a Pakistani American college student, did not wear the *hijab* herself, she best articulated how *hijabis* were largely viewed in the Muslim community:

> *Hijabis* are put—you know, because of their appearance—on this pedestal, to act a certain way or behave a certain way because they are seen as Muslims. And I guess *hijabis* feel more aware of what they are doing because of that. So even if they make mistakes or make a flaw, then people will generate rumors, gossip . . . bad-mouth Islam.

Indeed, activities usually frowned upon in the Muslim community, such as smoking or dating, if done by *hijabis*, generated harsher comments and became topics of community gossip. One time, I was having frozen yogurt with Shopna, Jahan, Taslima, and Raima—all Bangladeshi American college students—at a shop close to their college campus. We were sitting idly on an outdoor porch that overlooked a bustling street. Shopna wore a *hijab*, and Jahan her usual full sleeves and leggings. Taslima and Raima's clothes were more liberal: Taslima had on an off-the-shoulder top, and Raima a knee-length dress. Compared to Shopna and Jahan, Taslima and Raima were less strict about their daily prayers, were not *zabeeha*, and were open to dating, with Raima being engaged to her long-time boyfriend. All of them, however, self-identified as Muslim and claimed to have never consumed alcohol or pork. On this particular day, we were enjoying the sunshine and talking about a range of topics: from the current campus gossip, the plot of a recent episode of *Grey's Anatomy*, and a new restaurant opening, to more serious subjects like our marital aspirations and how we would react if our future children were gay (all four said they would be supportive). At one point, Shopna exclaimed, "Oh my god, you guys, like what is going on with Haseena and Javed?" I faintly recalled Haseena as a *hijabi* I had seen in the company of other Muslim students on campus. She was engaged to be married to Javed. But the couple was a recurring topic of gossip because of their dramatic, habitual falling-out and then getting back together. As the four women gossiped about the latest development, Shopna commented, "*Hijabis* can be crazy, y'all!" I asked, "What kind of crazy?" Shopna replied, "Like, they will wear the *hijab*, right? But that doesn't stop some of them from doing crazy stuff in parties. They'll do all kinds of stuff." The other three nodded. "Like what?" I asked, especially curious because it was Shopna, a *hijabi* herself, who was describing *hijabis* as "crazy." Taslima responded, "Like, I know *hijabis* who smoke, date . . ."

Despite also describing themselves as "moderates," the *hijabi* participants' self-presentation as "good Muslims" was markedly different than that displayed by those who did not wear an explicit marker of faith, like the headscarf. For one thing, *hijabi* participants were automatically marked as Muslims and thus could not distance themselves from their Muslim-ness as could Faizah and the rest. In addition, because their *hijabs* came with stereotypes that depicted them as oppressed women who'd been coerced into wearing a veil, the *hijabis* felt compelled to present themselves as "calm," "empowered," and "free to choose"—at times having to even overemphasize these universal but apolitical values. This often became burdensome and emotionally taxing to some of the *hijabi* participants because they felt pressure to represent Islam anywhere they went, all the time. Even their minute facial expressions and mannerisms carried potential repercussions in ongoing debates about Muslims.

Although primarily a symbol of faith, the *hijab* has come to carry multiple and, at times, even contradictory meanings based on historic and ongoing political discourses in both the national and global spheres.[59] Whereas to some segments of the U.S. population, the *hijab* symbolizes freedom of religious expression, to others it symbolizes an ever-looming threat of Islamic terrorism and the encroachment of Shariah law in the United States. Then again, while some view the *hijab* as a symbol of particularistic ethnoreligious identity,[60] others see it as a representation of an "American Islamic" identity and a symbol of anticolonial Muslim solidarity.[61] Conversely, others view it as an obstacle toward the integration of Muslim immigrants in Western societies.[62] The *hijab* is also intricately tied to gendered power relations. Whereas some see the *hijab* as a symbol of a patriarchal oppression inherent within Islam, others see it as a symbol of women's equal rights and empowerment.[63]

When one wears the *hijab*, she takes on all the different meanings attached to this piece of clothing and becomes an icon herself. Although only a small percentage of Muslim women in the West wear some sort of veil,[64] pictures of *hijabi* women have been used on posters protesting a "Muslim ban"—symbolizing resistance against nativism, racism, and right-wing nationalism—as much as they have been used to represent the "dangers" of Islamist fundamentalism and the risks of granting asylum to Muslim refugees. It is hardly a surprise, then, that the *hijab* has sparked contentious national and global debates about a whole host of issues that goes beyond a scarf being a mere marker of one's faith—debates about citizenship, national identity, secularism, multiculturalism, a "clash of civilizations," and the separation of church and state are but a handful of examples. Contentions over the *hijab* have also spilled over to other items of clothing that indicate Muslim faith, such as the *Burkini* (an all-coverage bathing suit for women). The controversy surrounding its ban in France in 2016 generated debates about Muslim integration in other Western countries, including the United States.[65] Together, these discourses have not only influenced public opinion about Muslims at large but also have shaped how Muslims perceive their collective position in the West.[66]

However, the *hijab*, like the label "moderate," is an inaccurate measure of one's religiosity and political views. I closely observed thirteen *hijabis* over the course of my fieldwork. Even within this small sample, opinions and experiences regarding the *hijab* varied widely. Some wore the *hijab* throughout the duration of the fieldwork; a few others had once worn the *hijab* but had stopped, choosing instead to wear modest clothing; and one wore it on and off before deciding to commit for the long term. While some viewed the *hijab* to be a step toward strengthening their faith, a couple of respondents had stopped wearing the *hijab* because they viewed it as an impediment to their spiritual development as Muslims. This latter group said they had been so preoccupied worrying about how others perceived them because of their *hijab* that the headscarf became too burdensome. They also said they felt more connected to Islam after they left the veil. Further, contrary to the popular view that veiled women are particularly strict about Islamic practices, some *hijabi* respondents had a more relaxed attitude about praying five times a day and eating *halal* than other women participants who had never worn the headscarf. With regard to political views, some *hijabis* espoused more progressive liberal views, such as advocating for gay rights, than other women without the veil.

Some *hijabis* also wore the veil to achieve goals beyond those related to religious devotion. While some liked wearing the *hijab* because they felt it protected them from the male sexual gaze, one young Bangladeshi woman I met during fieldwork had left the *hijab* because she was looking to get married and wanted to attract suitors. The *hijab* also served to help women gain respect in religious spaces and to widen their social networks. For instance, some older Bangladeshi *hijabi* women I met in Little Bangladesh wore the headscarf not only in devotion to their faith but also because they believed it to be the norm for older women in their ethnic society. One of these women said that the *hijab* garnered respect from her *deshi* peers. This was important for her, as she was well known in the enclave and used her social network for various worldly purposes, such as searching for a bride for her son.

Most of the *hijabi* participants, however, said they began wearing the headscarf of their own volition. Only a few—like Dina, a Bangladeshi American—started wearing the *hijab* at their family's behest. When I met her, Dina was a college sophomore planning to apply to medical school after graduation. Her family had come to the United States on a diversity visa when she was a month old. She had visited Bangladesh only once since then, when she was a child. Her wardrobe consisted of mostly denim jackets, light cardigans, full-sleeve tops, long skirts, jeans, scarves, and a few traditional *salwar kamiz*. She liked painting, sometimes applying henna designs on attendees at cultural events to earn pocket money. In her free time, she liked watching American sitcoms with her friends. Although she did not speak Bangla fluently, some of her friends came from Bangladeshi families. And though most of her friends were Muslim, they were ethnically diverse. She had met most of them through the Muslim Students Association in which she was an active member. Politically, Dina leaned more towards the left, although she said she was not "very interested" in American politics. She did not watch the news or subscribe to news apps on her phone. Rather, she preferred to keep up with only the news stories trending on social media. If she heard from her friends about important breaking news, however, she went on Google to learn more. Although Dina had been wearing the *hijab* regularly for the last few years, she didn't view it as defining every aspect of her life—and she didn't want it to. Instead, she viewed her decision to wear it as a continuous process in which she struggled with various aspects of her faith—a process that was shaped as much by Muslim stereotypes as by her own social interactions:

> *Hijab* was a process. My parents wanted me to wear it in middle school, and I firmly said no. I was very nervous about what people are going to say and stuff, remarks like, "You are terrorists," and that I am gonna be stigmatized. I was afraid of that. The middle school I went to, my friend group was diverse, and it wasn't the best neighborhood either. So, some people were very vocal about their opinions of us. My mom wears the *hijab*. So, I was scared that they would be vocal about me being outwardly Muslim. I actually wouldn't tell people I was Muslim growing up. It was something that I didn't talk about. I kind of hid it. I was sure that people were going to take my *hijab* negatively. Even one of my friends who I became really close to in high school, he would make jokes like, "Osama is your father." Nowadays, if someone says that, I wouldn't care. I would think them ignorant. It won't bother me. But back then, being a kid and knowing that people have these negative expectations of the person that you are even before they get to know you . . . I didn't want that. I wanted people to like me. I didn't want them to be like, "Oh, let's stay away from

her; let's make fun of her." I was really insecure about that. So, I chose not
to wear it in middle school. The high school I went to, I knew there were
many Muslims around. In my middle school there were no Muslims. In
high school, there were more Muslims, and the *masjid* was just across
the street. From what I had heard, the people there were a bit more open-
minded. So, I decided that I do want to wear the *hijab* and that this is the
point where I feel more comfortable doing it. Ever since then, I have been
really happy wearing it. In my first year, it was on and off sometimes.
I wore it at school, and I didn't wear it outside until later on in the year.
One day, I had it on and went outside, but I forgot that I had it on! At
that point, I realized that although this is a big thing, the *hijab* doesn't
define me completely—I am still myself. But even to this day, I struggle
a lot with still finding what I need to do in terms of finding my faith.

Despite Dina's concerns that the *hijab* would become the defining feature
of her identity, she nonetheless felt compelled to represent Islam in public.
Unable to distance herself from her visible Muslim-ness, the only strategy
often left at her disposal was to confront negative stereotypes about Muslims
directly. As such, to subvert the image of Muslims as aggressive and violent,
Dina often had to present herself as peace-loving, calm, and friendly, even in
interactions where one's normal, expected reaction would be to show anger:

> I make sure to smile . . . When you are wearing the *hijab*, you stand out.
> And if people have a perception of you from before because of your *hijab*,
> they might not be as open to talking to you initially. So, for me, a big
> thing is that *I* have to break that barrier. I just try to be myself around
> them [non-Muslims] and show them that I am not really different from
> someone who doesn't wear the *hijab*.

The "barrier" she was referring to was the idea that people from predominantly Muslim countries "are seen as the enemy" and that, to non-Muslims,
the behavior of one person from those countries might represent the behavior
of everyone from those countries. As Dina asserted, "It's all about perception."
She described feeling pressure to maintain her composure, in particular,
because she feared that any bad behavior she might be seen displaying would
then be assigned to all Muslims. Aware that she may be the only Muslim

person somebody has interacted with, she felt a burden of responsibility for putting her best foot forward in order to counteract negative media portrayals of Muslims.[67]

Asked to recall a specific incident in which she experienced this pressure, Dina explained,

> Yeah . . . let's see . . . umm, okay, so there was this one time when I was driving. There was a white guy who was driving a van. I had to go the lane behind him. I had to switch lanes and I could tell that he was looking at his rearview mirror to make eye contact with me. And I kept smiling. I was like, "This is stupid, but I am going to keep smiling." So, he comes to the other lane, drives next to me, and goes, "You motherf—ing Muslim!" And I just laughed, because I am not going to let him see me angry. So, I do feel that pressure . . . I do feel that, sometimes, when I meet new people, I have to put myself out there a little bit more to show them that I am interested in the same things as they are. Sometimes I sense that when people first meet me, they are a bit more reserved as opposed to when they get to know me. Then they are like, "Oh, I can be myself around her. We have similar interests."

Compared to Muslim women without veils, *hijabis* also encountered certain gendered stereotypes that stigmatized them as "un-American." In contrast to values widely accepted as "American" in U.S. society—such as freedom, equal rights, and empowerment—the *hijab* symbolizes to many Americans a backward, patriarchal Islamic culture that does not allow women the right to choose their clothing. Even in situations when *hijabi* women claim to have chosen to wear the headscarf, they are still viewed as being devoid of agency, incapable of thinking freely, and submissive to an oppressive religion.

These discourses were at the crux of Shehnaz's interaction with a fellow passenger on a bus to work. A first-generation immigrant from Pakistan, Shehnaz had traveled to various parts of the world before immigrating to the United States more than a decade before. When I first met her she was the founder of a nonprofit organization that moderated interreligious coalitions. As a naturalized U.S. citizen, she considered America her home. Even though Shehnaz described her family members as "relaxed" Muslims, she began wearing the *hijab* of her own volition when she started college in the United States. She was the only woman in her family to wear the headscarf. Even her grandmother who lived in Pakistan had discouraged her from wearing it because she saw *hijabis* as "too conservative." Shehnaz described her interaction on the bus as follows:

> I understand that people may have a lack of knowledge and information [about Muslims]. They may actually feel afraid at some level. The fear and concern that they feel may be expressed in anger, and so for me it makes sense to respond with as much compassion and empathy as I can. So, I just respond with calmness. There was one time where I was talking with a lady on the bus. And she was asking me why I was choosing to—well, she didn't use the word *choosing* to wear the headscarf—but she wanted to know why I was wearing the headscarf. And she told me that "You know, this is America. You don't have to do this—you are free here." And I was like, "Yes! I *am* free here, and that is why I choose to wear the headscarf. I am happy that America provides me the freedom to *choose* to wear my headscarf." And just hearing me, that I choose to do it, was a big surprise for her. And I was able to tell her that this is actually a way for me to empower myself. For me, I choose to do this because it's not just about the headscarf that I am wearing. The headscarf is just one part of how I dress. And the way I dress is just one part of how I behave and all of that—the reason that I choose to dress this way and behave this way is because, for me, it is a way to resist the sexual objectification of my body and, for me, that is a really empowering thing to do. And that was something that she could understand. Even if she didn't agree with the practice at the end of our conversation, my reason for empowering myself was something she understood, because she had the same values as an American woman.

The pushback against Muslim stereotypes from both Shehnaz and Dina was partly possible because of their positionality as young, U.S.-educated women who were fluent in English and exposed to the diversified American society. These resources allowed them to confront negative stereotypes with a level of ease that Hasna and Haleema, two older first-generation Bangladeshi *hijabis*, did not have.

Sisters Hasna and Haleema had very limited exposure to society beyond their small ethnic community. Neither of them had graduated from high school. Now widowed, their adult children were married and had their own families in Bangladesh, and the pair was living with their older brother and his family in a middle-class suburban neighborhood in the United States. He had sponsored them through the family reunification visa. Most of Hasna and Haleema's daily routine involved staying at home, where they cooked, cleaned, prayed, and watched Bangladeshi soap operas on YouTube. Their few outings were usually to the grocery store or to their relatives' house a few miles away. Although the area they lived in had a large South Asian and Arab population, most of their acquaintances were Bangladeshi, friends of their sister-in-law. The few non-Bangladeshis they knew were from their weekly English classes at a center near their home. Both knew very little English and seldom fully understood conversations in the language. Nonetheless, whenever they were treated differently than everyone else on the streets, they were aware it was because of their *hijab* and *burqa*.

In contrast to Dina and Shehnaz, however, who had the choice and the resources to inform non-Muslims about "real" Islam, Hasna and Haleema's only option when confronted with potential Islamophobia was to walk away. Neither of them could hold conversations in English. As such, they could not highlight their similarities with other Americans.

In our interview, I asked them how they felt they were perceived when they went out. Haleema answered that "people stare at us. They wonder what we are wearing, why we're wearing what we are." Hasna added, "They think we're Pakistani or Indian, but they don't know that we are actually Bangladeshi." She went on to explain,

> I don't get the feeling that they look at us in a good way. [Looking at Haleema for confirmation; Haleema nodding in agreement]. They look at our covering, and they sometimes clap, shout, make hand gestures, honk their cars. When they make a sound, we turn around and look at them once, but after that we don't pay them any attention. We just want them to know that we understand what they are trying to do to us, what they mean. Often, we hear them, but we don't pay attention, as if we didn't hear them. We just walk past them.

Compared to Dina and Shehnaz, Hasna and Haseena may appear unable to perform a "good Muslim" script. And yet, the fact that they did not engage when confronted with a possible hostile or Islamophobic situation is exactly what many South Asian Muslim Americans understand as enacting a "good Muslim" script. Doing nothing is, for them, a common strategy of navigating life in America as Muslims; however, their strategic silence comes with a price for Muslim Americans at large: Muslims are not only rendered politically passive but are also often collectively blamed for not speaking loud enough in condemnation of Islamist terrorism. At the same time, if Muslims do become politically vocal, they run the risk of associating themselves too closely with their Muslim-ness in public and, in some cases, being seen as politically deviant.

## ENACTING A "GOOD MUSLIM" SCRIPT AT THE ORGANIZATIONAL LEVEL

Islamic organizations, such as the Islamic Society of North America (ISNA) also strived to enact a "good Muslim" script, which involved adopting visibility strategies to help them appear "moderate." However, in contrast to the strategies deployed at the individual level, being visibly "moderate" was part of the organizations' larger project to construct a "Muslim American" identity that would allow members to actively participate in American public and political life. By portraying Islam as a peaceful and moderate religion that is compatible with American values, Muslim leaders aimed to establish an "American" brand of Islam that could overcome the limitations of political passivity and pave the way for Muslims' engagement in mainstream U.S. politics.

For instance, "constructing Muslim American identity" was one of the most recurring and extensively covered themes addressed in *Islamic Horizons*, ISNA's bimonthly magazine. This publication frequently included columns penned by Muslim scholars, educators, and activists who addressed the need to construct a Muslim identity specifically for the U.S. context, one that would highlight the compatibility between Islam and American values. For example, a Muslim leader and educator wrote in one of the issues, "Muslim Americans should accept and Islamize those cultural symbols and traditions of mainstream culture that do not contradict Islam."[68]

Growing the number of Islamic schools, which offer an alternative to public schools, was one key way that Muslim leaders aimed to inculcate a "Muslim American" identity. In their view, public schools did not help parents wishing to raise their children as Muslims—"at best they will ignore" that dimension of the children's identity.[69] In contrast, Islamic schools claim to teach students basic cognitive skills, like math, while also helping them to become "better Muslims" and "God-conscious Americans." To achieve those latter ends, students are taught the "universal" values of freedom, tolerance, and pluralism. From this view, Islam is a religion that promotes peace, pluralism, intellectual freedom, and tolerance for all—the same core values in the American ethos of freedom and democracy.

Thus, Islamic schools, according to Muslim leaders and educators, are spaces that can construct and distinguish an "American" brand of Islam—one that is "moderate" and tolerant (as opposed to religiously and politically extremist), respectful of freedom and pluralism (i.e., equal human rights for all), and in favor of democracy (as opposed to dictatorship and military autocracy). Muslim leaders' and organizations' efforts to define an "American" Islam based on these characteristics indicate the aim to differentiate the Muslim American community from other Muslims abroad, especially those in the politically turbulent and nondemocratic Muslim-majority countries in the Middle East. One issue of *Islamic Horizons* alluded to this aim by saying, "Transplanting a specific response to the colonialist threat in Muslim countries is not appropriate in the American context" and "Islamic schools must foster a healthy God-conscious identity that is compatible with America's pluralistic culture."[70] Moreover, Muslim community leaders claimed that Islamic schools act as "buffers against extremism" by inculcating in their students an interpretation of Islam specifically for the American context.

In fact, pluralism was one of the main aspects emphasized in the U.S. Muslim community's efforts to establish an "American" brand of Islam. For example, ISNA was aware that the Muslim American community is embedded in a racially charged political sphere in the United States and that this has produced fissures among different Muslim groups. Partly because of these contested group boundaries, ISNA at times struggled to present a unified front, which would presumably highlight its compatibility with America's pluralistic multicultural ethos. For example, ISNA usually downplayed the racial tensions that historically existed between immigrant and black Muslims. Then, after years of silence, ISNA made a hugely publicized gesture to "bridge" the divide between black and immigrant Muslims by publishing an *Islamic Horizons* issue showcasing African American Muslims. The issue reflected ISNA's overall aim to project a carefully carved image of the organization—and, thereby, a carefully carved image of the U.S. Muslim community at large—as a tolerant, multicultural group unified against Islamophobia.

With regard to the "Muslim American" identity, the main purpose of this category is to embed Muslims more firmly in U.S. civic and political life. So rather than distancing itself as an organization from politics, in order to avoid drawing attention to its Muslim-ness—as individual Muslims at times are compelled to do—ISNA used the Muslim American platform to encourage its readers to actively engage in local and national politics—to *highlight* their Muslim-ness and use it constructively instead of muting it. For instance, one issue of *Islamic Horizons* encouraged readers to engage in policy discussions and to lobby for the availability of *halal* food in fast food franchises, instead of silently consuming vegetarian alternatives. In another example, during presidential election cycles, issues of *Islamic Horizons* informed readers about how each candidate's platform impacted the Muslim community, encouraging them to actively participate in the elections.

Each year, ISNA sends envoys to meet political leaders in Washington to reinforce the image of Muslim Americans as a politically engaged constituency that is peace-loving, loyal, and law-abiding. Moreover, to foster political awareness among Muslim American youth, ISNA, along with other Muslim organizations, arranges annual Islamic youth conferences, scholarships, and internships that train young Muslims on how to gain leadership roles, engage in politics in Washington, forge coalitions, and advocate for civil rights.

Muslim American leaders also encouraged readers of its publications to voice their opinions on international politics concerning Islam and Muslims. Each issue of *Islamic Horizons* usually has two political sections: "Politics and Society," which covers domestic politics that ISNA thinks Muslim Americans should pay attention to, and "The Muslim World" or "Around the World," which covers Muslim-related issues abroad, in places like China, Palestine, Libya, Myanmar, France, and Australia. By spotlighting Muslim-related global issues like the Syrian refugee crisis and advertising charities that raise funds for such causes, ISNA has fostered the message that Muslim Americans—although distinctively "American" and "moderate"—are nonetheless part of the *Ummah*. This strategic platform allows Muslims in America to actively participate in Muslim-related issues in foreign places without running the risk of seeming "un-American."

Additionally, the community leaders urged Muslim individuals to strategically utilize their visibility to promote a positive image of Islam, to dispel ignorance about the religion, and to represent all Muslim Americans using the guidance of ISNA publications. For instance, one magazine issue focused specifically on ways that Muslim Americans could talk about Sharia law instead of remaining silent in fear of a backlash. The issue informed readers about parts of the Sharia that highlight democracy, equality, and freedom—values compatible with the U.S. Constitution.

Muslims in Houston volunteering after Hurricane Harvey and those in Tampa Bay offering to take in migrant children are just some examples of the Muslim American community's concerted efforts to insert Muslims into the public spotlight in a positive way. That said, Muslim American political mobilization still has a long way to go. Although there was a notable increase in grassroots activities in Muslim communities during the 2016 U.S. presidential election, overall, polls showed that Muslim voter registration and engagement lagged behind other religious groups.[71] Nonetheless, efforts to organize the Muslim American community saw great success in the 2018 midterm elections, where Muslims contested in unprecedented numbers, won 131 seats at the state and local levels, and—even more impressively—gained three congressional positions.[72] Arguably as a consequence of this wave, Rashida Tlaib and Ilhan Omar made history in the 2019 midterm elections by being the first Muslim women elected to U.S. Congress. However, despite these milestones, Muslim Americans at large continue to be racialized and conflated with Muslim-related politics abroad. The next chapter shows how Muslim Americans' insertion into U.S. politics interacts with their political orientation toward Muslim-related contexts "elsewhere."

# 5 | "MUSLIMS IN DANGER" BOTH HERE AND ELSEWHERE

ON THE EVENING of February 11, 2015, I was on a college campus in southern California. The Muslim Students Association (MSA) was organizing a community forum, to be held after the *Maghrib* prayer. The day before, three Muslim students in Chapel Hill, North Carolina—Deah Barakat, age twenty-three; his wife, Yusor Abu-Salha, twenty-one; and Yusor's sister, Razan Abu-Salha, nineteen—were killed in their home by their neighbor Craig Stephen Hicks, a white man. Hicks had shot the students in what Deah's father described as "execution style, a bullet in every head."[1] The shooting occurred just about a month after the *Charlie Hebdo* shooting. News of that terror attack had caught the world's attention and reignited debates in America about Muslims being threats to Western societies. Based on this broader context and the nature of the Chapel Hill shooting, the families of the victims described the incident as a hate crime. However, the police said the shooting appeared to have been motivated by an ongoing dispute between the neighbors over a parking space at their apartment complex.[2]

The Muslim American community was still reeling from the shock, especially because the mainstream media was slow to pick up the details and emotional resonance of the story. The local news had reported only that a man was arrested for a triple homicide.[3] Yet, my respondents, like many other

Muslim Americans, came to know about the shooting almost immediately through social media. Word went out on Facebook soon after the incident that the MSA would host a campus vigil to commemorate the victims. Respondents told me that some neighborhood mosques were also going to hold special prayers for the three students, indicating the incident had also struck a chord with Muslims beyond of the student community. A community forum, which I learned about from a Facebook post by one of my respondents, was set up for people to discuss what happened and how to move forward. As such, the atmosphere in the prayer area, where the forum was to be held, was noticeably somber.

The prayer area was actually an outdoor space on campus, adjacent to a parking lot behind a student activities building. During prayer times, students rolled out mats and carpets to pray. Behind them, the sound of delivery trucks unloading food for the campus cafeteria occasionally eclipsed the murmurs of student prayers. That evening it was already dark, but there were about forty students gathered in the area. Men and women were seated separately—the men in the front, and the women behind. The women's section had two rows. In the front row, the women were wearing *hijabs* or shawls to cover their hair. Everyone seemed to have come early so they could perform the *Maghrib* prayer before the forum began. In the back row a few women who had their hair uncovered were waiting for others to finish their prayers. People were still trickling in. I noticed that a few women who arrived late took scarves from their backpacks to cover their heads.

After the prayer, the men turned around so that they now faced the women, signaling the start of the forum. We were all sitting on the ground, with our feet bare and legs folded (we had to take off our shoes before entering the prayer space). The prayer mats did little to protect us from the cold, hard cement. From where I sat I recognized some faces in the audience: Daliah in the front row and Raima on the other side, toward the back. Hamzah, the president of the MSA, initiated the forum with some *Hadith* and verses from the Quran. After a few minutes a number of the students in the audience began to fidget—they seemed eager for the discussion to start. Hamzah ended his introduction by calling the three Chapel Hill victims "winners" because "they lived as Muslims and died as Muslims." Some of the audience nodded. He then asked everyone gathered, although they were in California and "not in the South where there is a lot of racism and Islamophobia," what they thought about their interactions with "others." "Should we be reactive or proactive?" he asked.

A woman from the front row responded by referring to the anti-Muslim backlash that followed the *Charlie Hebdo* attacks: "Even if we try to sympathize with those people, like those people in Paris perpetrating hate crimes against Muslims, it becomes alienating when they see you as 'others.' I have the question, like, how can we sympathize with people, when they don't do the same for us?"

Hamzah answered that "we" have to be nonetheless "proactive, because everyone on the other side is not the same." He then recounted a recent incident in which some Jewish students heckled MSA students after the student government passed a bill to divest Israel. The bill was part of the larger Palestinian-led Boycott, Divestment, and Sanctions (BDS)[4] movement on campus that advocated consumer boycotts from Israeli companies built in occupied Palestinian territories. The Muslim Student Associations in various campuses supported this movement. According to Hamzah, the MSA members did not react to the heckling. And later a Jewish student approached the hecklers and said that although he was from "the other side"—possibly referring to anti-divestment supporters and/or non-Muslims—the hecklers did not represent him in any way.

It is important to note that both Hamzah and the female audience member referred to Muslim-related issues rooted "elsewhere" to make sense of the Chapel Hill shooting in America. Indeed, although Hamzah's opening question was about the Chapel Hill shooting, the audience wanted to discuss a range of Muslim-related issues—not just here in the United States but also in places abroad where Muslims were stigmatized minorities. To them, Muslims in danger "elsewhere," especially in other Western societies, represented Muslims' collective "outsider" position here in the United States.

Similarly, at various times during my fieldwork, young South Asian Muslims often drew parallels between their collective and subjective experiences of growing up Muslim in post-9/11 America with Palestinians living under Israeli occupation. For instance, Bushra, the Pakistani American from chapter 3, said,

> I feel as Muslims, as a minority in this world,[5] we feel the discrimination against the Palestinians. Even here, Muslims feel the discrimination

against them . . . [Muslims] don't feel completely comfortable [here in America] as a white Christian person would. So, the fact that the U.S. and Israel are allies, it is obviously . . . so, our [Americans'] tax money [is] helping the occupation, which has a huge effect on us [U.S. Muslims], because we are basically helping kill people—Muslims—and settle into other people's homes, drive them away from their own homes, putting them in disastrous situations. That's kind of what is really great about the Muslim community is that we're unified on this issue because we understand it. Even if we [U.S. Muslims] are not Palestinian, you still understand how that feels, especially being in America. And I feel most people [Muslim Americans] have gone through some form of it, some form of discrimination, some sort of emotion that relates to it.

The South Asian Muslim American respondents, in fact, often strived to make sense of the politics surrounding Muslims in America using a globally informed lens. Sifat, the Pakistani American from chapter 2, believed that the conflict in Syria tied together Islamophobic contexts in various Western countries, such as the Muslim backlashes following ISIS terror attacks, Trump's calls for a "Muslim ban," and the discourse on immigration policy in light of the Syrian refugee crisis. This was made clear when I asked Sifat what she found interesting about the Syrian refugee crisis, a topic she said she was following on the news. She said,

I was actually discussing this with a friend recently. I don't know if you know this, but after the [November 2015] Paris attack happened, France didn't change its policy on letting Syrian refugees into the country, but the U.S. did. And even though the attacks didn't happen here, they [Americans] are pretty much going to keep an eye on how many Syrian refugees they are going to let into the country just because of that incident in Paris. I think that goes to show that America, or whoever that's controlling all of this in America, is looking for a reason to limit Muslims, limiting Middle Easterners, South Asian Muslims. I think they want to do that and this [the ISIS Paris attacks] gave them an excuse to do it.

In the days following the Chapel Hill murders, the emotional resonance surrounding the shooting intensified for Muslim Americans because of how the news media portrayed the incident. Many Muslims, including the interview participants, took note of the mainstream media's initial tepid response toward the murders, expressing their indignation on Facebook. Several posts included the hashtag #MuslimLivesMatter, referring to the Black Lives Matter movement. Muslims were especially outraged that the Chapel Hill police and the news outlets reported the incident as a parking dispute and not a hate crime.[6] Adding more fuel to their anger, some news outlets framed the incident as arising from the actions of a mentally disturbed individual.

This, however, was exactly how my participants and the larger Muslim American community had expected the U.S. media to respond. The day after the shooting, an op-ed titled "Chapel Hill Shooting and Western Media Bigotry" published in Al Jazeera, the Qatar-owned global news outlet, began to circulate among many of my respondents' Facebook pages. The author of the article, Mohamed Elmasry, an assistant professor of communications at the University of North Alabama, highlighted a pattern of Islam's representation in Western media and prognosticated that "Western media outlets will likely frame the most recent perpetrator of what some speculate is an anti-Muslim crime in the same way they frame most anti-Muslim criminals—as crazed, misguided bigots who acted alone."[7] He said that if past coverage gave any indication, the media reaction to the Chapel Hill shooting would provide "very little suggestion that the killer acted on the basis of an ideology or as part of any larger pattern or system." Indeed, that same day, Farhana, a Bangladeshi Muslim college student, shared on her Facebook page an NBC News story headlined, "Suspect's Wife: Shooting of Students Not Related to Race or Religion."[8] Using quotes from the video, Farhana posted:

> Welp, here we go. the shooter's lawyer has declared that in his personal opinion, "this highlights the importance of access to mental healthcare services and removing the stigma for people to ask for that type of help when they need it." as if the "mundane issue" of his parking frustrations justifies this heinous crime against humanity. ignorance frustrates me.

Faizah, also Bangladeshi American, then commented, "I was waiting for them to play the mental illness card." However, the coverage that sparked the most outrage from students was by CBS News's *Inside Edition*. Just one day after the Chapel Hill murders, the show's "Breaking the Code" segment featured a story on how to find parking space at the mall, referring to—and thereby legitimizing—the allegation that the shooting was the result of a parking dispute rather than a hate crime.[9] Deborah Norville, the host of the show, introduced the segment as follows:

> Three college students are dead. Their neighbor has been charged. Though initially some said it was a hate crime, the police say the dispute was over parking at the apartment complex. Now finding a parking space is one of those things that can push some people over the edge, but there is a way to always find a spot at the mall. Jim Moret helps you break the code.

A student made a video of the segment and uploaded it to her Facebook page with the comment "3 killed, but let us tell you how to find a great parking space. #muslimlivesmatter #chapelhillshooting #chapelhill #insideedition." Other students shared this clip calling it "sad," "disgusting," and "shameful." One of them used the hashtag #HateCrime. Although the participants thought a few journalists portrayed the Chapel Hill murders with the gravity it deserved—CNN's Anderson Cooper, for instance, was largely commended for his interview of Deah Barakat's sister—the insensitivity of the CBS News segment, along with the responses from the mainstream media overall, affirmed the view of many respondents that the media in the United States and the larger "West" was biased against—or, at best, indifferent toward—Muslims.

Of course, Muslims are by no means in conflict exclusively with the West, as world history offers countless examples of Muslims perpetrating violence against their coreligionists. The respondents themselves mentioned various such examples, such as the Sunni-Shia conflict, the Bangladesh-Pakistan war, the Saudi-Iran rivalry, and Bangladeshi and Pakistani domestic politics. And yet, in large part, examples of "Muslims in danger" around the world—such as incidents in France, the United States, and Israel—helped to reinforce the worldview of many of the respondents that the West was biased against Muslims.

As vectors of globalization, immigrants both produce and experience the interconnectedness of societies—not only those societies from which they come and to which they settle, but also those that occur beyond, or "elsewhere." Locating these immigrants' Muslim American identity on a global scale reveals how they situate themselves in relation to Muslim-related politics in foreign "elsewhere" places through their engagements in mainstream U.S. politics. For instance, many South Asian Muslim Americans are politically oriented toward places in the Middle East, like Palestine, Syria, and Turkey. As such, many of my participants supported Bernie Sanders during the 2016 presidential election because of his sympathy toward Palestinians.

Sometimes, Muslim-related issues "elsewhere" gained priority over those even in the participants' own homelands. For example, in late 2015, two refugee crises—both involving Muslims—were concurring in different parts of the world. One was the Syrian refugee crisis in the Middle East, and the other was that of Rohingyas in South Asia. Fleeing violent persecution in Myanmar, Rohingya Muslims were seeking asylum in Bangladesh. Yet whereas the South Asian Muslim immigrants avidly paid attention to the Syrian refugee crisis, the Rohingya crisis went largely unnoticed, even by the respondents who hailed from Bangladesh.

But why were these immigrants more oriented toward politics in the "elsewhere" Middle East than in their own homelands? And, relatedly, how did faraway foreign lands gain salience in South Asian Muslim Americans' political self-awareness? If their orientation toward politics "elsewhere" was indeed based on a sense of Muslim solidarity, then why did these immigrants not engage with Muslim-related politics "anywhere" in the world, such as Myanmar?

## POLITICAL AWARENESS TOWARD CONFLICTS
## INVOLVING ELSEWHERE

In the worldview of most respondents, the conflict that arguably stood as the most potent symbol of the West's continuing anti-Muslim attitude was that between Israel and Palestine. I inferred from conversations that the older, first-generation South Asians knew about the Palestinians before their migration to the United States, the issue's emotional resonance having been passed on to them by the prior generation. To them, Palestine was a reminder of the consequences of Western intervention in various parts of the Muslim world, including in their homelands, which had been under British colonization for over two centuries. In their view, around the same time Indians were fighting to oust their British colonizers (1947), so were their Muslim brothers in Palestine, which was a mandatory territory under British control. However, whereas South Asians succeeded in their anticolonial efforts, Palestinians did not. Although both regions were partitioned in 1947, these territorial divisions had a key difference. In the case of South Asia, despite the refugee crisis and the large number of deaths that resulted from the partition of Bengal, many natives from within the region (such as the All-India Muslim League and the Bengali Hindu Homeland Movement) desired the partitioning of the province between India and Pakistan based on religion. In contrast, the UN-approved partition of Palestine between Arabs and Jews was unwanted by the Palestinian Arabs and caused a civil and regional war, the effects of which seem to still generate headline-grabbing attention on almost an everyday basis.

The younger 1.5- and second-generation participants usually came to know about the specificities of the Israel-Palestine conflict after they entered college and encountered Palestinian classmates, activists, and human rights organizations. Before college they had been only somewhat familiar with Palestine based on glimpses of news headlines and snatches of their parents' conversations with Muslim co-ethnics. As a result, they thought of Palestine as just another conflict-ridden Muslim place in the Middle East. Most of these participants explained their concern for Palestinians as an expression of Muslim solidarity and viewed the Israel-Palestine conflict as one between a Muslim "us" and a non-Muslim "them." This attitude was exemplified by Dina and Jahan, two Bangladeshi Muslim college students. Dina wore the *hijab*, claimed to pray five times a day, and was actively engaged in the MSA. Jahan, in contrast, did not wear the *hijab* but wore "modest" full sleeves and leggings. She tried to pray if her class schedule allowed and participated mostly in cultural associations, particularly the Bangladeshi Students Association. Despite these differences in religiosity, Dina and Jahan came to care deeply for Palestinians based on an *Ummatic* sense of solidarity.

> DINA: I know people who are Palestinian, and there is also the religious aspect behind it. In the Quran, it says that Palestine will be free [according to her interpretation of the Quran]. We are supposed to help the oppressed. Again, them being Muslim is, I think, a big thing. When a Muslim brother or sister is in pain, you feel that too.[10]

JAHAN: I used to think it was a Palestinian issue and not a Muslim issue until I got to college and learned more about it, and then I considered it a Muslim issue as well. It's more of that we feel for the Palestinians, and a lot of Muslims take their side because Palestinians are Muslim. I think it's also basically because Israelis tend to be Jewish and Palestinians tend to be Muslims, and they are fighting over a land—horrible things are happening, Palestinians are dying, their homes are being destroyed, and they are our people. We are an *Ummah*, and we are supposed to support each other. I think it's our job to help them as much as possible. But I don't think the cause of the problem is only religion.

For both Dina and Jahan, their sense of Muslim solidarity also developed, if not emerged, in college, reflecting how exposure to the often-hyperpoliticized environment on college campuses shaped the political self-awareness of many of the young South Asian participants as Muslim Americans. In general, the younger respondents were U.S.-college-educated, fluent in English, plugged in to social media, and exposed to the larger American society far more than their parents. Particularly, they were exposed to campus student institutions, many of which espoused "color-blind activism," which is inclined to build solidarity among diverse racial and religious groups to advance a common cause, such as resisting Islamophobia and advocating for Palestinian rights.[11] Although most of these 1.5- and second-generation participants were members of the largely apolitical ethnic/cultural associations, they were nonetheless exposed (at times, even indirectly associated) to the more political activist student organizations through friends, roommates, classmates, and social media. For example, even though most of the young South Asian respondents were not members of the Palestinian rights organization on campus as college students, they had shown their support by participating in its demonstrations and forums, purchasing its organizational T-shirts, "liking" its posts on Facebook, and following its members' activities on social media. They had also supported the BDS movement, voting in favor of divesting Israeli companies during campus elections.

Although Palestine held symbolic importance for both the younger and older South Asian immigrants, an important contrast between the first generation and the more Americanized 1.5 and second generations was how much each group was willing to talk about their opinions on the subject. Whereas the younger generations were vocal about their thoughts on the Israel-Palestine conflict, often as a way to "speak up" against Islamophobia, their parents' generation was not only reluctant to publicly discuss their views but also instructed their children to stay away from organizations and conversations relating to this issue. These parents feared that becoming involved with this politically charged topic could "mark" their children as Muslims and put them on a "watchlist," which, in turn, could prevent them from getting jobs after graduation. This was reflected in a conversation I had with Ria, who had come to the United States from Bangladesh with her parents when she was about two years old. Her family was Sylheti, so when Ria spoke Bangla, she did so with a distinct regional accent. Ria wore a *hijab* and lived in Torrance, where her father ran a business supplying dry foods to South Asian and Persian markets. A fifth-year biology and philosophy major, she was working toward medical school when I met her through the Bangladeshi Students Association. As we were both active in the organization, we often spent hours together setting up cultural events. During that time, Ria and I talked about our families, our mutual friends, and the stresses that came with balancing personal life with work ambitions. I learned that she was a great cook, and on a trip to Artesia—the neighborhood known for its Indian clothing stores—I learned that she loved *desi* fashion and knew about all the big *haute couture* houses in India. Sometimes I shared findings from my fieldwork with her, to see if I was capturing nuances that were salient for long-time insiders of the community. In one such conversation I told Ria that I was having trouble recruiting first-generation respondents, as these "uncles and aunties" (referring to the older first generation) were usually not willing to be interviewed about their political views. She appeared to find their response familiar, saying that her parents did not let her talk about certain political topics, such as the Israel-Palestine conflict, even in the privacy of their own home:

> If I bring up topics like that or mention Palestine or BDS or the [Palestinian rights] organization, my mom will be like, "Hush! Hush! Don't say these things out loud." They told me to be very careful. Like, "If you are on their watchlist, they will find some way to take you down. You

understand this, right?" At my home, my parents watch a lot of Bangla-deshi news, so at home it's all very Bangladeshi. They are not really into American politics. But with this, they told me to be very careful.

When I asked Ria why her parents thought she needed to be careful, she said it was because of her Muslim background, which, when associated with Palestine, could render her "marked," presumably as a political dissident or an outsider. She said,

> You don't want to be marked. Actually, it is very common in a lot of South Asian families. So, you know the Muslim Students Association at UC Irvine? They are really political about this stuff [the Palestinian cause]. I know so many families who told their kids not to get involved with that MSA even though they are very religious. They just don't want their kids to get involved with politics and get marked.

The younger participants, of course, did not always listen to their parents' instructions. They usually openly expressed their opinions on Palestine as well as on other Muslim-related political topics during their conversations and recorded interviews with me. As such, I tried to learn about the first generation's views as much as I could through their children. Although frustrating at times, this strategy still proved useful. For instance, during my interview with Sifat (the Pakistani American from chapter 2), I asked her what her family members' views on the Israel-Palestine conflict were, and whether the crisis in Gaza, an issue she cared about, came up when she was away from campus, either in family gatherings or casual settings with older Pakistani men and women. Her response gave me insight into how the participants' reactions to "elsewhere" could vary based on their level of education. She said,

> These topics come up more in an educated setting, I would say. If you are with a group of people who haven't been to school, who haven't been to college, their main arguments would be either something that they have personally experienced or something they learned as they grew up. I have been in both kinds of settings, and when it's a setting with just a group of old people, just talking, sipping tea, it's always that the Jews hate us, and it sort of . . . the topic sort of begins and ends there. But when you

go to a more educated setting, if you go to where people sort of our age [and] Pakistani [are] talking, then they would go more into . . . they will bring up things that are happening in Palestine. They [the more educated individuals] will pull up things and show us, "Look, this is what"—not Jews, they wouldn't say Jews—they would probably say, "This is what Israel is doing in Palestine. This is what's happening, this house was blown up, this person was shot for no reason. But you will definitely feel in that room the vibe that everyone is really anti-Israel and very pro-Palestine in any Pakistani Muslim household across the board, I would say 100% of them. Some might be a little more aggressive about it, some might not want to give a straight answer, but majority believe that what's going on in Palestine is wrong. But unfortunately, 50–60% of them will say it just because its Muslims versus Jews, but the other 40% will give you a proper reasoning behind it. They will tell you, "This is happening here and here and here, and that is why I believe what I believe [pro-Palestine]."

Overall, the attitude of my respondents on the Palestinian issue largely reflected that of the overwhelming majorities in Arab and Muslim-majority countries: that the United States is believed to "favor" Israel "too much."[12] This perception has likely taken deeper hold in light of President Trump moving the U.S. embassy to Jerusalem in May 2018, despite mass Palestinian protest and loss of life, which the American and Israeli governments have said were instigated by Hamas.[13]

### ENGAGEMENT WITH THE ELSEWHERE MIDDLE EAST THROUGH MAINSTREAM U.S. POLITICS

Before the 2016 Democratic primary in California, Afroza, a Pakistani-American college senior, shared on her Facebook page the article "Why Muslims are Voting for Bernie Sanders," from a website called *Ummah Wide*. She encouraged her Muslim friends who were "advocating" for Hillary Clinton "without even doing their research" to read it. The article read as follows:

In the upcoming June 7 California primary, Muslim voters in the Golden State are consciously supporting Bernie Sanders, the one candidate that has explicitly and consistently condemned Islamophobia and bigotry. Sanders' vehement opposition to Islamophobia is far more than merely political posturing against the man who built much of his campaign upon it; nor pandering to a voting bloc that helped deliver the "Michigan miracle" [referring to Sanders's unexpected landslide win in the Michigan primary] to the Sanders campaign in March. But rather, a position consistent with a track record of siding with broad Muslim American interests, and against the "War on Terror" policies that curtail Muslim American civil liberties. . . .

Sanders, unlike Hillary Clinton, stood firmly against the PATRIOT ACT. And today, stands against Islamophobia while his Democratic Party competitor perpetuates "clash of civilizations" rhetoric that foreshadows a commitment to carry forward racial and religious profiling programs. . . .

With regard to foreign policy, Bernie Sanders is the far better candidate for Muslim Americans. Sanders vehemently stood against the War in Iraq, voting against it while Hillary Clinton favored it. In addition, Sanders brings an evenhanded and progressive stance on the Palestinian-Israeli conflict. During April's Democratic Debate in New York City, Sanders stated:

"In the long run, if we are ever going to bring peace to that region, which has seen so much hatred, and so much war, we are going to have to treat the Palestinian people with respect and dignity . . . I believe the United States and the rest of the world have got to work together to help the Palestinian people."

While unprecedented, these words reflect Sanders' humanitarian outlook, and outreach efforts to include Palestinian American leaders in his campaign, most notably Linda Sarsour and Amer Zahr, who serve as campaign surrogates. . . .

This inclusion also extends more broadly to Muslim Americans.[14]

An important finding of this book is that South Asian Muslim Americans, regardless of their immigrant generation, evaluate mainstream U.S. politicians based on those politicians' attitudes toward "elsewhere" conflicts. Said another way, how the politicians respond to Muslim-related issues "elsewhere" sends a signal about how those politicians would treat Muslims and their concerns here in America. This was made clear during the 2016 Democratic presidential primaries, when most of the participants favored Bernie Sanders over Hillary Clinton because, among other issues, they viewed Sanders as sympathetic toward Palestine. His willingness to "treat Palestinian people with respect and dignity" and his criticism of Israel for its "disproportionate" response in the Gaza Strip—as he famously declared during the Democratic primary debate in April 2016[15]—signaled to many of the respondents his openness toward Muslims at large. Conversely, many South Asian Muslim Americans viewed Clinton's Middle East policy as too pro-Israeli and thus biased against Muslim interests. The contrast between the two candidates on this issue was affirmed for many participants when Sanders criticized Clinton for "barely mentioning" the Palestinian people in her speech at a high-profile convention organized by AIPAC, the pro-Israeli lobby group.[16] Sanders, setting a sharp contrast to Clinton, had declined to either attend or speak in person at the convention.

Shortly after the Democratic primary debates, I went to interview Rahim and Rahila, a retired elderly Bangladeshi couple at their small, one-bedroom apartment in Little Bangladesh. Rahim and Rahila came to the United States when their daughter, a naturalized U.S. citizen through marriage, applied to bring them over to America. The couple now lived with their adult un-married son who worked full time while taking courses from a community college. Rahila usually spent the day cooking for the family and cleaning up the house. She knew several Bangladeshi families in the neighborhood and sometimes cooked food for them, which she took with her during house calls. Rahim, however, seemed not to have many friends, although he some-times went to the Bangladeshi restaurant nearby to watch cricket matches with other Bangladeshi men. Sometimes his son's *deshi* friends came over to their apartment to watch cricket matches together when Bangladesh was playing. Otherwise, he spent most of his day watching television, usually the Bangladeshi channels that catered to nonresident Bangladeshis (NRBs).

During my visit I sat with Rahim and Rahila in the tiny sitting area of their apartment, sipping fruit juice that Rahim had kindly offered. He had gotten up from the sofa to bring the drink from the refrigerator himself. With a shy but fatherly smile he had insisted I drink, saying *"Diet kora lagbe na. Eita foler rosh. Eita khele kichhu hoy na."* (No need to diet. This is fruit juice. You won't gain weight drinking it.) From where I sat, the apartment's narrow sliver of a balcony was on my left. Resting there was a chair on top of which was folded a *jaynamaj* (prayer mat). Rahila was cooking something on the stove, so she had to get up a few times to check on the food. She had a kind and friendly demeanor and asked about my family. Rahim was clearly the quieter of the two. Although he too seemed friendly and curious, he was a little shy about talking to me, a pattern I found common in Bangladeshi Muslim households, where older male members usually kept a distance from young women outside the family.

To break the ice before I asked Rahim's permission to interview him, I asked him what he usually watched on TV, which he then turned on mute. With a small smile, he gave a one-shoulder shrug and said, "*Eito, eita-sheita. Khobor.* Cricket." (You know, this and that. The news. Cricket.) I asked him if he watched news about the election. "Somewhat," he answered, saying that he mostly followed *deshi* news. I asked him what party he supported. He replied that of the two parties, the Democrats seemed to at least want "us" ("us" possibly referring to immigrants, Muslims, and/or Bangladeshis). When I asked him which one of the Democratic candidates he favored, he replied with a small smile, albeit reluctantly, "*Oi buratare beshi bhallagey,*" (I like the old man more,) referring to Sanders. When I asked why, he said, "*Oita tao to money hoy amader kotha shoney.*" (It seems like he at least listens to us.)

Conversations about American politics, particularly in regard to elections, primaries, race relations, and issues of social justice, were noticeably more frequent and pronounced among the younger, U.S.-college-educated 1.5 and second generations. A possible reason for that was their high level of connectivity to social media. Whereas the few older immigrants who used Facebook used it mostly to keep up with their *deshi* friends and family here and back home, the younger participants overwhelmingly used these platforms as their primary source for global, national, and local news. In addition to using social media to stay connected with friends, the South Asian Muslim youth used it to express their opinions on a wide range of subjects and to engage with various causes. This was particularly clear during election season, when they shared their views of the candidates on Facebook, sometimes posting live commentary about debates, town halls, forums, and primaries. For instance, many South Asian Muslim students watched the Democratic primary debate live on campus, where student organizations had arranged for projectors to screen the event in classrooms. Some of the students took pictures of the screen when Sanders was speaking about Palestine and posted them on Facebook, expressing their enthusiasm with the hashtag #feelthebern. Similarly, when Hillary Clinton and Bernie Sanders were locked in an intensely close race in the Iowa caucuses in February 2016, an Indian Muslim student posted, "make *dua* [an Arabic word for 'prayers'] for Bernie" as the results started coming in. These Facebook posts were an important way for me to gain insight into these students' political awareness and identification, because they were sharing them spontaneously in their own time, without my interference as a researcher to somehow prompt them to act in certain ways.

An important source through which the South Asian Muslim youth received news about the candidates and their platforms was the social media profiles of Muslim American activists, like Linda Sarsour, *ustadha* (teacher) Yasmin Mogahed, and Khalid Latif, the chaplain of the Islamic Center at New York University. Several of the young participants, for instance, admittedly did not stay tuned to the ups and downs of American or global politics. Few regularly read the major national newspapers like the *New York Times* or the *Washington Post*. In many of their houses, *desi* channels played in the background during family dinnertime instead of CNN or MSNBC. Even those who did show an active interest in politics received notifications of filtered topics from CNN, BBC, and Al Jazeera on their phones. Even then, some participants intentionally did not subscribe to American news outlets, often finding them "infuriating," "frustrating," and "too biased." As such, most young South Asian Muslims received their news updates from social media, namely Twitter and Facebook, rather than from traditional news outlets.

As such, during the 2016 U.S. presidential election, Muslim American activists like Sarsour, Mogahed, and Latif arguably played an influential role in shaping the South Asian Muslim youth's interpretations of the candidates. These kinds of personalities, with over a hundred thousand followers on Facebook each, are widely respected in the Muslim American community. In addition to providing spiritual guidance and motivational advice, these high-profile figures often write posts that express their political views. They encourage their followers to become "woke," or politically aware, about Muslim-related issues both in the United States and in places abroad, such as in Palestine, Pakistan, Bangladesh, and Yemen. Even prior to the 2016 election, in 2014 for instance, Yasmin Mogahed encouraged her followers to change their profile pictures to a photo that read "Save Gaza." She also made posts publicizing fundraising events for Syrians during the month of *Ramadan* in 2018 and drew attention to an Islamic relief tour in Canada that collected *zakat* (annual alms mandated in Islam) for arranging "emergency *iftaars*"[17] for Muslims fasting in Palestine. Similarly, in 2017, Khalid Latif posted pictures of himself in a Bangladeshi Rohingya refugee camp, encouraging his followers to make donations to supply food for their "brothers and sisters" in their "time of need." During the Democratic primaries, many of these personalities posted pictures, memes, and statuses indicating their support of Bernie Sanders because of his outreach to the Muslim American community. Figure 5.1 provides some examples of these posts, which were

**FIGURE 5.1.** Screenshots of Facebook posts of Muslim American public figures in support of Bernie Sanders. *Source*: Public Facebook pages of Linda Sarsour and Yasmin Mogahed.

liked and shared by thousands of Facebook users, including some of my participants. In the first example, Bernie Sanders tweeted in Arabic, calling for a united stand against "racism, hatred and bigotry" with the English hashtag "#AmericaTogether." His use of Arabic and Linda Sarsour's retweet not long after suggest that the post was referring specifically to Islamophobia. In the second example, Yasmin Mogahed posted a meme that depicted Bernie Sanders as the more favorable alternative to both Trump and Clinton.

In large part, these posts aimed, if not served, to mobilize Muslim Americans to participate in mainstream U.S. politics, and more specifically, to vote for Bernie Sanders. The fact that Bernie Sanders was a Jew who, in his youth, spent several months volunteering in a *kibbutz* in Israel[18] did not dampen the participants' or the larger Muslim American community's favorable view of him. His foreign policy toward the Middle East, sympathy for Palestinians, and outreach to Muslims in the United States seemed to outweigh his personal affiliations with Israel. Indeed, when voters in Dearborn—a city in Michigan where over 90 percent of the population is Arab and Muslim— overwhelmingly supported Sanders, a Jewish candidate, in the Democratic state primary, reporters flocked to interview the residents, to shed light on this seeming contradiction. When one reporter asked a young Arab American Muslim why he supported Sanders, the young man replied that his support was based on Sanders's "good foreign policy record."[19] Moreover, many Arab and Muslim voters did not seem to care about the candidates' personal religious backgrounds. In fact, they deemed the media and political analysts' bafflement over Muslims supporting a Jew to be based on a stereotype that all Muslims are somehow anti-Semitic.[20]

After Sanders lost the Democratic presidential nomination to Clinton, Nilufer, an Indian American Muslim college student, shared a post that listed all the reasons why she would rather vote for third-party candidate Jill Stein than Clinton. Among the reasons were, "[Hillary] is partial when it comes to Israel and Palestine. She is openly hostile towards Palestinian human rights and does not care about the occupation and colonialism Palestinians face that have led to apartheid conditions." I later learned that a few of the participants had indeed voted for a third-party candidate in the main election.

These orientations based on a sense of solidarity with Palestinians reveal a form of cross-border political tie that goes beyond the existing homeland-hostland framework. Scholars have long studied long-distance nationalism and political transnationalism—specifically, how immigrants have sought to participate in homeland nation-building, regime change, or democratic political processes from their hostlands.[21] However, the South Asian Muslim Americans were engaging in anticolonial efforts directed at "elsewhere." They did so as individuals in everyday forms such as sharing and liking social media posts and buying T-shirts from activist organizations; but they also did so in more organized collective ways, such as by demonstrating, voting for consumer boycotts, participating in calls for economic sanctions, and engaging in mainstream politics.

### PRIORITIZING ELSEWHERE OVER THE HOMELAND

That many South Asian Muslim Americans engaged in some form of political activity targeted at Muslim-related conflicts in foreign lands would not have been as surprising had they been equally engaged in similar ongoing events that involved coreligionists and co-ethnics in their homelands. Yet, many of the young participants were unaware of some of the deep-seated conflicts in their countries of origin—even those who regularly tuned in to Muslim-related world news based on a sense of solidarity and subscribed to homeland-oriented ethnic and cultural identities (such as *desi* or Bangali). Their political engagements were, rather, overwhelmingly aimed toward "elsewhere" Middle Eastern places, such as Syria, Palestine, and Turkey.

For example, in late 2015, around the same time that the world turned its attention to the Syrian refugee crisis, when the body of three-year-old Aylan Kurdi washed ashore on a beach in Turkey, another refugee crisis was unfolding in South Asia—that of Rohingya Muslims in Myanmar. And yet it would take two more years and the chilling photograph of another child washed up, facedown, on a muddy riverbank—this time sixteen-month-old Mohammed Shohayet—for the global public to finally take notice of the more than half a million Rohingyas fleeing violent religious persecution in their homeland.[22] A distinct Muslim ethnic group in the Rakhine province of Myanmar, the Rohingyas have long suffered apartheid-like conditions. Although they have lived in the country for centuries, the Myanmar government views Rohingyas as Bangladeshi economic migrants and stripped them of their Burmese citizenship in 1982, effectively rendering them stateless.

These tensions reached a critical level in 2012, resulting in violent clashes and the displacement of over 140,000 Rohingyas.[23] Since then, much like their Syrian counterparts, almost a hundred thousand Rohingyas set sail on boats, in dangerous attempts to escape their homeland by sea.[24] The International Organization for Migration estimated in 2015 that eight thousand Rohingyas were stranded at sea.[25] So great was the exodus of Rohingyas attempting to cross the Malacca Strait and the Andaman Sea into Malaysia, Indonesia, and Thailand that the international community dubbed them the "boat people."[26] Also called the world's "most friendless people" because their plight has been overlooked by the global community,[27] these refugees were caught in international "human ping-pong," when none of the neighboring countries wanted to grant them asylum.[28] Most of the refugees were taken into Bangladesh, where they now continue to live in dire conditions in refugee camps. Since 2017, pleas for aid and visits to the sprawling Rohingya camps in Bangladesh—the largest refugee camp in the world[29]—by international humanitarian organizations, celebrities, and public figures have helped to bring political and public attention to this crisis, leading to increased public interest in the United States.[30] Interestingly, it was also in late 2017 that I observed some concerted effort within the *desi* Muslim community to raise funds for the Rohingyas, but that was only because a Bangladeshi American who had recently graduated from college had taken the initiative through her community mosque. During the remainder of my fieldwork, from 2012 to 2017, however, this ongoing crisis was overwhelmingly overlooked. Unlike in the case of Syrian refugees, news of Rohingyas hardly ever "trended" on social media. For instance, a Google Trends search of the terms "Rohingya refugee" and "Syrian refugee" yields a flatline for the former and huge spikes for the latter, indicating the disparity in American public interest toward the two crises over the course of my fieldwork.[31]

Even while my participants avidly paid attention to events in Syria—following social media trends, posting statuses on Facebook, organizing forums, discussing the news with family and friends, donating and raising funds to help Syrians flee for safety—the plight of the Rohingya refugees went virtually unnoticed. Indeed, many of the Bangladeshis were unaware of who the Rohingyas even were, despite sharing with them not only a common religion but also a common ethnicity. While I heard the older, first-generation

Bangladeshis express sadness about Syrian refugee children dying, I never heard them mention Rohingyas in their conversations. And as it was mostly the young, college-educated respondents who appeared to keep up and engage with Muslim global politics, I was surprised to find that only one of the younger participants, Taslima, a Bangladeshi college senior, mentioned the Rohingya crisis. In the comments section of a news post about Rohingya refugees on Facebook, Taslima criticized Bangladeshi Prime Minister Sheikh Hasina's initial refusal to grant asylum to the Rohingyas. Even then, her critique mainly addressed the widespread corruption of Bangladeshi politicians rather than the plight of the Rohingya people. These examples show how, for the South Asian Muslim immigrants, the salience of persisting divisions based on homeland dynamics appears to fade, replaced by concerns oriented toward "elsewhere."

My interview with Faizah, the second-generation Bangladeshi from chapter 4, offers another example of respondents being more attuned to Muslim-related crises "elsewhere" than to those in their homelands. When I met Faizah, she was a year away from graduation, after which she planned to go to optometry school. She regularly participated in the Bangladeshi Students Association where many of her closest friends were board members. Although Faizah could not speak Bangla fluently, she described herself as "culturally Bangali." When I asked her what she meant, she listed a string of things she liked, such as "wearing *desi* clothes, eating homemade Bangali food, and watching Bollywood movies," indicating a sense of symbolic attachment to her Bangladeshi ethnicity. Faizah did not wear a *hijab* but, like her older sister, took care to wear "modest" clothes that covered her arms and legs. Her mother, a homemaker, also did not wear a *hijab* but wore *salwar kamiz*, even at home. It was from her mother that Faizah and her sister had learned to pray *namaaz*. As a self-labeled "practicing" Muslim, Faizah claimed to try to perform all five prayers and to fast during *Ramadan*. She had also been active in the MSA since her first days in college. There, she had found a supportive group of friends who helped her with information about classes and professors, loaned her iClickers and textbooks, and introduced her to people and associations on campus.

One of the organizations she came to know through her MSA friends was the Palestinian rights organization. Although she was not an active member, she often went to its events and town hall meetings. Like many other young respondents, she also shared and liked the organization's posts on social media. Her Facebook timeline showed news stories from the BBC and Al Jazeera about outbreaks of violence in Gaza, indicating that she kept informed about Palestine. Sometimes—usually during campus elections—she posted statuses that urged students to vote in favor of BDS. When I interviewed Faizah in late 2015, she described how she first came to learn about Palestine as follows:

> So yeah, when I came to college and joined the MSA, I started hearing about this issue called divestment, which was to divest from companies that we are currently invested in and that contribute to what's happening in Gaza right now. So [initially], I had no idea about what any of that was or what that meant. I honestly was pretty ignorant about what was happening in Gaza. But by going to the divestment hearings, because it's such a big deal [on campus], and learning more and more about what it was, and hearing people's personal anecdotes—[from] Palestinians or Muslim people, [from] people who cared in general—hearing their anecdotes about how what's happening in Gaza was so unacceptable and how we are all complicit in it by not acting on it or trying to stop it, I became very, very guilty, and so I started looking into it more and more. And then now it's just something that I care a lot about.

I asked Faizah why she cared about a faraway foreign place like Palestine, especially as it produced little impact in her life in America. Much like Dina and Jahan, Faizah expressed a sense of "groupness" with fellow Muslims there. Yet, when I asked her if she felt the same sense of belonging with Rohingya Muslims, I found her unaware of the Rohingya refugee crisis. She replied, "Umm . . . I am sorry, but I don't know about that." I gave a brief overview about Rohingyas and their struggle to receive asylum in Bangladesh, to which she responded, "Oh, wow, that's so sad. I know this is bad, but I didn't see this news. I don't follow the news that religiously actually. But this is very bad what's happening. If something bad happens to Muslims or anyone else, basically we all [Muslims] need to step up."

I observed a similar contrast in the way some participants responded to the political dynamics in Pakistan and Turkey. Both countries had conducted genocide against an ethnic minority in their respective territories—Turkey against Armenians from 1915 to the early 1920s, and Pakistan against

Bangladeshis in 1971. Further, the governments of both countries still deny having conducted the mass killings. Yet, whereas many South Asian Muslim Americans engaged in divestment efforts to force the Turkish government to recognize the Armenian genocide, there was no similar pushback against Pakistan for its denial of the mass killings of Bangladeshi civilians, who were citizens of East Pakistan at the time.

This became clear to me when Daliah (the Bangladeshi American from chapter 2) and I were preparing for a bake sale for the Bangladeshi student organization at my apartment. It was busy work, so we kept ourselves entertained with conversations about the Bollywood superstar Shah Rukh Khan, the latest spat between the Palestinian and Jewish student organizations, and the most recent cases of aunties[32] pushing us to get married. Finally, after a long day of mixing and baking, all of the batches of brownies were in the oven and Daliah and I were able to catch a breath. We had more of the same to do, but we were waiting on other Bangladeshi students from the organization who would arrive soon to help. After a few moments of silence, Daliah, who was relaxing on a recliner, asked me if I would support a movement to divest Turkey. I was caught off-guard, because the only divestment movement I was aware of was that toward Israel. When I asked her why one would divest from Turkey, she replied that the Turkish government's denial of the Armenian genocide was "wrong" and that "we should stand up and make them recognize what they did." I knew Daliah was actively engaged in the BDS movement, so I asked her if she did not think that divesting from Turkey would be a conflict of interest, given that Turkey is a predominantly Muslim state and a major provider of humanitarian resources to Palestine. Daliah replied that, even then, "we Muslims can't be blind" to our own wrongdoings. She added,

> We [Muslims] have to stand up to all human rights abuses—not only to those against us. We have to own up to what we do. If we don't, we can't expect others to own up to theirs. Besides, I know many Armenians, and the Armenian student association supported BDS.

In the following weeks and interviews, I inquired about the matter further to find out whether other South Asian respondents shared Daliah's views. I learned that the Palestinian rights organization and several South Asian cultural associations had signed and released official statements regarding divestment from Turkey. When asked about their motivations, some of the members of these organizations emphasized the need to build coalitions centered on the BDS movement against Israel. As the Armenian Students Association was considered an "ally" because of their support for BDS, Muslim students were inclined to return the favor by signing the divestment resolution against Turkey. Other college-going participants supported the divestment from Turkey based on a sense of humanitarian and religious obligation as "good Muslims." For instance, Bushra (the Pakistani American from chapters 3 and 4) said it was the "duty of a good Muslim" to stand up to any injustice.[33] Yet, when I asked Bushra why she then did not also divest from Pakistan, because of its denial of the mass killings of Bangladeshis in 1971, Bushra looked embarrassed. She replied that she was "not very familiar" with that part of her homeland's history but thought that the Pakistani government should apologize to Bangladesh. Like Bushra, I found that many of the young Pakistani Americans did not know about the Bangladeshi genocide before they entered college. Moreover, whereas Bangladeshis—even those of the 1.5 and second generations who had mostly symbolic ties to their ancestral homeland—understood their country's independence as "gaining liberation" through the 1971 war, the Pakistani Americans were vaguely informed about Bangladesh just "seceding" from West Pakistan. These young Pakistanis appeared to be encountering the history of the Bangladeshi genocide for the first time at cultural events on campus in which Bangladeshi students gave presentations on their homeland.

### ELSEWHERE AND POLITICAL SELF-IDENTIFICATION

So why had these immigrants given more attention to Muslim-related contexts in the "elsewhere" Middle East than in their own homelands? My findings from chapter 3 show that these immigrants came from homelands where religious politics is used as a lens to inform boundaries both within and between the homelands and between the so-called Muslim world and the West. The national, political, and religious lives in these countries are still deeply influenced by the subcontinents' direct conflict with the West during British colonization. Moreover, the general public of that region is largely aware, if not informed, of the various instances of Western intervention in the Muslim world, such as in Palestine, Iran, Iraq, Afghanistan, and Pakistan.[34] Arab influence over Islam and religious institutions in South Asia added a global dimension to these historic and ongoing conflicts, shaping the homelands' internal religious-political dynamics as well as the worldview of many segments of these countries' Muslim populations.

South Asian immigrants brought these homeland contexts with them to the United States, but upon their arrival, they encountered the heightened Islamophobic context that had arisen after 9/11, as shown in chapter 4. The immigrants' homeland contexts, their Islamophobic encounters in the hostland, the American media's portrayal of Muslim Americans and the ongoing contentions between the United States and the Middle East all combined to reinforce the worldviews of many South Asian Muslim Americans that "the West" was biased against "the Muslim world." However, as Muslim Americans, these South Asian immigrants were able to now influence U.S. policies toward the Muslim world by voting and engaging in mainstream U.S. politics—something they were not able to do back in their homelands despite having sympathy for their fellow Muslims. In fact, engaging in mainstream politics not only in the U.S. context but also toward Muslims in other countries has been one of the key goals of Muslim leaders and organizations in constructing a "Muslim American" identity (as was shown in chapter 4). And as this chapter has shown, many South Asian Muslim Americans indeed favored mainstream politicians who they viewed as sympathetic to Muslims both here and abroad. Figure 5.2 below presents a visual representation of this analysis using the multicentered relational framework.

With regard to why Muslim-related contexts, particularly those in the Middle East, had salience for the participants—at times even more so than similar contexts in the homelands—I argue that South Asian Muslim Americans engaged with the Middle East not just based on a sense of groupness with fellow Muslims but also because Muslim-related conflicts in the Middle East are more influential than regional South Asian events in how they are identified in the United States. For example, whereas the Syrian refugee crisis impacted U.S. immigration policies and border control, the Rohingya refugee crisis—despite also involving Muslims—did not have any direct impact on the United States. Further, the participants' homeland-oriented engagements may have been absent partly because any confrontation over conflicts occurring in the sending countries, such as in the 1971 Bangladesh-Pakistan war,

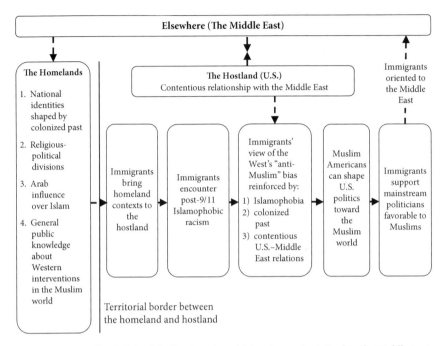

**Elsewhere (The Middle East)**

**The Homelands**

1. National identities shaped by colonized past

2. Religious-political divisions

3. Arab influence over Islam

4. General public knowledge about Western interventions in the Muslim world

**The Hostland (U.S.)**
Contentious relationship with the Middle East

Immigrants bring homeland contexts to the hostland

Immigrants encounter post-9/11 Islamophobic racism

Immigrants' view of the West's "anti-Muslim" bias reinforced by:
1) Islamophobia
2) colonized past
3) contentious U.S.–Middle East relations

Muslim Americans can shape U.S. politics toward the Muslim world

Immigrants oriented to the Middle East

Immigrants support mainstream politicians favorable to Muslims

Territorial border between the homeland and hostland

**FIGURE 5.2.** South Asian Muslim Americans' "elsewhere orientation" to the Middle East. *Source:* Created by the author.

would create divisions among the South Asian American community and run against panethnic and pan-religious platforms, like *desi*. Therefore, sweeping aside those aspects of homeland history that are unpleasant and not pertinent to life in a foreign land becomes an easier, more peaceful approach than the alternative. Rather than blaming each other, a more favorable strategy for immigrants to develop a sense of group-ness is to fight a common opponent for a cause that is both detached from their homelands and without direct impact on their day-to-day lives. In this context, engaging with causes rooted far away in the Middle East—such as the Israel-Palestine issue, Turkey and the Armenian genocide, and the Syrian refugee crisis—served as an effective group-generating course of action that both highlighted a shared Muslim identity among the three South Asian national groups and paved the way for building cross-ethnic coalitions and friendships with other immigrant and native groups in America. However, "elsewhere"-based politics may create new forms of boundaries within the *desi* Muslim community, as I show below.

## CLEAVAGES BASED ON ELSEWHERE POLITICS

Despite having sympathy for the Palestinians as fellow Muslims, some college-going South Asians did not find engaging with the Israel-Palestine issue appealing. For example, Atif, the first-generation Pakistani from chapter 3, represented the small handful of South Asian Muslim students who were reluctant to get involved with the issue although many of their *desi* friends were actively involved in divestment efforts against Israel. In Atif's view, this "elsewhere" issue was divisive for the college community, with the student-led divestment against Israel producing little impact on actually improving the conditions for Palestinians. In his words,

> Personally, I don't see a point of divesting. Because by doing that, you are actually excluding a part of campus community who actually thinks we shouldn't divest. And you are walking away from them. Even though I am Muslim and obligated [he laughs] to not be in favor of the Jews, but if you think rationally you have to think from their side as well. I don't know if you've ever seen a Pakistani passport before. So, on every page it says this passport is valid for every country except the republic of Israel. So anyways, students here are not responsible for the killings in Palestine. The Palestinian students should have their say, and this organization is good that they give them that platform. Of course, the Israelis obviously do horrific things to Palestine and there should be an organization to support the Palestinians, but at the same time we also have to think about the student organizations on campus that represent the Jews because they are a big part of the college community as well. So, I don't think there should be animosity between us. Obviously, you are not Israel and Palestine yourself. You are just organizations—students—you are the future of the world. And if you continue with those views, if you don't get along, it's not gonna get better anytime soon.

Sometimes, these differences of opinion led to tensions among the *desi* Muslim campus community. This became the case with Yunus, a newly arrived college student who started participating in various *desi* events while I was conducting fieldwork. Yunus had come to the United States from Bangladesh with his family when he was five years old. Both his mother and sister wore *hijab*, and he described himself as an observant Muslim. The first time

I met Yunus was at a South Asian cultural event. Like many other college-going participants, he thought the student organizations would be a good way to make new friends. Tall and handsome, with a charming, easy-going personality, he soon became a popular name within the campus Muslim and *desi* circles. However, his popularity began to decline when Yunus decided to run for student government on a party platform many respondents described as "anti-BDS" and "pro-Israel." Yunus soon became a subject of gossip, even among those who had once gone out of their way to invite him to parties. Some labeled him a "social climber" because of his chosen party platform. Adding more fuel to the fire, it became known that Yunus would be going to Israel as part of a sponsored trip for college students. It was around this time that I interviewed Yunus. We decided to meet on campus. At our scheduled time, Yunus arrived looking fairly distraught. I learned that he was worried that the Muslim and South Asian students would "ostracize" him if he visited Israel. He had thought he could rely on the *desi* and Muslim students for their votes during the upcoming student election, but now he wasn't so sure. Although sympathetic toward Palestinians, Yunus wanted to know "the other side of the story" and felt that the BDS issue was dividing the campus community. However, his decision to visit Israel had induced backlash from even his close Muslim friends on campus. He said, "I don't feel I am doing anything wrong. My religion is important to me. But they [the Muslim and South Asian students] think that I am going to be the token Muslim [in the party], you know?"

These "elsewhere"-based cleavages were not present in the homelands but emerged in particular immigrant communities in the hostland, usually in places with sizeable Muslim and South Asian populations. For instance, I did not observe these forms of mobilization in my prior research on South Asian Muslims in Mississippi, where Muslims comprise a very small minority.[35] This contrast also highlights how institutions shape Muslim Americans' political identities and their ties to "elsewhere." For example, whereas Muslim organizations both on and off campus in California reacted to the Chapel Hill murders, based on my phone conversation with the *Imam* in the small community mosque in Mississippi, I garnered that there was no such response to the shooting in this latter state. In contrast to respondents in California, who were able to come together as a community and commemorate the lives of the three victims, Muslims in Mississippi did not have such an opportunity.

Although the mostly student-led activities described in this chapter reflect, to some extent, the politicized environment on college campuses, which may not persist after graduation, they nonetheless show the means through which many South Asian Muslim youth become politically aware as "Muslims" as well as the salience of the "elsewhere" Middle East in the formation of their political identities. Indeed, participants who had already graduated from college no longer engaged in organizational activities directed at Palestine. Yet, their sentiments and views toward the issue remained unchanged, and they continued to subscribe to news related to Palestine and other "elsewhere" places in the Middle East. Moreover, Muslim-related issues continued to shape these participants' interpretations of U.S. politics and foreign policies. For instance, respondents who had already graduated and were young professionals at the time of their interviews expressed their enthusiasm for Bernie Sanders for the same reasons as respondents still in college. So it seems that the on-campus organizations to which these young South Asians were exposed at one point or another during college were arguably influential in shaping their political identities as Muslim Americans.

## THE ROLE OF CAMPUS ORGANIZATIONS

When I began fieldwork, campus organizations promised both the opportunity to meet South Asian Muslims from diverse locations in California and a methodological trap for collecting data from individuals who were arguably already predisposed to "elsewhere" affinities. As such, I did not recruit participants from political and religious organizations, namely the MSA and the Palestinian rights organization. Instead, I collected data from South Asian organizations that were explicitly founded upon secular and cultural platforms, such as the Bangladeshi Students Association, the Pakistani Students Association, and the Indian Students Association. My entrée into these associations, particularly the Bangladeshi Students Association, was largely a stroke of good fortune. The Bangladeshi association needed a cultural adviser, and as none of the founding board members, who were mostly from the 1.5 and second generations, felt they were sufficiently informed about

Bangladesh's history to take this role, they invited me to fill that position. In this advisory capacity, I was eventually able to branch out and recruit participants from the other South Asian cultural associations. The main aim of these cultural organizations was to increase awareness of their respective national group's culture and history on campus, through events in which "elsewhere" issues were almost never mentioned.

However, I soon learned that many students were members of both these cultural organizations and the MSA, which staunchly supported and often collaborated with the Palestinian rights organization. These overlapping memberships became particularly important during student government elections, when the overall campus environment grew explicitly polarized, especially with regard to candidates' attitudes toward BDS. In these situations, students who had overlapping memberships or friends in the Palestinian rights organization informed the board members of the cultural associations about the platforms of the different candidates. I discovered that these South Asian organizations, especially the Pakistani and Bangladeshi associations, overwhelmingly supported BDS, expressing a sense of humanitarian obligation and Muslim solidarity. This support was especially clear when candidates came to speak with board members and ask for their organizations' endorsement. One recurring question the president of a South Asian cultural association asked of these candidates was what their views were on BDS and sponsored student trips to Israel. For all these reasons, in order to trace the day-to-day lives of the South Asian Muslim youth, I sometimes attended events organized by the on-campus political and religious associations with my respondents.

With members from diverse ethnic/national backgrounds who are supposedly bound by a common identity, the Muslim student associations and the Palestinian justice groups allowed respondents like Faizah, Dina, Daliah, and Jahan to tangibly experience being part of a global community of Muslims, or the *Ummah*. They also created spaces for Muslim students to gather as a community and make sense of various Muslim-related events as they unfolded, as was the case after the Chapel Hill murders. Moreover, using social media and organizational events, these on-campus institutions exposed the students to Muslim-related contexts abroad, providing them with information, symbols, rhetoric, and lenses that indicated what they should care about as Muslim Americans. Relatedly, these organizations helped mobilize students to participate in mainstream politics in ways that spoke to Muslim Americans' collective interests, like voting for Bernie Sanders in the 2016 Democratic primaries.

### FROM SELF-IDENTITY TO BEING "OTHERED"

That South Asian Americans lead rich political lives is hardly surprising. Sangay Mishra, in his book *Desis Divided*,[36] has documented the various modes of mobilization and transnational political engagements in which Indian, Pakistani, and Bangladeshi immigrants have long partaken as they have settled into U.S. society. Based on interviews and surveys of community members, leaders, and activists, his book shows how political participation in both the home countries and host countries is, in many ways, part of the South Asian American experience, at least for the elites in the *desi* diaspora. What is new about my findings, then, is their revelation that South Asian Muslim Americans engage in politics *beyond* their homelands and hostland—in places "elsewhere." Overall, this chapter tells only one half of a two-part story about how different "elsewhere" places shape not only how the South Asian Muslim Americans view themselves, but also how others in the hostland view these immigrants. In addition to understanding how the participants self-identify *with* "elsewhere," it is also important to get a sense of how these immigrants are identified *by others* in relation *to* "elsewhere." South Asian Muslim Americans' identification with "elsewhere" places in the Middle East often has little impact in how they are largely perceived by the larger U.S. society. Rather, it is the exogenous shocks in "elsewhere" Europe that determine how these immigrants are viewed as Muslims in America.

# 6 | TAKING PRECAUTIONS HERE FOR "MUSLIMS IN CONFLICT" ELSEWHERE

ON NOVEMBER 13, 2015, tensions on the ground in the United States became palpable as news broke online and across television screens that ISIS had conducted mass terror attacks in Paris, killing 130 people and injuring 413 more. It were as if the attacks had taken place not in France thousands of miles away, but right here in America. Global and national public response was almost immediate. World leaders, along with American politicians and commentators, swiftly condemned the attacks and expressed their solidarity with France. Facebook users worldwide, including many in the South Asian Muslim communities I observed, temporarily changed their profile pictures to the French flag or to the phrase *"Je suis Paris"*—a direct reference to *"Je suis Charlie,"* the slogan widely shared after the *Charlie Hebdo* attacks in January of that same year. Many others posted photos of themselves in front of the Eiffel Tower taken on previous visits to France.

The attacks revitalized political debates in America over Muslims being national security threats.[1] National political figures asserted that if Islamist attacks could take place in France, they could happen again in the United States. It was on this thread that Ted Cruz, then vying for candidacy in the Republican primaries, proposed religious tests for Syrian refugees; meanwhile, Donald Trump famously announced his plans for a "Muslim ban" and proposed to register Muslims already in the country.[2] These platforms were met with widespread public support from many segments of U.S. society. As such, fears and tensions among Muslim Americans were particularly high—reasonably so, as reports showed a spike in the number of anti-Muslim threats and hate crimes across America after the attacks.[3] Effects of the backlash spilled over to affect even "Muslim-looking" non-Muslims, such as Latinos.[4]

However, my participants had expected this sort of backlash from at least some segments of American society. For instance, as soon as Tasneem, a journalist born in the United States to a Pakistani mother and an Indian father, learned about the breaking news at work, she texted her "*desi* Muslim" friends: "Oh god. Get ready for a worse or an equivalent Muslim backlash since 9/11." I spoke with Tasneem about the incident over Skype, just after she had returned from buying groceries. She was wearing a white sleeveless T-shirt and had her hair in a ponytail. Tasneem told me that even though the identities of the attackers were not yet released, she instinctively knew that the perpetrators were Muslim, specifically ISIS:

> Because it was all coming in slowly, right? We knew there was some shootings at restaurants and some explosions outside of the stage . . . then we found out about all the hostages at the concert hall, and the next thing you know are these numbers, and you are like . . . and even before they said anything, I kind of knew it was ISIS because it was France, because of everything. . . . So wasn't surprised when I found that out.

However, Tasneem, despite anticipating an ensuing anti-Muslim back-lash, did not encounter any Islamophobia firsthand. In contrast, Ahmed, a first-generation Pakistani immigrant who owned a fast food restaurant in Los Angeles, directly felt the impact of the Paris attacks. With ethnic facial features, a brown complexion, and a heavy accent, Ahmed's appearance was much more stereotypically "Muslim-looking" than Tasneem's. He, too, had instinctively known the attackers would be Muslim when the news first broke. Yet, he had waited apprehensively in front of his television for the confirma-tion, all the while hoping he was wrong. Ahmed's apprehensions about an Islamophobic backlash were confirmed when a few days after the attacks, a white male customer walked into his restaurant and, while placing his order, asked where Ahmed was from. Ahmed replied that he was an American. "No, where are you originally from, like what's your real country?" the customer asked. Given the multicultural backdrop of Los Angeles, these questions are quite common and generally reflect a cosmopolitan curiosity by Angelenos about each other's diverse backgrounds. However, in light of another mass-scale Islamist terrorist attack in the West at a time when anti-Muslim sentiments in America were already on the rise, this seemingly innocuous question posed by a white customer to a brown, bearded man with a foreign accent carried latent connotations of "us" and "them." Ahmed seemed to understand these nuances as he replied, "I was born in Pakistan, but I have been here for the last forty years." The customer responded, "Oh. So, you are also like one of those immigrants who did that in Paris." Ahmed responded that he was from Pakistan, whereas the attackers had come from Syria, referring to the news of Syrian passports being found at the scene of the attacks. "But even then," Ahmed added, "that doesn't mean all Syrians are bad." "But you are Muslim?" the customer asked. Ahmed then replied in a way that many Muslim Americans tend to do when associated with terrorism—he distanced Islam and "moderate" Muslims from "extremists." He responded, "What they [the attackers] did is not real Islam. They are extremists. Real Muslims do not condone any kind of violence. We are moderate. Peaceful."

The participants' expectation of an anti-Muslim backlash after these attacks in a foreign country was again exemplified a week later, when I asked Shehnaz, a *hijabi* first-generation immigrant from Pakistan, about her experiences as a "Muslim-looking" woman in the now tense environment. She said that, much like after 9/11, there was an uptick in people approaching her with questions about her thoughts on ISIS and "why Muslims hated us," with "us" referring to Americans and Westerners more broadly. She recalled a particular incident in the aftermath of the Paris attacks that reminded her of her experiences after 9/11:

> I was just standing at a traffic light, waiting to cross . . . and there is this car full of guys, but there may have been girls there too. They were acting a little rowdy, and I saw someone throwing trash out onto the street. And I didn't actually say anything, but something might have shown on my

expression in a way, like, "Why are you throwing trash in the middle of the street?" Because they noticed me standing there and then felt necessary to shout out to me, calling, "Osama! Osama!"

When I asked her how she responded, she said, "I reacted as I did before [referring to 9/11]—I calmly walked away."

Study participants were not the only ones who likened the aftermath of the Paris attacks to that of 9/11—so great was the intensity of the public and political reaction that global and U.S. media centers drew comparisons as well.[5] For example, an article in *Newsweek*, published on the two-year anniversary of the Paris attacks, described the event as follows: "If 9/11 was known as the 'day that everything changed,' this [November 13] was the day of reckoning for both the political bloc known as the European Union and Europe as a whole."[6] Another powerful symbolic show of solidarity, which also highlighted this parallel, was that after news broke about the Paris massacre, the One World Trade Center in New York, built on the site of the 9/11 attacks, was lit up in red, white, and blue—the colors of both the French and American flags.

Concerned by the overwhelming public response to the Paris attacks, many South Asian Muslim parents who still vividly remembered the anti-Muslim backlash after 9/11, reiterated instructions to their children not to respond to comments about Islam. And other participants who usually wore markers associated with Islam in public chose not to do so in the days that followed the attacks. For instance, on Wednesdays, when she attended organizational meetings on campus, Nargis, a Pakistani American graduate student and a BDS activist, usually wore a *keffiyeh*—a checkered black-and-white scarf that symbolized Palestinian solidarity that was often mischaracterized as an expression of sympathy for terrorism. The week after the attacks, however, Nargis decided to leave her *keffiyeh* at home, because she felt it would explicitly mark her as a Muslim in the same way the *hijab* would. She made this decision when she arrived on campus and observed that tensions were "running pretty high." She said her social media feed was inundated with the same debates that television was—about Muslims being unassimilable and posing threats to national security in France and the West at large, and about the West, at best, disregarding Muslim beliefs and practices. Even students in her Arabic and ethnic studies classes broke into arguments about the situation during class discussion. On one side, students argued that France had "ghettos" and "all the Muslims are in there"—a view made popular among conservative circles earlier that year by Bobby Jindal, the then Republican governor of Louisiana. Students on the other side protested the French *laïcité* laws that banned Muslim women from wearing the *hijab* and practicing their faith in public.

Nargis's strategy to leave Islamic markers at home as a precaution was a practice also advocated in public forums and vigils, where speakers advised women who wear the headscarf to be careful about their clothing. For example, at one campus vigil, a South Asian Muslim speaker said, "To my *hijabi* sisters, this is not the time to show resistance, but to be safe," echoing the advice of Muslim American leaders on social media—advice that many study participants had already shared widely on Facebook. One such post read, "To all my Muslim sisters who wear *hijab*, if you feel your life or safety is threatened in any way because of your dress, you have an Islamic allowance (*darura*/ necessity) to adjust your clothing accordingly. Your life is more important than your dress." Some *hijabi* college students indeed wore caps instead of their headscarves in the week after the Paris attacks. Many strategically traveled in groups, coordinating with friends who were either male or non-*hijabi* female to walk home together after dark. And others did not attend classes on religious or political topics, to avoid being put on the spot.

Interestingly, on November 12, 2015, just one day before the Paris attacks, ISIS had also claimed responsibility for two coordinated suicide bombings in a Shia-majority neighborhood in Beirut, which killed forty-three people and injured over two hundred others. Yet, in sharp contrast to the attacks in Paris, the bombings inspired little sympathy among Americans. In addition, neither the global public nor world leaders provided the same outpouring of sympathy and condemnation of the attacks. Facebook users did not change their profile pictures en masse to the Lebanese flag in a show of solidarity. And, although the major U.S. newspapers and news networks reported the incident, the coverage was not nearly as extensive as the weeklong wall-to-wall analysis of the Paris attacks and their aftermath.[7] Figure 6.1 indicates the sharp contrast between the levels of U.S. public interest in the two attacks.

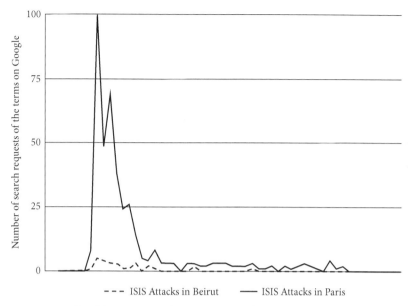

**FIGURE 6.1.** U.S. public interest in the 2015 Beirut and Paris ISIS attacks, November 8, 2015, to December 31, 2015. *Source*: Reproduced by the author using data from Google Trends 2018d.

Puzzlingly, even the participants for whom the Middle East seemed to be salient responded with silence. They did not take any safety precautions; nor did they condemn the attacks and express solidarity with Beirut on Facebook as they had after Paris. This absence of response was particularly noticeable given how active they usually were on social media regarding Muslim-related issues, especially in the Middle East (see chapter 5). I initially thought the participants were unaware of the attacks. Yet interviews later revealed that many of them were indeed informed of the bombings. Many even reported that they had turned to alternative news outlets, namely Al Jazeera and the BBC, for further coverage of the bombings, as they felt these latter outlets provided more in-depth and "less biased" coverage of Muslim-related events than American news channels. Moreover, many participants noted the contrast between U.S. media and public interest in the Beirut bombings and that in the Paris attacks, interpreting it as America's general anti-Muslim bias and overall indifference toward the plight of Muslims. This same theme regarding U.S. interest was reflected in my interview with Rashed, a Shia Muslim from Pakistan and a recent college graduate. He compared today's Islamophobia and the "othering" of Muslims by Trump with the stigmatization and persecution of Jews before and during World War II, a comparison that several other 1.5- and second-generation participants made at different times during my fieldwork.

> I actually got angry at the fact that everyone was like, "Paris attack! Paris attack!" as if nothing happened before that. *Beirut* happened before Paris! It bothered me. Again, Beirut was also Shia. The suburb belonged to Hezbollah, which is listed as a terrorist organization. Anyways, so I guess it was then, you just saw the biased nature of reporting, you know? Nobody wants to talk about it because it's [Beirut] a war zone, whereas Paris is a "civilized" [used hand quotes] city because it belongs to the Western world. Yes, but people are still trying to be normal in that war zone . . . Paris was an unfortunate event—don't get me wrong. It was the way we [Americans] reacted to it [the Paris attacks]. Like, Donald Trump comes on the news and says Muslim people should have an emblem to identify as Muslims. Is this a post-WWII world or not? Are we turning the wheel back on itself?

It is interesting to note that, despite feeling bitter and frustrated with the U.S. reaction (or lack thereof) to the Beirut attacks, Rashed nonetheless identified as an American—indicated by his use of "we" when referring to Americans.

These vignettes show that immigrants, as vectors of globalization, feel the aftermath of events transpiring thousands of miles away—but not *all* events and not *anywhere* in the world. Rather, immigrants seem to "instinctively" anticipate which events will produce an exogenous shock to the hostland and the rest of the world, and they consequently take precautions against those events they predict will produce a backlash. What is not so clear, however, is *why* immigrants respond to some events with anticipatory precautions and not others? Specifically, in the example above, why were the study participants—despite being so emotionally affected and despite usually being concerned for "Muslims in danger" in the Middle East—silent about the Beirut bombings when they were explicitly vocal about the attacks in Paris? This is the puzzle that is at the heart of this chapter.

Whereas the previous chapter showed that many South Asian Muslim Americans self-identify with "Muslims in danger" in the "elsewhere" Middle East, this chapter will show how others in the hostland identify these immigrants in relation to "Muslims *in conflict*" in "elsewhere" *Europe*. I will make this argument based on an analysis of six ISIS attacks that happened during my fieldwork—two in "elsewhere" Europe (Paris and Brussels), two in the "elsewhere" Middle East (Beirut and Istanbul), and two in the hostland United States (San Bernardino and Orlando). In the duration of my fieldwork from 2015 to 2017, ISIS conducted or inspired fifty-eight attacks across the world.[8] Not all fifty-eight of these attacks, however, appeared to impact U.S. society or the participants' day-to-day lives. Like my participants, I, too, remained unaware of all these events. The attacks that did grab the whole world's attention, however, were also reflected in the participants' day-to-day routines and interviews. As such, I selected six of the events, either because the participants mentioned them in their interviews and conversations or because there were observable changes in the participants' daily lives as a result of the events' widespread impact on the larger U.S. society.

## VARIATIONS IN HOSTLAND REACTIONS TO ATTACKS ELSEWHERE

Like the reactions of the larger U.S. society, participants' reactions to the six ISIS attacks fell into a pattern based on where the events had taken place: attacks that occurred in Europe and the United States had either "high" or "very high" salience, causing moderate to extreme reaction, whereas attacks in the Middle East had "low" salience, causing little to no reaction (see table 6.1).

For all four of the attacks that took place in Europe and the United States, the participants correctly anticipated backlash. Further, the safety precautions they took after the Paris and Brussels attacks resembled those after San Bernardino and Orlando. Overall U.S. responses to ISIS attacks in Europe and America were also similar, with the Paris, Brussels, San Bernardino, and Orlando attacks all producing a spike in anti-Muslim sentiment (see figure 6.2).

TABLE 6.1

*Variations in the Level of Salience of Different Elsewhere and Hostland Events*

| Event | Date of Event | Location of Event | Level of Salience | Where Are Most Victims From? | Participant Precautions | Reactions of U.S. Host Society and Participants | | |
|---|---|---|---|---|---|---|---|---|
| | | | | | | National and Global Outcry? | Anti-Muslim Backlash in the United States? | Level of Media Coverage? |
| Beirut Bombings | November 12, 2015 | The Middle East | Low | The Middle East | No Precaution | No | No | Low |
| Paris Attacks | November 13, 2015 | Europe | Very High | The West | Extra Precaution | Yes | Yes | High |
| San Bernardino Shooting | December 2, 2015 | The United States | Very High | The West | Extra Precaution | Yes | Yes | High |
| Brussels Bombings | March 22, 2016 | Europe | High | The West | General Safety Precaution | Yes | Yes | High |
| Orlando Shooting | June 12, 2016 | The United States | High | The West | General Safety Precaution | Yes | Yes | High |
| Istanbul Airport Attack | June 28, 2016 | The Middle East | Low | The Middle East | No Precaution | No | No | Low |

*Source:* Created by the author.

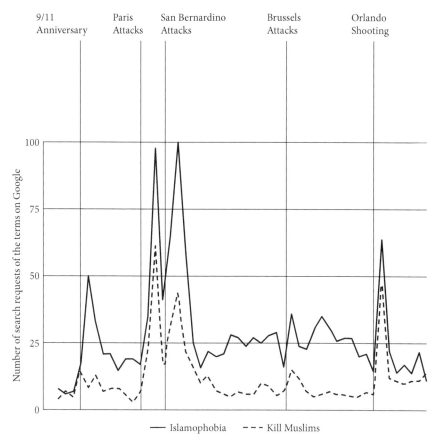

FIGURE 6.2. U.S. public response to Islamist terror attacks in the United States and Europe, August 16, 2015, to May 29, 2016. *Source*: Reproduced by the author using data from Google Trends 2019b.

Conversely, the "low" salience of both Islamist attacks in the Middle East meant participants neither predicted backlash nor took anticipatory precautions. It could be argued that the salience of the Beirut bombings was low because the incident was subsumed by the overwhelming response to the Paris massacre just the day after. However, that would not explain the similarly low level of response to yet another terrorist attack in the Middle East in June 2016. Seven months after the Paris attacks, ISIS was suspected to have conducted mass shootings and explosions in the Istanbul Ataturk

Airport in Turkey. Although there was some coverage of the events by major U.S. news outlets, the attacks did not generate any public outpouring of sympathy for the Turkish victims or any anti-Muslim backlash. Neither was there much visible reaction from the participants in either their day-to-day routines or social media activities. Yet some participants, during their interviews, mentioned the Istanbul attacks in passing, indicating that they were indeed aware of the incident. A few participants also liked Facebook posts by other Muslim public figures and commentators. These posts admonished ISIS for inflicting violence against Muslims, especially during the Islamic holy month of Ramadan, which was going on at the time of the Turkey attacks; the posts also offered the usual critiques about the U.S. news media associating ISIS with Islam. One such post that a handful of participants liked read as follows:

> The fact that ISIS would carry out terror attacks in Turkey during the Holy Month of Ramadan reveals just how pointedly sacrilege their motives are, and how profusely anti-Muslim their mission is.
>
> The overwhelming majority of their victims are Muslims. Both in terms of fatalities (90%), and the millions more victimized by the displacement, stereotyping, surveillance and xenophobia their monstrous actions encourage.
>
> The mainstream media's incessant association of ISIS with Islam obscures this—and adding great insult to grave injury—erases the recurring realities of mass Muslim tragedy and victimhood.
>
> Prayers with Turkey.

One trend to note, however, is the variation in the level of salience between the two "elsewhere" European places. In March 2016, ISIS coordinated suicide bombings in Brussels, killing thirty-one people and injuring three hundred others. Although these attacks had a "high" level of salience in the United States, that differed from the "very high" level of salience after Paris. Said another way, even though Islamophobic sentiments in the United States spiked in response to the Brussels bombings, that spike was not as high as the spike after the Paris massacre. Indeed, U.S. public interest in the Brussels attack was, overall, lower compared to that of the Paris attacks.[9] Further, whereas many political commentators, bloggers, and news personnel—and even the participants themselves—drew parallels between the Paris attacks and 9/11, these comparisons were noticeably missing in the public discourse after the Brussels bombings.[10] Although globally, some Facebook users changed their profile pictures to the Belgian flag, the number of users who took this action was nowhere near as high as after the Paris attacks. I also did not observe any of my participants changing their Facebook pictures to stripes of red, black, and yellow (the colors of the Belgian flag) as an expression of solidarity with the victims.

These variations may be partly based on how Belgium and France are located in the American public perception. Although both France and Belgium are friendly Western countries and part of the "we," Belgium does not have the same level of historical significance, emotional salience, and cultural proximity with the United States as France. In the global sphere as well, Paris, being an iconic city, is arguably more influential than Brussels. The magnitude of the Paris attacks was also greater than the attacks in Brussels in terms of the number of people killed and injured and the impact on world politics. Moreover, by the time the Brussels bombings took place, there had been a series of high-profile ISIS attacks in the West and across the world, rendering the threat of Islamist terrorism and Islamophobia what then–FBI director James Comey called "the new normal."[11] In this worldview, Western societies have to cope with the presence of Islamic terrorism on the one hand, and Muslims have to find ways to live within an Islamophobic atmosphere on the other.[12] After ISIS struck Brussels, an article published in the *Economist* summarized the now "normal" stages of Europe coming to terms with yet another Islamic terrorist attack:

> Over the next few days Europe will once again pass through terrorism's stages of grief: despair over innocent lives cut short; anger towards the young men and women (some of them citizens) who will kill in the name of *jihad*; questions about the grip of the police and intelligence services; and eventually, as news bulletins and headlines subside, a weary resignation.[13]

The "normalization of fear" discourse explained the participants' reactions as well. In my interviews and conversations soon after the Brussels bombings, some participants sounded resigned rather than anxious, as they had after Paris. "It feels so numbing now," said Hamid, the Indian Muslim college student from chapter 3, describing his reactions to the Brussels attack. "Whenever we hear something now, it's like, oh no, not this again." Similarly, Soraya, a Pakistani American elementary school teacher said, "It's just the way it is now. And sadly, we just have to find ways to live with it." Indeed, I did not find people within the South Asian Muslim communities as visibly anxious as they were after the Paris attacks. So while the day-to-day impression management necessary to be "good Muslims" remained after the Brussels attacks, I did not find South Asians going to extra lengths, such as leaving their religious markers at home.

Overall, these on-the-ground observations suggest that not all "elsewhere" places have the same level of salience. Rather, variations in salience are moderated by multiple hostland-centric factors, such as geographic location, prevailing public imaginary, and the hierarchy of power among different regions at the global level. Specifically, I argue that the ISIS attacks in Europe generated a strong emotional reaction in America because of Europe's location in the prevailing public imaginary of "the West," which also includes the United States. Europe, hence, is seen not as a foreign place but as part of the "we"—a "we" that is presumably different from the seemingly homogenous Muslim "outsiders." Thus, the U.S. public generally sees an Islamist attack in Europe as an attack against "us" by "them." In contrast, a similar Islamist attack in the predominantly Muslim Middle East—a region that is also at the periphery of the core Western countries, both in the general American public's mental map and in the current world order—does not invoke that feeling.

To some extent, these reactions, especially the "normalization of fear," are driven by the media cycle. Today's news is old news by tomorrow: so even though the Brussels attacks were heavily covered in the news, by the time these bombings took place, the paradigm of "Muslims in conflict" with the West—a long-standing paradigm in American public perception[14] that has only been reinvigorated because of ISIS—was old news. In other words, the Brussels bombings did not seem to have the sense of novelty that the Paris attacks had as a breaking news story that captured audience attention.

Even though the Paris attacks are now "old news," the story appears to have continued cultural and sociopolitical impact on the world, driven by popular media. Netflix, for instance, released a three-part documentary series in 2018 on the events that transpired just before, during, and after the Paris attacks, called *November 13: Attack on Paris*.[15] On the one hand, movies and news stories such as this, which commemorate the Paris attacks, perpetuate the salience of the incident by keeping it relevant. On the other hand, these popular media are products that are influenced by the invisible hand of the marketplace.[16] They are produced to capture the attention and satisfy the demands of a certain kind of audience market. As such, the media arguably determines, at least to an extent, the salience of different "elsewheres" in the hostland.

For example, one likely reason the Beirut bombings had little salience in U.S. society was because of the American media's scant coverage of the attacks, which translated into the American public being largely unaware of the event. Conversely, another reason could be that the American public is largely uninterested in news of Muslims killing other Muslims in the Middle East,[17] and thus U.S. news outlets diverted its resources to covering issues that were closer to home and of more interest to its target audience, such as issues "here" and in "elsewhere" Europe. Hashem, a Bangladeshi American student, reflected this latter view when he said,

> When a terrorist act happens outside the U.S. by a Muslim person, I think it somehow affects all Muslims in the U.S. But I also think it depends on how much exposure it gets, and the amount of exposure it gets depends on how Europeanized the place has been. So something like Paris got 24/7 media coverage but not Beirut, not Baghdad where there was also an attack two days before Paris, or the thing that happened in Turkey—that is not getting any media coverage . . . I think attacks in the non-European countries like in the Middle East add to the bigger picture, but it doesn't stir up as much as, say, an attack in a European country or like a global power. ["What is this bigger picture?" I asked.] You know, of Islam and terrorism or Muslim countries being volatile and dangerous.

Social media arguably also moderates the overall impact of an exogenous shock—namely, what people, places, and topics matter to the host society. It was Facebook, for instance, that prompted its users to temporarily change their profile pictures to the French flag. Popularly labeled "solidarity filters," this option allowed Facebook users to lay a translucent French flag over their profile pictures along with the hashtags #prayforparis and #jesuisparis.

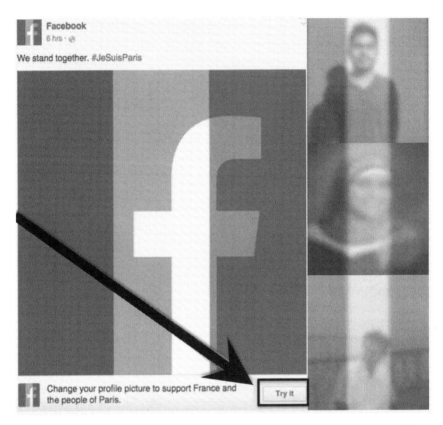

**FIGURE 6.3.** Facebook's "solidarity filter" option after the 2015 ISIS terror attacks and three examples of participants' Facebook profile pictures. *Source*: Reproduced by the author using modified images from Bonarenko 2017 and Facebook. Faces have been blurred to protect anonymity.

Figure 6.3 shows how Facebook advertised the solidary flag to its users[18] and some of the participants' profile images after using the filter.

Facebook introduced this feature after the Paris attacks and with much success, as more than 120 million people used the French flag overlay in the first three days.[19] Contrastingly, Facebook did not offer this compassionate gesture to help users express solidarity with the victims of the crises in Lebanon and Syria.[20] Consequently, those Middle Eastern events, including the Beirut bombings, did not produce any visible impact on people's social media feeds and thus did not generate much public awareness.

However, while these factors provide an explanation of American public reactions to "elsewhere" events, they do not fully capture why the participants—for whom instances of "Muslims in danger," especially in the Middle East, tended to be salient—were silent with regard to the Middle East ISIS attacks. I argue that the participants' contrasting reactions to the Middle East and Europe attacks are rooted in the sociopolitical contexts regarding Muslims in the United States and the relationship between those contexts with the different "elsewheres."

## "MUSLIMS IN CONFLICT," BOTH HERE AND ELSEWHERE

In December 2015, less than one month following the Paris attacks, two Muslim Americans of Pakistani background conducted a mass shooting in San Bernardino, California, killing fourteen people and injuring twenty-two others. The shooters were a married couple and self-radicalized. Before the attacks, they had jointly pledged allegiance to ISIS on Facebook. The couple was reportedly in the last stages of planning an even bigger assault and had a stockpile of ammunitions in their home. Even more shocking to the American public, the shooters had been living in the United States for several years, with the husband being a U.S. citizen and having no prior criminal record.

Because the incident occurred so soon after the Islamist attacks in France, the media coverage of San Bernardino and Paris together lasted for months. With anti-Muslim right-wing support already gaining momentum during the 2016 U.S. presidential election, these back-to-back attacks reshaped the political debate about Muslims in America as well as the overall election cycle. Several high-profile politicians, including Trump, along with many segments of the U.S. population, held Muslim Americans collectively accountable for not reporting the shooters' suspicious behavior, renewing calls for profiling Muslims.[21] Later that same month, as Trump proposed to shut down mosques, anti-Muslim attacks tripled in the United States, with nearly half of those being targeted against mosques.[22] Anti-Muslim sentiment soared in America, reaching its highest level since 9/11.[23]

On the ground, the atmosphere in the South Asian Muslim communities in California was fraught with tension, especially given the close proximity of the shooting. In the week that followed the attacks, several participants said they did not go out of their homes unless needed. Even Hashem, who identified himself as agnostic, was cognizant about his "Muslim-looking" appearance and how that might affect his public interactions. His parents, after watching the news about San Bernardino with what Hashem described as a combination of disbelief and resignation, reiterated their instructions to "never get in fights" and "just walk away" if anyone asked him about his religion. Many other South Asian Muslim Americans just continued with the precautionary measures they had been taking since the Paris attacks, such as not using or wearing religious markers in public. Families and friends called or messaged each other to check in. I, too, received messages from a few people I became close with during my fieldwork, asking if I was safe and offering their support. One such message read, "How are you? Stay safe! Making *dua* [prayer] for you and your family!" Curiously, I noticed that some of the participants who were usually vocal about Muslim-related issues on social media, such as issues related to Palestine or other places where they perceived Muslims to be in danger, stayed relatively quiet. Their few posts were somber in tone, usually offering prayers for the victims and their families.

Another event in the United States that produced a shockwave through American society was the ISIS attack in Orlando, Florida on June 12, 2016. Omar Mateen, an Afghan American Muslim, conducted a mass shooting at a gay nightclub, killing fifty people and wounding fifty-three others. At the time this attack was the largest loss of life in the United States after 9/11. Mateen was reported to have pledged allegiance to ISIS while conducting the attack.[24] The event took place just three months after the Brussels bombings, in the midst of America's "new normal." But the ensuing nationwide response and virulent anti-Muslim backlash were hardly normal, indicating that while European places, such as Belgium, were deemed important, events transpiring inside the United States had far more immediate impact. Indeed, anti-Muslim sentiment after Orlando spiked much higher than after the Brussels attacks, although still not to the same level as after the Paris and San Bernardino massacres (see figure 6.2).

Yet, compared to the other ISIS terror attacks, the Orlando shooting had an added layer of connotation related to domestic U.S. politics: in addition to being viewed as further proof of the presence of ISIS in America, the Orlando attack was largely deemed as a targeted hate crime against homosexuals, with Mateen reportedly expressing outrage after seeing two men kissing in Miami before the attacks.[25] These two contexts are relevant for analyzing the participants' responses, given that homosexuality is a taboo topic in the South Asian and Muslim communities. The younger generations were relatively more open and accepting of the LGBTQ community than the older South Asian Muslims, who would have considered it an affront had I asked them about their views toward gay rights during interviews. This contrast was reflected in the participants' varying reactions to the Orlando shooting. While I did not hear the older participants condemn the attack as a homophobic hate crime, they were aghast at yet another violent attack in their hostland that, in their view, misrepresented their religion and gave Muslims a "bad name." In contrast, the younger 1.5 and second generations viewed the shooting as a hate crime against gays and expressed their outrage accordingly on social media.

However, even those participants who identified themselves as queer questioned Omar Mateen's ties to ISIS. They did not see him as a self-radicalized member of an Islamist terrorist group; rather, they viewed him as a "mentally unstable" and "homophobic" person. As such, they criticized the U.S. news media's coverage of the story, arguing that it highlighted Mateen's connection to ISIS rather than his unstable mental condition.

Some younger participants also viewed the attack as an outcome of flawed gun-control laws. Wasim, a Bangladeshi college student who identified himself as bisexual, expressed these views in a Facebook post that received over a hundred likes, many from other study participants. Part of his post said,

> Radical Islam undoubtedly played a role in this massacre—the monster pledged allegiance to IS. Make no mistake, though, the gun laws of this country played a much larger role. WHY does a civilian have access to artillery, and extra bullets to spare? HOW is someone that has no ties to the police, military, any form of national defense organization, have access to enough ammo to hit more than a hundred people, and have more to be able to hold them hostage? . . . My religion condemns murder. It says that murdering an innocent human is a murder of humankind itself. Why are we hearing about him [Mateen]? Because he fits the media and the US political institutions' definition of a "terrorist". Born to Afghan parents, raised Muslim—so easy to rally the masses against him. Nothing that hasn't been done before. What about James Wesley Howell, the white man who had a collection of guns and was headed for LA Pride? Why

do I have to scroll down 5 paragraphs to read "the police have identified the potential shooter as James Wesley Howell" when every single article about Orlando starts by reading "Omar Mateen, the Orlando shooter."

These were also some of the key themes addressed at a campus vigil organized by the Muslim Students Association. Interestingly, I observed that not as much emphasis was given to safety concerns at this vigil as was given at vigils after San Bernardino. For instance, I did not hear speakers and participants mention *darura*. An Arabic word, *darura* translates to "necessity." Muslims tend to understand this as an idea that urgent or life-threatening necessity can allow for violating explicit prohibitions in Islam. In the climate of fear and Islamophobic backlash that ensued the Paris and San Bernardino attacks, religious authorities at vigils, local mosques, and social media dispensed advice to *hijabi* women to observe *darura* if they felt they were in harm's way. Emphasis at the Orlando vigil, rather, was given to broader and less urgent topics like the media's seeming double standard in portraying Muslim and non-Muslim terrorists, gun control, and tackling homophobia and mental health issues in the *desi* community. This contrast indicated to me a variation in the level of salience based on geographic proximity of the San Bernardino and Orlando attacks. Although the Orlando attacks arguably produced a shockwave throughout U.S. society, it was still on the other side of the country for the Muslims and immigrants I observed in California. As such, the South Asian Muslim respondents did not respond with the same level of intensity or fear for their immediate safety as they had after the attacks in San Bernardino, which was about an hour drive from where the participants and their loved ones lived. This is evident when conversely in Florida, levels of public interest in the San Bernardino attacks far away in California was much lower than their interest in the Orlando attacks close to home.[26]

This was the overall U.S. sociopolitical context in which I observed the South Asian Muslim Americans respond to "elsewhere" attacks in the Middle East and Europe. The participants were largely silent about the Beirut ISIS bombings because, despite sharing a sense of group-ness with fellow Muslims in the Middle East, these immigrants and their descendants reside in the United States and are thus directly exposed to the sociopolitical contexts within it. The embeddedness of the participants in U.S. society is often reflected by many of them viewing themselves as "Americans"—as being part of the "we" or "us"—just as did Rashed in the quote earlier in the chapter. In fact, according to a survey conducted by the Pew Research Center, 89 percent of U.S. Muslims say that they are both proud to be American and proud to be Muslim.[27] However, the heightened Islamophobic U.S. context puts the identity categories "Americans"—"us"—and "Muslims"—"them"—at odds with each other, with the participants having to prioritize or balance their seemingly bifurcated sense of selves as "Americans" and "Muslims" in moments of crises. This is evidenced by Rashed's explanation below on why he and the Muslim community at large remained silent on social media about the Beirut bombings. Note that while in his previous quote Rashed used "we" to refer to Americans, here he is using that same pronoun to refer to Muslims, implicitly referring to the predominantly non-Muslim American public as "them":

> In our [Muslim] community, there is a sense of paranoia, so we [Muslims] don't actually talk about politics very much. We [Muslims] are very . . . it [politics] only stays in your [Muslims'] home, when you are sipping on your cup of tea and you're talking to your family members, which is basically preaching to the choir. How much difference of opinion can you have in a family? And even if you do, how much would it matter? It's just gonna stay there.

I inferred from this conversation with Rashed that in light of the highly charged sentiments at the time, the participants explicitly associating themselves to an ISIS-related conflict in the Middle East by showing solidarity with Beirut or publicly critiquing the U.S. media as biased against Muslims on social media would have highlighted their "Muslim-ness," thus potentially exposing them to Islamophobic backlash.

Yet, as Muslims are collectively held responsible and called to account for the actions of their coreligionists, many respondents feel "forced" to talk about their religion in moments of Muslim-related crises in the United States and Europe, despite their usual reluctance to do so with their non-*desi* and non-Muslim friends (see chapter 4). Muslim individuals' choice to remain out of the public spotlight by remaining silent in these tense situations could be misperceived as silently supporting and enabling Islamist terrorism. In the words of Tabassum, a young Pakistani American nonprofit employee,

If we [Muslims] don't, if we just keep quiet, then people [non-Muslims] are like, "Oh, you are quiet because you agree with what they [Islamist terrorists] are doing." Then we [Muslims] have to be like, "No, no, that's not true! What they are doing is not real Islam. We are just like you [Americans]. We hate what they are doing!"

Social media gives the participants an outlet to vocally condemn Islamist attacks and highlight their similarities with other Americans as these platforms are publicly accessible while still being within the user's control. This is reflected in Alisha's (the Pakistani American from chapter 3) lengthy Facebook post ten days after the Paris attacks, excerpts from which are as follows.

Hello Facebook friends! In light of the recent Paris attacks, the vilification of Syrian refugees, and Trump's Muslim ID idea, I wanted to reconnect and reintroduce myself to you all. . . .

[She describes here her mundane day-to-day life: her work as a physician's assistant, her love for Harry Potter and *Downton Abbey*, her hobby of traveling, and her difficulty waking up early in the morning.]

All in all, my life is pretty status quo. In my eyes, the only real difference between [many of] you and me is that my choice of religion automatically casts my life into suspicion. I can't just be my normal introverted self; my initially shy demeanor must mean that I'm submissive and oppressed. I can't just be cranky because I didn't get enough sleep or got into an argument with a family member; I must have anger issues because I'm a Muslim, and Muslims are angry people. I can't walk with my hands in my pockets or in my purse for too long; such behavior means I'm hiding a gun that I will use to shoot random people. I can't speak too much about how I have to go pray before the time runs out; too open of adherence to my religion might be seen as fanatical. I can't possibly wear the headscarf of my own accord; some male figure in my life must have brutally threatened me until I consented to wear it. I can't be speaking in Urdu on a flight, saying phrases like "*insha'Allah*" or "*Allah hafiz*," because I'm speaking to my parents; I must be secretly communicating some terrorist plot!

It's simultaneously depressing and frustrating to know that my just being my normal self makes others feel unsafe and in danger. Like damn I'm just trying to figure my life out—get my career on track, lose those last five pounds, battle my demons, and become a better wife/daughter/sibling/

friend/human—same as you. I wish I could carry a sign that reads something along the lines of this: Please stop assuming. Please stop over-analyzing
my actions. Please stop branding me as a terrorist. Please stop holding
me accountable for the actions of terrorists. I'm no alien, but I do come in
peace. Talk to me. Ask me questions. Humble yourself. Educate yourself.

In the above post, Alisha, in reaction to the Islamophobic backlash following the Paris attacks, "reintroduced" herself to over one thousand of her
Facebook friends, but on her own terms, according to how she wants to be
viewed—which is as an American, like many of her Facebook friends, and
as a Muslim, who "come(s) in peace." Unlike many of her other posts, which
were usually set to "friends only," Alisha set the privacy of this post to public,
thereby allowing anyone—friends, acquaintances, and strangers alike—to
read it. Alisha could not have shared these details about herself at such great
length or with so many people through her daily face-to-face interactions. Thus,
Facebook provides a semipublic platform for participants like Alisha to selec-
tively and strategically voice their opinions on various Muslim-related issues.

This could explain why many of the participants were highly vocal in con-
demning the attacks and sympathizing with victims after ISIS struck Paris, but
not after it exacted similar attacks in Beirut or Istanbul. Because the Beirut and
Istanbul attacks took place in the Middle East, Muslims were not collectively
called upon to account for the attacks, so participants did not feel the need
to use social medial to vocally condemn the attacks. Thus, the participants'
relative inactivity on social media after Beirut compared to their activity after
Paris suggests they might use self-expression on social media as yet another
form of precaution against the stigma attached to their Muslim identity.

These sociopolitical contexts of the hostland make Europe another
"elsewhere" center in the identification processes of South Asian Muslim
Americans. The participants do not necessarily think of European places as
their homes, nor do they feel any diasporic affinity to their co-ethnics and
coreligionists living there. Rather, South Asian Muslim Americans feel tied
to Europe because in the prevailing public perception of "us against them,"
Europe is not a foreign place but a part of the West, which includes the
United States. On that note, Paris would not be considered a foreign city but a
familiar place in the West that Americans like to visit. Conversely, the seemingly indistinguishable Muslims are all categorized as "them." Thus, the U.S.

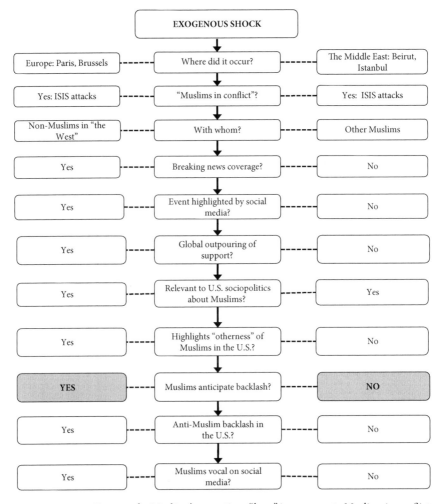

**FIGURE 6.4.** Contexts for Muslims' precautions "here" in response to Muslims in conflict "elsewhere." *Source:* Created by the author.

public generally sees an Islamist attack in Europe as an attack against "us" by "them"—a perception that comes to shape how Muslims are identified by others in the United States in the wake of Muslim-related conflicts in Europe.

In contrast, an Islamist attack in the predominantly Muslim Middle East does not invoke the feeling of "us" being attacked by "them." In addition, Beirut is largely viewed as a "war zone" far from the United States, both geographically and culturally. For these reasons, after the Beirut bombings Tasneem did not send her *desi* Muslim friends a text saying that she anticipated another 9/11-like backlash the way she had after the Paris attacks. When I asked her why not, she replied by saying that Beirut was "far away in the Middle East. . . . And," she added, "it was kind of like Muslims killing Muslims." Using the Paris, Beirut, Brussels, and Istanbul attacks as examples, figure 6.4 shows how exogenous shocks stemming from contexts where Muslims are in conflict filter down and under what conditions Muslims in the United States anticipate backlash and take precautions in response.

## A GLOBAL HIERARCHY

Broadly, contrasts in hostland responses are in part a reflection of the hierarchy of power across the regions of the world. Because of America's position as a core country in the global political order, its domestic issues tend to impact the rest of the world. As such, people in the periphery regions pay attention to events in the United States, as exemplified by Indian Hindus closely following the outcome of the 2016 U.S. presidential election or people in Afghanistan, Iraq, and Iran evaluating the American presidential candidates based on their Middle East policy platforms.[28] Similarly, a Gallup poll assessing whether the rights of Muslims in the West were important for Muslims globally showed that six in ten respondents said it was "very important" to them that "the West treated Muslims fairly in the policies that affect them, protect the rights of Muslim minorities in these societies, accurately portray Muslims in the Western media, and work with Muslim societies as equal partners on issues of mutual interest."[29] Conversely, internal conflicts in developing, non-Western countries seldom affect the world political order unless they are used as proxies for fights between global powers; the wars in Syria, Yemen, and Afghanistan are a few notable examples. In contrast, the West's general public seems little concerned about conflicts ensuing in the faraway peripheral outskirts. For instance, whereas many Facebook users in Bangladesh had changed their profile pictures to the French flag in a show of solidarity after the 2015 ISIS attacks in Paris—indicating yet again the extent to which social media can moderate global response to certain events—Westerners were largely indifferent to the ISIS attacks that had taken place in Dhaka, Bangladesh's capital, a few months later.[30]

# 7 | HERE, THERE, AND ELSEWHERE

ALTHOUGH PERHAPS not in these exact words, my father is what many people would describe as "Muslim-looking." In fact, he has heard similar comments about his looks at his workplace, a state-run mental health facility where he has been working for over a decade. With a dark brown complexion, a full beard and mustache that he grooms patiently every day, deep-set eyes and bushy eyebrows, a thick Bengali accent, in which he pronounces each syllable with equal emphasis, he easily cuts an unusual figure among his mostly white and African American colleagues in the Deep South. He tells me that his appearance is the first thing patients usually notice about him, and some ask him questions like, "Are you Muslim?" or "Do you read the *Kor-Anne* [Quran]?" One of his patients once told another patient, while pointing at my father, "He is f—king ISIS, man. He's gonna kill us, man, he's gonna kill us."

Once, even a colleague refused to cooperate with my father. When a mutual coworker asked the colleague—a black military veteran—why, he answered, "I don't compromise with terrorists." Most of his colleagues, however, have been far less explicit and far more diplomatic when expressing curiosity about my father's Muslim-ness. Every so often, after there had been breaking news about an Islamist attack, they would ask for his opinion: As a Muslim, what did he have to say about what ISIS was doing? This was, in fact, what happened in 2016, when he was at work and heard the news on television about a church in Egypt being attacked by a Muslim suicide bomber.[1] He was doing his rounds when his colleague, a white coworker, asked him about his thoughts on why ISIS would blow up a church.

My father sometimes shares these interactions with us at home. And sometimes I ask him if he feels angry about being associated with Islamist terrorists. In most cases, he tells me that he is not surprised, but that rather than anger, he feels a sense of resignation. Yet, when I am at home during semester breaks, I see that, before going to work, my father routinely turns on the news and listens to the highlights. On the occasions when there is breaking news about a Muslim-related conflict, he makes sure to google the details on his iPhone so that he is armed with facts and figures in case he needs to tackle, yet again, comments or questions based on his religion and, in response, present himself as a "good Muslim."

I observed this same mix of anxiety and resignation in the South Asian Muslim Americans whose lives I explored in this book—in Ahmed, who waited in front of his television to confirm his fears that the terrorists were Muslim; in Tasneem, who texted her Muslim friends to warn them of an Islamophobic backlash; and in the many who used Facebook posts to urge *hijabis* to be careful about their clothing choices after the ISIS terror attacks in France. Although instances of Islamophobic violence were rare, with hostile interactions few and far between, I observed my respondents' repeated concerns that such interactions might nonetheless occur, reflecting an overall climate of fear based on the prevailing global discourse on Islam and Muslims. When news broke on July 22, 2016, of a shooting in Munich, Germany,[2] Naser, the first-generation Pakistani immigrant (from chapter 2) posted on Facebook, "Please don't tell me this shooter in Germany is Muslim or Muslimish." The shooter, a German-Iranian teenager named David Sonboly, was in fact not a Muslim but presumably secular or a convert to Christianity, according to news sources.[3] But it was not long before the media associated his "Muslimish" background—that his parents were Muslim immigrants from Iran—with Islam and ISIS. The *Wall Street Journal*, for instance, ran the following headline the next day: "Munich Gunman Had Interest in Mass Shootings,

No Apparent Islamic State Ties."[4] Right-wing media outlets like Breitbart ran another story accusing BBC of "scrubbing" the Munich Gunman of the "Muslim" bit of his name—Ali.[5]

None of the places mentioned above—Egypt, France, or Germany—are either the homeland or hostland of my father or the South Asian Muslim Americans I have studied in this book. Yet, Muslims in conflict in those places shaped how Muslims in the United States were perceived, even when neither the perpetrators nor the victims were these immigrants' compatriots. Many scholars have described this homogenization of Muslims as a form of racism. Erik Love called it Islamophobic racism.[6] However, Muslim Americans are stereotyped as perpetrators of terror not only because of their race or even because of what they wear or how they speak; also important are their real or perceived ties to other Muslims abroad and the global geopolitics between those foreign lands with the immigrants' homelands and hostland.

Foreign places also come to shape how immigrants understand themselves. The South Asian respondents often interpreted and understood their experiences as Muslims in America based on their perceptions of the conditions their fellow Muslims were living under in other Western countries. Moreover, many of the immigrants felt a sense of solidarity with their core-ligionists in various parts of the Muslim world, but especially in the Middle East—the birthplace of Islam—and in places where the participants perceived Muslims to be in danger or living in oppressed conditions, such as in Palestine and Syria. This sense of solidarity propelled many Muslim Americans to engage in U.S. politics with the hope of bringing about change that was favorable not just for Muslims "here" but also for those abroad.

These places that are neither the immigrants' homelands nor hostland but are nonetheless important for their sense of selves comprise "elsewhere." Together, the homelands, hostland, and "elsewheres" shape these immigrants' identities—both in terms of how they view themselves and how they are viewed by others. In tracing the effects of "elsewhere" through a new, multi-centered relational framework, my goal was to address a theoretical gap in the scholarship of international migration. Although the sociology of migration has traditionally been devoted to studying the processes of cross-national connections through migrants and their offspring, I argue that this view is largely limited within a dyadic framework, in which the sending society stands on one end and the receiving society on the other. The field contends that as immigrants leave their homelands to settle in a new society, they bring with them the values, practices, and societal boundaries of their sending country, which then continue to shape their lives in the hostland. Inversely, these ties to their homelands and to the people they have left behind motivate immigrants to stay informed about ongoing developments in those homelands and to remit resources back to the sending countries from the hostland. Further, scholarship shows that where these immigrants came from and how they came are consequential factors in determining the kinds of opportunities these immigrants and their children have in the receiving country.

In each of the preceding six chapters I have posed a challenge to this dyadic paradigm by showing the influence of not just two societies—the homeland and hostland—but also the influence of "elsewhere" on immigrants' identity-making. In chapter 1 I described immigrants broadly, and South Asian Muslim Americans specifically, as vectors of globalization who both produce and experience the interconnectedness of societies. In chapter 2 I showed how faraway foreign places become "elsewheres" for immigrant identities. In chapter 3 I explored how "elsewhere" dynamics gave global dimensions to immigrants' homeland ties. And in chapter 4 I traced how Muslim immigrants navigated hostland-"elsewhere" interactions. I continued that story in chapter 5 to show how many South Asian Muslim immigrants self-identified with "elsewheres," interpreting their lives here based on their views of Muslims' conditions in the Middle East and Europe. Conversely, in chapter 6 I showed how events transpiring in "elsewhere" European countries often determined how Muslims were identified in America.

But is the multicentered relational framework generalizable? I do not wish to contend that "elsewhere" is somehow always salient to immigrants' identities. Rather, I hope to have shown that its salience is determined by larger geopolitical contexts: the presence of exogenous shocks, homeland-hostland relations, the collective position of immigrants in the hostland, and the worldviews immigrants bring with them from their homelands. The West is the developed, geopolitically powerful, core region of the world, and as such, people from different corners of the globe pay attention to what goes on in Western countries. Muslims from all over the world, for instance, pay attention to how Muslims are treated in Western societies.[7] Ongoing developments in the non-Western developing nations usually matter little to the general Western public, unless exogenous shocks from those far-off places affect the global political order or produce domino effects in their own societies. Whereas the United States and European countries are "elsewhere" centers to many, faraway peripheral places like Nigeria and Myanmar matter to relatively few.

By exploring "elsewhere" effects on immigrant identity formation for the first time, this book introduces substantive questions for race and migration scholars about how "elsewhere" can influence group relations, political participation, and a sense of belonging for diverse immigrant groups in different national contexts. For instance, studies conducted by Canadian sociologists showed that South Asian Muslim immigrants in Canada also experienced Islamophobia in their local communities in response to 9/11 in the United States.[8] And from 2012 to 2015, anti-Muslim hate crimes more than tripled in Canada—a rise that mirrored the increase of Islamophobic hate crimes in the United States at around that same time.[9] These findings suggest that contexts emanating from "elsewhere"—in this case the United States—shape immigrant identities in Canada as well. Despite both countries being neighbors in the West, the United States and Canada have wide differences in immigrant integration, Muslim incorporation, racial dynamics, and sociopolitics that can shape how they respond to global geopolitics. For example, although both countries are currently responding to the same global crisis—the Syrian refugee crisis—they are doing so in diverging ways. Whereas the United States is enacting a "Muslim ban," Canada is seemingly embracing Syrian refugees. Just how these diverging reactions to the same global conflict shape the identity formation of the same immigrant group—South Asian Muslims—in two different nation-state contexts would need to be addressed in future research.

Another possible question to explore: Since South Asian Muslim Americans respond to Muslim-related contexts in the Middle East, are places in South Asia that have Muslim majorities also "elsewheres" for Arab and Middle Eastern Americans? If not, why not? And, what does the answer to these questions mean for the emergence of a "Muslim panethnicity" and civil rights coalitions at the organizational level? With panethnicity being a response to adverse hostland contexts, and with 43 percent of Americans harboring some degree of prejudice against Muslims,[10] the post-9/11 Muslim backlash in the United States should have led to the solidification of a pan-ethnic identity encompassing the two largest Muslim immigrant groups— South Asians and Middle Easterners. Yet such coalitions have not occurred, and scholars are just beginning to investigate why that is the case.[11] I did show that there are some forms of panethnicity between South Asians and Middle Easterners based on "elsewhere" politics in places like Palestine and Turkey; however, "elsewhere" conflicts can conversely suppress panethnicity by deterring these immigrant groups from interacting out of fear of drawing attention to their Muslim-ness. These findings suggest that, contrary to burgeoning state-centric explanations, the answer to the puzzle of Muslim panethnicity might not lie solely within the receiving country but be tied to ongoing global politics that spill across state borders. The multicentered relational framework can make a timely intervention in these research pursuits.

Further research could also examine whether and to what extent "elsewhere" effects vary based on geographical location within the same country. For instance, I conducted this study in California's cosmopolitan milieu, where one only has to step out for lunch to see the effects of globalization around them. But the Deep South, despite emerging as a new destination for immigrants, presents a very different America, one that is predominantly white, Christian, and politically conservative. In Mississippi, for instance, Muslims comprise less than 1 percent of the state's total population.[12] An online search for religious centers in Mississippi produced only sixteen mosques in contrast to over 1,100 churches. In this context, Muslims are not organized as a collective and cannot mobilize like the Muslim Americans in California. They, too, are exposed to Islamophobia, however—and arguably more intensely than their coreligionists in big, urban centers[13]—so how they navigate "elsewhere" ties and to what extent global geopolitics reaches their daily lives need to be explored.

It is also up to future research to explore whether "elsewhere" is solely an immigrant phenomenon or whether it also applies to nonimmigrant groups. For example, does it also apply to black Muslims, for whom the racialized religious experience has been largely bound within the U.S. context? Indeed, research has shown that black Muslims' preoccupation with domestic issues and immigrant Muslims' preoccupation with foreign affairs have produced tensions between these two groups.[14]

Relatedly, the multicentered relational framework also introduces new questions about whether there are "elsewhere" effects for predominantly non-Muslim but racialized "Muslim-looking" groups, like Latinos/as.[15] Indeed, while the 9/11 backlashes against terrorism primarily targeted Arabs and Muslims (real or perceived), they also affected Latinos/as. This latter group was initially deemed safe from the War on Terror, but it was not long before preexisting racial stereotypes of Latinos/as as "violent," "criminal-minded," and "disloyal" brought them into the fold of being perceived as terrorist threats.[16] Donald Trump, in fact, kicked off his presidential bid by talking about the dangers that Mexicans, Middle Easterners, and South Asians brought to the United States. Latinos/as have also been victims of misdirected Islamophobic attacks because of their physical resemblance to Muslim groups.[17] Even at the institutional level, Latinos/as as a group have been affected and further racialized as a result of the changes in U.S. immigration policy and border control brought on by 9/11.[18] Since the September 11 attacks, the United States has looked at its immigration policy mainly from a national security lens, giving rise to new measures and initiatives not just across and outside its borders but also within them. While, in name, these interior immigration policies were about fighting terrorism, in practice they were concerned about undocumented labor migration across the U.S.-Mexico border.[19] Based on this context, in which Latinos/as are homogenized with other "Muslim looking" groups of color, it is possible that conflicts concerning Islam and Muslims in "elsewhere" places also produce exogenous shocks for the Latino/a hostland experience.

The multicentered relational framework allows one to trace the different ways in which global politics in and between multiple places becomes salient and shapes immigrant identities in the hostland. Immigrants embody the interconnectedness of societies through their various ties to places across the globe. Scholars of transnationalism have particularly argued that immigrants—also conceptualized as "transnational migrants"[20] and "transmigrants"[21]—build and maintain multiple networks of connection to their countries of origin while simultaneously settling in a new country.[22]

Peggy Levitt went further, saying that "studies of the South Asian experience in the United States cannot look only at the immigrant experience in America. The American experience is also a product of what goes on in India, the United Kingdom, South Africa, and other countries where South Asian immigrants live."[23]

Yet, South Asian immigrants are also connected to places and contexts that are not part of the South Asian diaspora. Rather, reflecting the geopolitical interplay of states at the global level, immigrants are connected to places that extend beyond the borders of societies of origin and reception, or "elsewhere." The South Asian immigrants in this study did not necessarily think of "elsewhere" places in Europe and the Middle East as their "homes." Nor did they feel any particular sense of diasporic connection to these places. Nonetheless, these societies were salient in the ways South Asians both self-identified and were identified by others in the hostland as Muslims. Moreover, the participants' sense of solidarity with their coreligionists from other ethnic/national backgrounds sometimes gained priority over their membership to co-ethnics back home and abroad. Yet, despite this sense of a unified global Muslim community, Muslims from all places did not attract the same level of solidarity from participants. Where Muslims were located, the geopolitical relationship of those locations to the hostland, and relevant homeland orientations together determined the level of salience of that "elsewhere" place in the immigrants' identity formation.

Thus, by breaking away from a dyadic homeland-hostland paradigm and introducing a new "multicentered relational framework," I hope to have highlighted the truly transnational aspect of these "transmigrants" while simultaneously considering the limitations imposed on transnational social fields by nation-state borders. Indeed, it is because the South Asian Muslim immigrants are located within the United States and are thus subject to the sociopolitical dynamics within its territories that various places around the world become relevant to their identification processes.

Since I completed my fieldwork for this book, the world has continued to be assailed by a nativist and Islamophobic backlash, brought on by right-wing populism and, perhaps, most prominently by the Trump presidency. At the same time, immigrants and Muslim Americans are running for office in highest numbers since 9/11,[24] and with great success: in 2019, for the first time in American politics, two Muslim women—Rashida Tlaib, a daughter of Palestinian immigrant parents, and Ilhan Omar, a refugee from Somalia— made history by being elected to U.S. Congress. Even so, Muslims running for political office are confronted with formidable challenges because of their religion and their racialized status.[25]

In this rapidly changing world order, Facebook and Twitter have become tools for meeting geopolitical ends, and global politics is being filtered down to an image or a few phrases, connecting individuals to distant foreign places with a mere touch of a screen. This makes it all the more crucial for migration and race scholars to begin analyzing how immigrants' lives and worldviews are shaped by contexts "here," "there," and "elsewhere." However, as I have shown, "elsewhere" is hardly a new phenomenon; nor are its effects limited to only Muslims. Rather, various moments in immigration history involving different groups reflect the enduring need to bring this thus-far-overlooked piece of the puzzle into our research paradigm. I hope this book takes us one step closer in that enterprise.

# *Notes*

CHAPTER 1

1. Healy and Barbaro 2015.

2. The Bridge Initiative 2016.

3. Kishi 2016.

4. Identity formation is the collective struggle among social actors over recognition as members of an identity category. Recognition is required from both those who claim to be members and non-members of that category. As such, identity formation has two halves—self-identification and identification by others—with social actors being located at the intersection of these two processes (Lamont and Molnár 2002; Brubaker 2004).

5. Pew Research Center 2017.

6. Pew Research Center 2011.

7. The percentages of Muslims in Bangladesh, Pakistan, and India are 90.4 percent, 96.4 percent, and 14.6 percent respectively (Pew Research Forum 2011).

8. Pew Research Center 2015.

9. Zong and Batalova 2016.

10. Shams 2017.

11. Cesari 2005; Levitt 2007; Wuthnow and Offutt 2008.

12. Lichterman 2008.

13. "Islamist"—as opposed to "Islamic," which means something relating to Islam—refers to something or someone in support of Islamic militancy or fundamentalism.

14. Google Trends 2019b.

15. A diasporic term to refer to things from South Asia.

16. BUFLA 2012.

17. Author's translation. All translations of non-English quotes in this book were provided by the author.

18. A long, loose garment covering the whole body from head to foot, worn in public by many Muslim women.

19. According to some conservative interpretations of Islamic principles and in certain Arab cultures, men and women are expected to lower their gaze and avoid sustained eye contact with each other. This practice is considered respectful and observant of the partition between genders.

20. I discussed this ethnographic snippet about the Bangladeshi family in an earlier work, although for a different analysis (Shams 2017).

21. Guhin 2014.

22. Aslan 2005.

23. Schmidt 2005; Mandaville 2011.

24. Cesari 2004: 92; see also Bowen 2004; Schmidt 2005; Leichtman 2010.

25. Aslan 2005: 137–38.

26. Bowen 2004; Grillo 2004.

27. Leichtman 2010.

28. Bowen 2004: 880.

29. Eickelman and Piscatori 1996; Grillo 2004; Waldinger and Fitzgerald 2004; Zubaida 2004; Yilmaz 2010; Mandaville 2011.

30. Soysal 1994; Koenig 2005.

31. van der Veer 2002a, 2002b.

32. Mas 2010; Joppke and Torpey 2013.

33. Connor 2010.

34. Waldinger 2015; Shams 2017.

35. GASTAT 2018.

36. Al Jazeera 2019.

37. Bunt 2009.

38. Chebib and Sohail 2011; Atlanta and Wiest 2011; Wilson and Dunn 2011.

39. Wynbrandt 2004.

40. Bianchi 2008.

41. Petersen 2012: 128.

42. Bakalian and Bozorgmehr 2009; Cainkar 2009.

43. Whine 2007.

44. Zhou and Bankston 1998; Alba and Nee 2003; Telles and Ortiz 2008.

45. Kim and White 2010.

46. Glick-Schiller, Basch, and Blanc-Szanton 1992; Glick-Schiller, Basch, and Szanton Blanc 1995; Portes, Guarino, and Landolt 1999; Waldinger 2015.

47. Burawoy 1998.

48. Desmond 2014.

49. Desmond 2014: 548.

50. Landler and Harris 2018.

51. Rana 2011.

52. American Community Survey 2016.

53. Topics explored: friends, families, and colleagues; everyday routines; workplaces and other regularly visited spaces; favorite television shows; the news; hobbies; parents' concerns about raising children; food and clothing preferences; families back in the homeland; opinions on politics; religious practices; thoughts about spirituality, gender, and sexuality; future aspirations; and more.

54. Brubaker (2013: 6) calls taking for granted the participants' Muslim-ness as a continued form of self-identification a "trap" or "methodological Islamism."

55. Yildiz and Verkuyten 2013.

56. The time frame used was from 2001 (when 9/11 occurred) to 2016 (when I was completing fieldwork). Because of its bimonthly schedule, the number of *Islamic Horizons* issues was large for qualitative analysis. So, I selected ten issues that focused on the Muslim American community's identity concerns across different spheres, from national politics to interpersonal communication. The topics: the legacy of African American Muslims; the role of faith communities against anti-Muslim bigotry; the spying by the NYPD on Muslim Americans; the role of Muslim leaders in responding to Muslim American needs; discussion about Sharia law to non-Muslims; the role of Muslims in the U.S. presidential election; the embrace of diversity within the Muslim community; the role of Islamic schools in developing Muslim American identity; the Syrian refugee crisis; and hate crime law.

57. Camarota 2012.

58. Pew Research Forum 2017.

59. Levitt 2007: 104.

60. See Spielhaus (2010) on self-identification as "cultural" or "secular" Muslims.

## CHAPTER 2

1. McCoy 2014; Google Trends 2018a.

2. McCoy 2014.

3. Google Trends 2019a.

4. Porto's is a popular bakery in California. Students often drove to its stores to buy cakes, rolls, and tarts, which they then sold on campus to raise funds for their organizational events.

5. Gonzales 1986.

6. See Leonard 1994.

7. Jensen 1988; Sohi 2014.

8. Abdullah 2013.

9. Glick-Schiller, Basch, and Blanc-Szanton 1992: 1.

10. Brubaker et al. 2006: 201.

11. Bernstein 2014; Santana 2014.

12. However, the left has not long been an advocate for immigrant rights. Prior to the 1980s, for instance, several labor unions that many would describe as major actors on the left instigated or supported measures to restrict immigration (Briggs 2001).

13. Bruce 2016.

14. Bouie 2014.

15. Similarly, in 2019, ultra-orthodox Jews were perceived as the harbingers of a measles outbreak in New York because of their anti-vaccination stance, leading to Anti-Semitism (Nir and Gold 2019).

16. Kraut 2004.

17. Markel and Stern 2002: 778.

18. Bouie 2014.

19. Higham 1994.

20. See Liu n.d.

21. Zeitz 2015.

22. Coben 1964.

23. Powell 2011; Silva 2017.

24. See Darden and Thomas 2013.

25. Hassan 2006: 312.

26. Ibid.

27. Shams 2017.

28. Ibid.

29. Although I attended only Bangladeshi *dawats*, this tradition exists for Pakistanis and Indians as well.

30. I refer to this observation in Shams (2017).

31. Name changed to protect anonymity.

32. I refer to this observation in Shams (2017).

33. Manik, Anand, and Barry 2016.

34. India TV 2015.

35. Desilver 2014.

36. Peters 2016.

37. Bennett 2017.

38. Paul and Choksi 2016.

39. Leidig 2016; Bennett 2017.

40. Bennett 2017.

41. Kurien 2010.

## CHAPTER 3

1. Massey et al. 1987; Levitt 2001.

2. Waldinger and Fitzgerald 2004; Waldinger 2015.

3. Hondagneu-Sotelo 1992; Duval 2004; Tannenbaum 2007.

4. Shams 2017.

5. Uddin 2006; Tunzelmann 2007.

6. Uddin 2006: 48.

7. Khan 2008.

8. Ashraf 2017; "At the Stroke of Midnight My Entire Family Was Displaced," 2017.

9. Riaz 2010.

10. Pew Research Center Global Attitudes and Trends 2011.

11. In 2008, ten Pakistanis associated with Lashkar-e-Taiba stormed buildings in Mumbai, killing 164 people during a four-day-long siege (CNN 2017). The memories of this attack are still present in Indian national consciousness, indicated by the many Bollywood movies on the event that have been made since then.

12. Ibid.

13. Bangladesh Genocide Archive 2018.

14. Aydin 2017.

15. From 2012 to 2016 there were an estimated 6.9 million Indian, 3.2 million Bangladeshi, and 3.2 million Pakistani workers in the Middle East (Gulf Labour Markets and Migration 2019).

16. United Nations 2013; Doherty et al. 2014; World Bank 2014.

17. Levitt (1998) calls this form of cultural transfusion from the hostland to the homeland "social remittances."

18. Nazli Kibria 2011: 135–36.

19. Keay 2004.

20. Dalrymple 2015.

21. Metcalf 2009.

22. A fundamentalist interpretation of Islam prevalent in Saudi Arabia.

23. Rashid 2012; Shane 2016; Jaffrelot and Louër 2017.

24. Abedin 2017; "Bangladesh to Build Hundreds of Mosques with Saudi Cash," 2017; *Dawn* 2017.

25. Lichtblau and Schmitt 2010; Georgy 2011; Choksy and Choksy 2015.

26. In 2013, gathering almost half a million supporters, this group launched violent marches and rallies on the streets of Dhaka, demanding the government enact a thirteen-point charter, which included an "anti-blasphemy law." Other points included the banning of candlelit vigils (a common form of peaceful mass protest in Bangladesh), men and women mixing in public, and erecting sculptures in public places. Canceling the country's women development policy, ending "shameless behavior and dresses," sentencing to exemplary punishment all bloggers and others who "insult Islam," and declaring the Ahmadiyya sect (a persecuted Muslim minority in Bangladesh) "non-Muslim" were also included in the charter (Mustafa 2013).

27. Barry and Manik 2017.

28. Tharoor 2010; Cafiero and Wagner 2015.

29. In February 2018, for instance, Saudi Arabia asked for—and received—military assistance from Pakistan to stem the influence of Iran in the Yemen conflict, which many analysts view as a proxy war between Iran and Saudi Arabia (Reuters 2018).

30. McNally and Weinbaum 2016.

31. Rana 2011.

32. Landler and Harris 2018.

33. Pew Research Center Global Attitudes Project 2011.

34. Ibid.

35. Pew Research Center Global Attitudes and Trends 2012.

36. I noticed Atif's use of "we" and "they." While he, like most other informants, usually referred to the United States as "we," in this instance, he used "they" when talking about the United States. I interpreted this discrepancy as a reflection of the dissonance he felt from America in light of its foreign policies toward his homeland and other Muslim countries.

37. A *salwar kamiz* is worn by both men and women in Bangladesh, India, and Pakistan. It consists of two pieces—the *salwar*, a pair of baggy trousers—and the *kamiz*, a fitted long shirt. Women sometimes also wear a *dupatta*—a long, flowing piece of cloth—around their neck, hair, or shoulders.

38. A *kurta* is a long upper garment for both men and women in South Asia.

39. This has since changed. In 2017, Saudi women were allowed to drive under the orders of Crown Prince Muhammad bin Salman.

40. Islamic law derived from the Quran and *Hadith* (the teachings of Prophet Muhammad).

41. Most of the Muslim population in Pakistan, roughly 85 to 90 percent, is Sunni (Central Intelligence Agency 2016), with just about 15 percent of Pakistani citizens being Shia (Council on Foreign Relations 2014). This demographic breakdown of Pakistani Muslims along the Sunni-Shia divide is representative of the global Muslim population—Shias comprise only 15 percent of the 1.6 billion Muslims in the world, whereas Sunnis are the overwhelming majority (Pew Research Center on Religion and Public Life 2011). This proportion is also representative of this study's sample; although I recruited participants who simply identified as "Muslim," upon interviewing, I found that only three out of the sixty participants were Shia and that all of them came from a Pakistani background.

42. For instance, they grew up learning that Shias are different from Sunnis: that despite all being Muslims and believing in one Allah and the Prophet Muhammad, they go to different mosques, have different religious rituals and festivals, believe in different symbols, and revere different religious figures than do their Sunni friends.

43. Kibria 2011.

44. Ibid.

45. Citing financial irregularities and unpaid taxes, the Bangladeshi government nationalized Grameen Bank and forced Dr. Yunus to resign. Many Bangladeshi political analysts say that his ousting was the result of his trying to organize a rival political party back in 2007.

46. Manik, Anand, and Barry 2016.

47. DAESH is a transliteration of the Arabic acronym formed of the same words that make up ISIS in English.

48. BUFLA 2016.

49. Ullah entered the United States with an F43 visa, which is issued to children of immigrants who are sponsored by a direct relative who is a U.S. citizen (Ballesteros 2017). Ullah obtained the visa by being the son of an F41 visa recipient who was sponsored by a U.S. citizen sibling.

50. Baker and Weiser 2017.

51. Hajela and Dobnik 2017.

52. Just over 14 percent of the total Indian population is Muslim, whereas almost 80 percent is Hindu (CIA 2016). Muslims also make up a small percentage of the country's emigrant population to the United States—only 10 percent compared to 51 percent of Hindus (Desilver 2014).

53. An opinion poll from 1993 revealed that 78 percent of Hindus believed that separate Muslim personal laws are divisive, over half of them believed that Indian Muslims "consider themselves Muslims first and Indians later," and a solid majority viewed Muslim leaders to be generally fundamentalist extremists.

54. Ashraf 2017.

55. Ibid.

56. Ibid.

57. *Aarti* is a Hindu ritual of worship. Light from wicks soaked in *ghee*, or purified butter, is offered to deities. Songs are sung in praise of the gods or goddesses. Sometimes a coconut is broken as a sign of humbling oneself to god.

58. Mishra 2016.

59. As Muneer Ahmed (2004) puts it, all "Muslim-looking" individuals are racially profiled into the same "Muslim" category based on two assumptions: (1) all "Muslim-looking" people are Muslims, and (2) all Muslims are associated with terrorism. Many scholars have even argued that the religion of Islam itself has been racialized as inherently flawed and prone to violence, and not just the people who subscribe to it (Cainkar 2009).

60. Dhingra 2007; Shams 2015; Shams 2017.

61. Mathew and Prashad 2000; Kurien 2001, 2004,

62. See Kurien 2016.

63. Peters 2016.

64. Bennett 2016.

65. Chaldean Christians in the United States provide another example. They supported Trump's "Muslim ban," which they interpreted through the lens of religious sectarian conflicts in Iraq.

66. Choksi and Paul 2016.

67. Haberman 2016.

68. As of April 30, 2019, the date this chapter was completed, the image is also the publicly visible and publicly accessible profile picture of the Hindus for Trump Facebook group.

69. See Choksi and Paul (2016) and Paul and Choksi (2016) for news coverage of the event.

70. Kibria 1998; Prashad 1998; Mishra 2016.

71. Masud 2002.

72. In Levitt's (2007) terms, "symbolic faithfuls" (see chapter 1).

73. Pew Global Attitudes Project 2003.

## CHAPTER 4

1. I analyzed this and other examples in this chapter using a different analytical lens in a previous publication, *Sociological Forum* (Shams 2018).

2. Prashad 2000, 2012.

3. Said 1979.

4. Bakalian and Bozorgmehr 2009; Cainkar 2009; Selod 2018.

5. Apuzzo and Goldman 2011.

6. Human Rights Watch 2014.

7. Lichtblau 2016.

8. Shaheen 2001; Powell 2011; Silva 2017.

9. Bail 2015.

10. Ibid.

11. Ibid.

12. Powell 2011; Silva 2017.

13. Powell 2011.

14. Powell 2011: 106.

15. Kearns, Betus, and Lemeaux 2017.

16. Department of Homeland Security 2017.

17. Patel and Koushik 2017.

18. Houry 2017.

19. MACLC et al. 2013.

20. Hamilton 2016.

21. Tabassum's appearance in her own words:

People never know where I am from. I have had so many people tell me that I don't look *desi*. What's the new term—ethnically ambiguous? That's being thrown around a lot, especially in our [*desi*/South Asian] community. I get that a lot. People think I am mixed, and when I say that both my parents are from Pakistan, I would get, "Oh, I could never tell, you are so ethnically ambiguous." I think it means that you fall short of the stereotype of how a South Asian should look like. Most people think I am Persian or Latina.

22. See BBC News 2013; De Sondy 2016.

23. Lewin 2001.

24. Basu 2016.

25. Dhingra 2007.

26. ACLU n.d.

27. Mogahed and Mahmood 2019.

28. Several others, however, drank alcohol. Some claimed to be "social drinkers," meaning they would not seek out drinks, but if offered, they would not refuse. In South Asian Muslim communities, drinking alcohol is usually perceived as a sign of immorality. As such, some respondents seemed embarrassed when they responded yes to my question about whether they drank alcohol.

My question about drinking habits was aimed at understanding the practicing aspects of lived religion.

29. Semple 2015b.

30. Hennessy-Fiske 2017; Murdock and Jeltsen 2017; Wax-Thibodeaux and Hauslohner 2017.

31. Murdock and Jeltsen 2017.

32. Hennessy-Fiske 2017.

33. Interestingly, these stories about Muslims—the so-called un-American violent outsiders—providing relief to hurricane victims ran in sharp contrast to another news story that appeared in news headlines around the same time: that of Joel Osteen, a multimillionaire televangelist pastor in Houston who refused to open his church's 16,800-seat indoor arena to flood victims (Blumberg 2017). His refusal drew criticism from many Americans until he was compelled to open his church as a shelter (McKirdy and Park 2017).

34. Rogers and Stolberg 2018.

35. Ilmfeed 2018.

36. Ibid.

37. Rabasa et. al. 2007; Rashid 2011; Ibrahim 2016.

38. Hubbard 2016.

39. Ibid.

40. Rubin 2016.

41. Leiken and Brooke 2007.

42. Rizvi 2014.

43. Manzoor 2015.

44. Rabasa et. al. 2007.

45. Pew Research Center 2017.

46. Ibid.

47. Mamdani 2002: 766.

48. Mogahed and Mahmood 2019.

49. Brubaker et al. 2006: 211.

50. This categorization of Latinos/as as white in some instances of everyday colloquialism is interesting. Latinos/as are sometimes "white" for *desis*, but they are at times also conflated as "Muslim-looking" in the larger U.S. society, especially in moments of increased national security. However, as I did not see the Latinos/as in Faizah's friend group, I could not observe exactly who she conflated as "white."

51. Bennhold 2015.

52. The concerns of these South Asian Muslim parents are not groundless. Arifa, the Pakistani from chapter 3, received similar advice from her parents, but disregarded it and became involved in Palestinian activism. One day, I was volunteering at a *samosa* (fried pastry) sale when she dropped by. "So, I just found out that I am on Canary," she abruptly told those of us at the table. Puzzled, I asked, "What's Canary?" I learned that it is an open-access website that documents people and groups allegedly promoting anti-Semitism and anti-American sentiments on U.S. college campuses (Canary Mission n.d.). According to the *Guardian*, the website was launched by an unknown group to "profile[s] people affiliated with pro-Palestinian student groups . . . in an effort to dissuade potential employers from hiring them" (Holpuch 2015). I analyze these findings with more data and in-depth analysis in Shams 2020.

53. Cruz 2011.

54. Medina 2011.

55. Cruz 2011; Esposito 2011.

56. Medina 2011.

57. Cruz 2011.

58. Benchemsi 2015.

59. Bullock 2003.

60. Bullock 2000.

61. Haddad 2007.

62. Read and Bartkowsky 2000.

63. Williams and Vashi 2007.

64. Chalabi 2013.

65. Bilefsky 2016.

66. "The Burkini Debate," 2016; Dremeaux 2016.

67. Polls have indeed shown that knowing a Muslim personally is linked to lower Islamophobia (Mogahed and Mahmood 2019).

68. Salahuddin 2016.

69. Joseph and Keyworth 2010.

70. Ibid.

71. Mogahed and Mahmood 2019.

72. CAIR, Jetpac, and MPower Change 2019.

CHAPTER 5

1. Stancill et al. 2015.

2. Katz and Pérez-Peña 2015.

3. Grubb 2015.

4. BDS is a Palestinian-led, nonviolent, international pressure group that promotes various forms of boycott against Israel until it ends "occupation and colonization of all Arab lands," recognizes the rights of Arab-Palestinian citizens of Israel, and protects the rights of Palestinian refugees "to return to their homes" (BDS n.d.).

5. Although Bushra thought so, with a population of over 1.6 billion (nearly equaling the number of Christians) and comprising the second largest and fastest growing religious group in the world (Pew Research Center 2015), Muslims are hardly a global minority.

6. See Ose 2015; Stancill et al. 2015.

7. Elmasry 2015.

8. NBC News 2015.

9. Inside Edition 2015.

10. Dina is implicitly referring to a popular *Hadith* about the *Ummah*. The *Hadith* goes that the global Muslim community is like one cohesive human body. If a finger hurts, the whole body feels ill.

11. Love 2017.

12. Pew Global Attitudes Project 2003.

13. Berenson 2018; Landau and Khoury 2018.

14. Bazian and Beydoun 2016.

15. CNN 2016.

16. Lachman 2016; LoBianco and Diamond 2016.

17. *Iftaar* is the meal that Muslims eat after sunset to break their fast during Ramadan.

18. Erlanger 2016; Ripley 2016.

19. Warikoo 2016.

20. Abbey-Lambertz 2016; Dardai 2016.

21. See Anderson 1983; Itzigsohn 2000; Glick-Schiller and Fouron 2001; Smith 2003; Smith and Bakker 2008; Eckstein 2009.

22. Wright 2017; UNICEF 2018.

23. "The Rohingya Boat Crisis," 2015.

24. Human Rights Watch 2015a.

25. Kapoor and Hamzah 2015.

26. Pearlman 2015.

27. Tharoor 2017.

28. Human Rights Watch 2015b.

29. Sengupta and Fountain 2018.

30. Google Trends 2018c.

31. Google Trends 2018b.

32. Although not related by blood, older women in the *desi* community are referred to as aunties. Young *desis* viewed aunties as the purveyors of community gossip.

33. Despite their sense of standing up against "any injustice," Bushra, like other respondents, appeared unaware or indifferent to the fact that Turkey is governed by an Islamist party, evidenced by their silence on the topic.

34. Pew Global Attitudes Project 2003.

35. See Shams 2015.

36. Mishra 2016.

## CHAPTER 6

1. "Europe's Response to the Paris Attacks Is Different This Time," 2015.

2. Haberman and Pérez-Peña 2015.

3. Levin 2016; Southern Poverty Law Center 2016.

4. Semple 2015a.

5. Doucet 2015.

6. Moore 2017.

7. Phillips 2015; Sullivan 2016.

8. Yourish et al. 2016.

9. Google Trends 2018e.

10. Even then, the level of interest among the American public after the Brussels bombings was much higher than that after the Beirut attacks (Google Trends 2018h).

11. Sussman 2015.

12. Gonzalez 2015; Semple 2015b; "Bombings in Brussels," 2016; Mudde 2016; Pape 2016.

13. "Bombings in Brussels," 2016.

14. Said 1979.

15. Naudet 2018.

16. Napoli 2003.

17. Barnard 2015.

18. The top image of the Facebook filter advertisement was reported by Bonarenko (2017) for *Business Insider*. The participants' profile images have been blurred to protect their anonymity.

19. Bonarenko 2017.

20. Barnard 2015.

21. Wilkie 2016.

22. The Bridge Initiative 2016.

23. Lichtblau 2016; Stack 2016.

24. Perez et al. 2016.

25. Ellis et al. 2016.

26. Google Trends 2018f; Google Trends 2018g.

27. Pew Research Center 2017.

28. "How the World Views the U.S. Elections, from Israel to North Korea," 2016; Parvaz 2016.

29. Gallup 2011.

30. Barnard 2016.

CHAPTER 7

1. On December 11, 2016, a suicide bomber killed twenty-nine people and injured forty-seven others at the El-Botroseya Church. ISIS claimed responsibility.

2. On July 22, 2016, a shooting near the Olympia shopping mall in Munich killed ten people, including the perpetrator, and injured thirty-six others.

3. Mekhennet, Witte, and Booth 2016.

4. Troianovsky, Alessi, and Wilkes 2016.

5. Kassam 2016; Spencer 2016.

6. Love 2017.

7. Gallup 2011.

8. Jamil and Rousseau 2012.

9. Statistics Canada 2017.

10. Gallup 2015.

11. Bozorgmehr, Ong, and Tosh 2016.

12. Pew Research Religion and Public Life 2013.

13. Shams 2015.

14. Mazrui 2004.

15. According to a Pew Research Center survey from 2007, Hispanics comprise just 4 percent of all Muslim Americans, but make up 10 percent of the Muslim population born in the United States.

16. Bender 2002.

17. Semple 2015a.

18. Romero and Zarrugh 2017.

19. Coleman 2007; Chishti and Bergeron 2011.

20. Levitt 2004.

21. Glick-Schiller, Basch, and Szanton Blanc 1995: 48.

22. Glick-Schiller and Fouron 2001.

23. Levitt 2004.

24. Raphelson 2018.

25. Marans 2018.

# References

Abbey-Lambertz, Kate. 2016. "Yes, Muslims Voted for a Jewish Candidate. No, Pundits Shouldn't Be Surprised." *Huffington Post*, March 10. https://www.huffpost.com/entry/dearborn-muslims-arab-americans-bernie-sanders_n_56e16b5ae4b0860f99d7ea1f.

Abdullah, Zain. 2013. "American Muslims in the Contemporary World." In *The Cambridge Companion to American Islam*, edited by Julianne Hammer and Omid Safi, 65–82. Cambridge: Cambridge University Press.

Abedin, Syed Zainul. 2017. "Saudi to Pay Big Money to Mosques." *Dhaka Tribune*, April 20. http://www.dhakatribune.com/bangladesh/nation/2017/04/20/saudi-pay-big-money-mosques/.

ACLU (American Civil Rights Union). n.d. "Surveillance under the USA/Patriot Act." https://www.aclu.org/other/surveillance-under-usapatriot-act. Accessed July 14, 2018.

Ahmed, Muneer. 2004. "A Rage Shared by Law: Post–September 11 Racial Violence as Crimes of Passion." *California Law Review* 92(5): 1259–330.

Alba, Richard, and Victor Nee. 2003. *Remaking the American Mainstream: Assimilation and Contemporary Immigration*. Cambridge, MA: Harvard University Press.

American Community Survey. 2016. "FactFinder: 2016 American Community Survey 1-Year Estimates." Washington, DC: U.S. Census Bureau.

https://factfinder.census.gov/faces/tableservices/jsf/pages/productview.xhtml
?pid=ACS_16_5YR_B02015&prodType=table.

Anderson, Benedict. 1983. *Imagined Communities: Reflections of the Origin and Spread of Nationalism.* New York: Verso.

Apuzzo, Matt, and Adam Goldman. 2011. "Inside the Spy Unit that NYPD Says Doesn't Exist." Associated Press, August 31. http://www.law.uh.edu/faculty /eberman/security/AP%20reporting%20on%20NYPD%201.pdf.

Ashraf, Ajaz. 2017. "India's Muslims and the Price of Partition." *New York Times,* August 17.

Aslan, Reza. 2005. *No God but God: The Origins, Evolution, and Future of Islam.* New York: Random House.

"At the Stroke of Midnight My Entire Family Was Displaced." 2017. *New York Times,* August 14.

Aydin, Cemil. 2017. *The Idea of the Muslim World: A Global Intellectual History.* Cambridge, MA: Harvard University Press.

Bail, Christopher. 2015. *Terrified: How Anti-Muslim Fringe Organizations Became Mainstream.* Princeton, NJ: Princeton University Press.

Bakalian, Anny, and Mehdi Bozorgmehr. 2009. *Backlash 9/11: Middle Eastern and Muslim Americans Respond.* Berkeley: University of California Press.

Baker, Al, and Benjamin Weiser. 2017. "'I Did It for the Islamic State,' Bombing Suspect Told Investigators." *New York Times,* December 12.

Ballesteros, Carlos. 2017. "New York Terrorism Suspect Got into the Country on a Family Visa Donald Trump Wants to End." *Newsweek,* December 11.

Bangladesh Genocide Archive. 2018. http://www.genocidebangladesh.org.

"Bangladesh to Build Hundreds of Mosques with Saudi Cash." 2017. *Dawn,* April 27. https://www.dawn.com/news/1329553.

Barnard, Anne. 2015. "Beirut, Also the Site of Deadly Attacks, Feels Forgotten." *New York Times,* November 15.

Barnard, Anne. 2016. "After Attacks on Muslims, Many Ask: Where Is the Outpouring?" *New York Times,* July 5.

Barry, Ellen, and Julfikar Ali Manik. 2017. "To Secular Bangladeshis, Textbook Changes Are a Harbinger." *New York Times,* January 22.

Bazian, Hatem, and Khaled A. Beydoun. 2016. "Why Muslims Are Voting for Bernie Sanders." *Ummah Wide,* June 6. https://ummahwide.com/why-muslims -are-voting-for-bernie-sanders-f482c7865869.

BBC News. 2013. "Decoding Facial Hair in the Arab World." February 2. https://
www.bbc.com/news/magazine-20877090.

BDS (Boycott, Divestment, and Sanctions). n.d. "Overview." https://bdsmovement
.net/what-is-bds. Accessed May 24, 2018.

Benchemsi, Ahmed. 2015. "Why Will No One Let the Muslim World Be
Secular?" *Time*, January 26. http://time.com/3675429/muslim-world
-secularization/.

Bender, Steven W. 2002. "Sight, Sound, and Stereotype: The War on Terrorism
and Its Consequences for Latinas/os." *Oregon Law Review* 81: 1153–78.

Bennett, James. 2017. "Donald Trump, Narendra Modi Parallels Excited Conservative Hindu Nationalist Group." ABC News, June 25. http://www.abc
.net.au/news/2017-06-26/conservative-hindus-see-parallels-donald-trump
-narendra-modi/8650404.

Bennhold, Katrin. 2015. "Jihad and Girl Power: How ISIS Lured 3 London Girls."
*New York Times*, August 17.

Berenson, Tessa. 2018. "The White House Blamed Hamas after Israeli Troops
Shot and Killed Palestinians." *Time*, May 14. http://time.com/5276896/hamas
-gaza-strip-israel-white-house-raj-shah/.

Bernstein, Sharon. 2014. "With U.S. Ebola Fear Running High, African Immigrants Face Ostracism." Reuters, October 24. https://www.reuters.com/article
/us-health-ebola-usa-xenophobia/with-u-s-ebola-fear-running-high-african
-immigrants-face-ostracism-idUSKCN0ID1J420141024.

Bianchi, Robert. 2008. *Guests of God: Pilgrimage and Politics in the Islamic World*.
New York: Oxford University Press.

Bilefsky, Dan. 2016. "France's Burkini Debate Reverberates around the World."
*New York Times*, August 31.

Blumberg, Antonia. 2017. "Joel Osteen's Houston Megachurch Blasted for Clos-
ing as Thousands Are Displaced." *Huffington Post*, August 28. https://www
.huffpost.com/entry/joel-osteen-lakewood-church-hurricane-harvey_n
_59a45aa4e4b0821444c513d8.

"Bombings in Brussels: The New Normal." 2016. *Economist*, March 26.

Bonarenko, Veronika. 2017. "Facebook Quietly Stopped Offering Flag Profile-
Picture Filters after Terrorist Attacks." *Business Insider*, June 10. http://www
.businessinsider.com/facebook-stops-offering-flag-profile-picture-filters-after
-terrorist-attacks-2017-5.

Borzorgmehr, Mehdi, Paul Ong, and Sarah Tosh. 2016. "Panethnicity Revisited: Contested Group Boundaries in the Post-9/11 Era." *Ethnic and Racial Studies* 39(5): 727–45.

Bouie, Jamelle. 2014. "America's Long History of Immigrant Scaremongering." *Slate*, July 18. http://www.slate.com/articles/news_and_politics/politics/2014/07/immigrant_scaremongering_and_hate_conservatives_stoke_fears_of_diseased.html.

Bowen, John R. 2004. "Beyond Migration: Islam as a Transnational Public Space." *Journal of Ethnic and Migration Studies* 30(5): 879–94.

The Bridge Initiative: A Georgetown University Research Project. 2016. *When Islamophobia Turns Violent: The 2016 U.S. Presidential Elections*. May 2. http://bridge.georgetown.edu/wp-content/uploads/2016/05/When-Islamophobia-Turns-Violent.pdf.

Briggs, Vernon M. 2001. *Immigration and American Unionism*. Ithaca, NY: Cornell University Press.

Brubaker, Rogers. 2004. *Ethnicity without Groups*. Cambridge, MA: Harvard University Press.

Brubaker, Rogers. 2013. "Categories of Analysis and Categories of Practice: A Note on the Study of Muslims in European Countries of Immigration." *Ethnic and Racial Studies* 36(1): 1–8.

Brubaker, Rogers, Margit Feischmidt, Jon Fox, and Liana Grancea. 2006. *Nationalist Politics in Everyday Ethnicity in a Transylvania Town*. Princeton, NJ: Princeton University Press.

Bruce, Tammy. 2016. "When Foreigners Bring Disease across the Border." *Washington Times*, January 25.

BUFLA (Bangladesh Unity Federation of Los Angeles). 2012. Bangladesh Day Parade 2012. April 1. http://bufla.com/Multimedia/BDParade/BDParade2012Picture.aspx.http://bufla.com/Multimedia/BDParade/BDParade2012Picture.aspx.

BUFLA (Bangladesh Unity Federation of Los Angeles). 2016. "News/Press Note Archive." July 1. http://bufla.com/NewsMedia/NewsPressReleaseDB.aspx?Param1=1010.

Bullock, Katherine. 2000. "Challenging Media Representations of the Veil: Contemporary Muslim Women's Re-veiling Movement." *American Journal of Islamic Social Sciences* 17(3): 22–53.

Bullock, Katherine. 2003. *Rethinking Muslim Women and the Veil: Challenging Historical and Modern Stereotypes*. Herndon, VA: International Institute of Islamic Thought.

Bunt, Gary R. 2009. *iMuslims: Rewiring the House of Islam*. Chapel Hill: University of North Carolina Press.

Burawoy, Michael. 1998. "The Extended Case Method." *Sociological Theory* 16(1): 4–33.

"The Burkini Debate: Muslin Modesty vs. French Norms." 2016. *New York Times*, August 26. https://www.nytimes.com/2016/08/27/opinion/the-burkini-debate -muslim-modesty-vs-french-norms.html.

Cafiero, Giorgio, and Daniel Wagner. 2015. "Saudi Arabia and Pakistan's Evolving Alliance." *The National Interest*, November 19. http://nationalinterest.org /feature/saudi-arabia-pakistans-evolving-alliance-14391?page=show.

Cainkar, Louise. 2009. *Homeland Insecurity: The Arab American and Muslim American Experience after 9/11*. New York: Russell Sage Foundation.

CAIR, Jetpac, and MPower Change. 2019. *The Rise of American Muslim Changemakers: Political Organizing in the Trump Era*. https://www.jet-pac.com/wp -content/uploads/2018/11/Rise_of_the_changemakers_2.pdf.

Camarota, Steven A. 2012. *Immigrants in the United States: A Profile of America's Foreign-Born Population*. Center for Immigration Studies. https:// cis.org/sites/cis.org/files/articles/2012/immigrants-in-the-united-states -2012.pdf.

Central Intelligence Agency. 2016. "The World Factbook." https://www.cia.gov /library/publications/the-world-factbook/.

Cesari, Jocelyn. 2005. "Religion and Politics: Interaction, Confrontation, and Tensions." *History and Anthropology* 16(1): 85–95.

Chalabi, Mona. 2013. "How Many Women Wear the Niqab in the U.K.?" *Guardian*, February 20.

Chebib, Nadine Kassem, and Rabia Minatullah Sohail. 2011. "The Reasons Social Media Contributed to the 2011 Egyptian Revolution." *International Journal of Business Research and Management* 2(3): 139–62.

Chishti, Muzaffar, and Claire Bergeron. 2011. "Post-9/11 Policies Dramatically Alter the U.S. Immigration Landscape." Migration Policy Institute, September 8. https://www.migrationpolicy.org/article/post-911-policies-dramatically -alter-us-immigration-landscape.

Choksi, Mansi, and Sonia Paul. 2016. "Hindus for Trump." *Slate*, October 17. http://www.slate.com/articles/news_and_politics/roads/2016/10/scenes_from _a_hindus_for_trump_rally_in_new_jersey.html.

Choksy, Carol E. B., and Jamsheed K. Choksy. 2015. "The Saudi Connection: Wahhabism and Global Jihad." *World Affairs*, May/June. http://www.world affairsjournal.org/article/saudi-connection-wahhabism-and-global-jihad.

Chughtai, Alia. 2019. "Hajj 2019: An In-Depth Look at the Sacred Journey." Al Jazeera, August 9. https://www.aljazeera.com/indepth/interactive/2017/08 /hajj-2017-depth-sacred-journey-170824132159144.html.

CNN. 2016. "Full Transcript: CNN Democratic Debate." April 15. https://www .cnn.com/2016/04/14/politics/transcript-democratic-debate-hillary-clinton -bernie-sanders/index.html.

CNN. 2017. "Mumbai Terror Attacks Fast Facts." December 12. https://www.cnn .com/2013/09/18/world/asia/mumbai-terror-attacks/index.html.

Coben, Stanley. 1964. "A Study in Nativism: The American Red Scare of 1919– 1920." *Political Science Quarterly* 79(1): 52–75.

Coleman, Mathew. 2007. "Immigration Geopolitics beyond the Mexico-U.S. Border." *Antipode* 39(1): 54–76.

Connor, Phillip. 2010. "Contexts of Immigrant Receptivity and Immigrant Religious Outcomes: The Case of Muslims in Western Europe." *Ethnic and Racial Studies* 33(3): 376–403.

Council on Foreign Relations. 2014. "The Sunni-Shia Divide." https://www.cfr .org/interactives/sunni-shia-divide#!/sunni-shia-divide.

Cruz, Nicole Santa, Lauren Williams, and Mike Anton. 2011. "Irvine 11: 10 Students Sentenced to Probation, No Jail Time." *Los Angeles Times*, September 23.

Dalrymple, William. 2015. "The Great Divide: The Violent Legacy of Indian Partition." *New Yorker*, June 29.

Dardai, Bilal. 2016. "Bernie Sanders Won Arab Americans in Michigan. The Media Is Wrong About Why." *Vox*, March 11. https://www.vox.com/2016/3 /11/11193030/bernie-sanders-muslims.

Darden, Joe T., and Richard W. Thomas. 2013. *Detroit: Race Riots, Racial Conflicts, and Efforts to Bridge the Racial Divide*. East Lansing: Michigan State University Press.

Department of Homeland Security. 2017. "Countering Violent Extremism." https://www.dhs.gov/countering-violent-extremism.

Desilver, Drew. 2014. "FactTank: 5 Facts about Indian Americans." Pew Research Center, September 30. http://www.pewresearch.org/fact-tank/2014/09/30/5-facts-about-indian-americans/.

Desmond, Matthew. 2014. "Relational Ethnography." *Theory and Society* 43: 547–79.

De Sondy, Amanullah. 2016. "The Relationship between Muslim Men and Their Beards Is a Tangled One." *Guardian*, January 28.

Dhingra, Pawan. 2007. *Managing Multicultural Lives: Asian American Professionals and the Challenge of Multiple Identities.* Stanford, CA: Stanford University Press.

Doherty, Meghan, Brian Leung, Katie Lorenze, and Amanda Wilmarth. 2014. *Understanding South Asian Labor Migration.* Robert M. La Follette School of Public Affairs. Madison, WI: University of Wisconsin, Madison.

Doucet, Lyse. 2015. "Paris Attack: From 9/11 to 1/11." BBC, January 12. https://www.bbc.com/news/world-europe-30786552.

Dremeaux, Lillie. 2016. "The Way People Look at Us Has Changed: Muslim Women on Life in Europe." *New York Times*, September 2.

Duval, David Timothy. 2004. "Linking Return Visits and Return Migration among Commonwealth Eastern Caribbean Migrants in Toronto." *Global Networks* 4(1): 51–67.

Eckstein, Susan. 2009. *The Immigrant Divide: How Cuban Americans Changed the US and Their Homeland.* New York: Routledge.

Eickelman, Dale, and James Piscatori. 1996. *Muslim Politics.* Princeton, NJ: Princeton University Press.

Ellis, Ralph, Ashley Frantz, Faith Karimi, and Elliot C. McLaughlin. 2016. "Orlando Shooting: 49 Killed, Shooter Pledged ISIS Allegiance." CNN, June 13. http://www.cnn.com/2016/06/12/us/orlando-nightclub-shooting/.

Elmasry, Mohamed. 2015. "Chapel Hill Shooting and Western Media Bigotry." Al Jazeera, February 11.

Eltantawy, Nahed, and Julie Wiest. 2011. "Social Media and the Egyptian Revolution: Reconsidering Resource Mobilization Theory." *International Journal of Communication* 5: 1207–24.

Erianger, Steven. 2016. "Bernie Sanders's Kibbutz Found. Surprise: It's Socialist." *New York Times*, February 5.

Esposito, John L. 2011. "The Irvine 11: Student Freedom of Speech and Dissent under Siege." *Huffington Post*, June 16.

"Europe's Response to the Paris Attacks Is Different This Time." 2015. *Economist*, November 14.

Gabaccia, Donna R. 2000. *Italy's Many Diasporas*. London: Routledge.

Gallup. 2011. "Islamophobia: Understanding Islam in the West." http://www.gallup.com/poll/157082/islamophobia-understanding-anti-muslim-sentiment-west.aspx.

Gallup. 2015. "Perceptions of Muslims in the United States: A Review." December 11. https://news.gallup.com/opinion/gallup/187664/perceptions-muslims-united-states-review.aspx.

GASTAT (General Authority for Statistics: Kingdom of Saudi Arabia). 2018. "GASTAT: The Total Number of Pilgrims in 1439H *Hajj* Season Reached (2.371.675) Pilgrims." https://www.stats.gov.sa/en/news/280.

Georgy, Michael. 2011. "Saudi Arabia, UAE Funded Jihadi Networks in Pakistan." Reuters, May 21. https://www.reuters.com/article/us-pakistan-saudi-uae/saudi-arabia-uae-funded-jihadi-networks-in-idUSTRE74L0ER20110522.

Glick-Schiller, Nina, Linda Basch, and Cristina Blanc-Szanton. 1992. "Transnationalism: A New Analytic Framework for Understanding Migration." *Annals of the New York Academy of Sciences* 645: 1–24.

Glick-Schiller, Nina, Linda Basch, and Cristina Szanton Blanc. 1995. "From Immigrant to Transmigrant: Theorizing Transnational Migration." *Anthropological Quarterly* 68(1): 48–63.

Glick-Schiller, Nina, and Georges Eugene Fouron. 2001. *Georges Woke Up Laughing: Long-Distance Nationalism and the Search for Home*. Durham, NC: Duke University Press.

Gonzalez, Edgar. 2015. "The New Normal?" *Harvard Political Review*, March 31. http://harvardpolitics.com/world/47575/.

Gonzales, Juan L. 1986. "Asian Indian Immigration Patterns: The Origins of the Sikh Community in California." *International Migration Review* 20(1): 40–54.

Google Trends. 2018a. https://trends.google.com/trends/explore?date=2009-01-01%202018-01-11&geo=US&q=Boko%20Haram.

Google Trends. 2018b. https://trends.google.com/trends/explore?date=2015-06-30%202016-06-30&geo=US&q=Rohingya%20refugee,Syrian%20refugee.

Google Trends. 2018c. https://trends.google.com/trends/explore?date=2016-01-01%202018-01-01&geo=US&q=Rohingya%20refugee.

Google Trends. 2018d. https://trends.google.com/trends/explore?date=2015-11
 -08%202015-12-31&geo=US&q=ISIS%20attacks%20in%20Beirut,ISIS%20at
 tacks%20in%20Paris.

Google Trends. 2018e. https://trends.google.com/trends/explore?date=2015-11
 -01%202016-04-30&geo=US&q=ISIS%20attacks%20in%20Paris,ISIS%20at
 tacks%20in%20Brussels.

Google Trends. 2018f. https://trends.google.com/trends/explore?date=2015
 -12-01%202016-06-30&geo=US&q=ISIS%20Orlando,ISIS%20San%20Ber
 nardino.

Google Trends. 2018g. https://trends.google.com/trends/explore?date=2015-12
 -01%202016-06-30&geo=US-CA&q=ISIS%20Orlando,ISIS%20San%20Ber
 nardino.

Google Trends. 2018h. https://trends.google.com/trends/explore?date=2015-11
 -01%202016-04-01&geo=US&q=ISIS%20Brussels,ISIS%20Beirut.

Google Trends. 2019a. https://trends.google.com/trends/explore?date=2009-01
 -01%202018-01-11&geo=US&q=Boko%20Haram.

Google Trends. 2019b. https://trends.google.com/trends/explore?date=2015-08
 -16%202016-05-29&geo=US&q=Islamophobia,Kill%20Muslims.

Grillo, Ralph. 2004. "Islam and Transnationalism." *Journal of Ethnic and Migration Studies* 30(5): 861–78.

Grubb, Tammy. 2015. "Chapel Hill Police Arrest Man in Triple Homicide." *News
 and Observer*, February 10.

Guhin, Jeffrey. 2014. "Religion as Site Rather Than Religion as Category: On the
 Sociology of Religion's Export Problem." *Sociology of Religion* 75(4): 579–93.

Gulf Labour Markets and Migration. 2019. "GCC: Estimates of the Figures of
 Foreign Nationals (Selected Nationalities), by Country of Residence in the
 GCC (2012–2016)." https://gulfmigration.org/gcc-estimates-figures-foreign
 -nationals-selected-nationalities-country-residence-gcc-2012-2016/.

Haberman, Maggie. 2016. "Trump Says He's a 'Big Fan' of Hindus." *New York
 Times*, October 16.

Haberman, Maggie, and Richard Pérez-Peña. 2015. "Donald Trump Sets Off a Fu-
 ror with Call to Register Muslims in the U.S." *New York Times*, November 20.

Haddad, Yvonne Yazbeck. 2007. "The Post-9/11 'Hijab' as Icon." *Sociology of
 Religion* 68(3): 253–67.

Hajela, Deepti, and Verena Dobnik. 2017. "Bangladeshis Worry They'll Pay Price for NYC Subway Bomb." *U.S. News and World Report*, December 16.

Hamilton, Matt. 2016. "Donald Trump Repeats False Claim that Neighbors Saw Bombs All Over before San Bernardino Attack." *Los Angeles Times*, October 9.

Hassan, Riaz. 2006. "Globalization's Challenge to the Islamic Ummah." *Asian Journal of Social Science* 34(2): 311–23.

Healy, Patrick, and Michael Barbaro. 2015. "Donald Trump Calls for Barring Muslims from Entering U.S." *New York Times*, December 7.

Hennessy, Fiske. 2017. "Muslim Volunteers Spend *Eid* Helping Houston Hurricane Recovery." *Los Angeles Times*, September 1. https://www.latimes.com/nation/la-na-houston-muslim-volunteer-20170901-story.html.

Higham, John. 1994. *Strangers in the Land: Patterns of American Nativism 1860–1925*. New Brunswick, NJ: Rutgers University Press.

*Hindus for Trump* blog. 2020. http://hindusfortrump.blogspot.com.

Hindus for Trump Facebook Group. 2015a. Posted December 15, 2015. https://www.facebook.com/HindusForTrump/photos/a.814764598646555/814764658646549/?type=1&theater.

Hindus for Trump Facebook Group. 2015b. Posted October 28, 2016. https://www.facebook.com/HindusForTrump/photos/a.814784248644590/1023196171136729/?type=3&theater.

Holpuch, Amanda. 2015. "Website Targets Pro-Palestinian Students in Effort to Harm Job Prospects." *Guardian*, May 27.

Hondagneu-Sotelo, Pierrette. 1992. "Overcoming Patriarchal Constraints: The Reconstruction of Gender Relations among Mexican Immigrant Women and Men." *Gender and Society* 6(3): 393–415.

Houry, Nadim. 2017. "Trump's CVE Program: Going from Bad to Worse." Human Rights Watch, February 23. https://www.hrw.org/news/2017/02/23/trumps-cve-program.

"How the World Views the U.S. Elections, from Israel to North Korea." 2016. *Guardian*, October 31.

Hubbard, Ben. 2016. "A Saudi Morals Enforcer Called for a More Liberal Islam. Then the Death Threats Began." *New York Times*, July 11.

Human Rights Watch. 2014. "Illusion of Justice: Human Rights Abuses in U.S. Terrorism Prosecutions." *Human Rights Watch*, July 21. https://www.hrw

.org/report/2014/07/21/illusion-justice/human-rights-abuses-us-terrorism
-prosecutions.

Human Rights Watch. 2015a. "Southeast Asia: Accounts from Rohingya Boat
People." May 27. https://www.hrw.org/news/2015/05/27/southeast-asia
-accounts-rohingya-boat-people.

Human Rights Watch. 2015b. "Southeast Asia: End Rohingya Boat Pushbacks."
May 14. https://www.hrw.org/news/2015/05/14/southeast-asia-end-rohingya
-boat-pushbacks.

Ibrahim, Raymond. 2016. "Radical vs. Moderate Islam: A Muslim View." Gate-
stone Institute International Policy Council. https://www.gatestoneinstitute
.org/8101/radical-moderate-Islam.

Ilmfeed. 2018. "Tampa Bay Muslim Community Offers to Host Migrant Children
Separated from Their Families." June 26. https://ilmfeed.com/tampa-bay
-muslim-community-offers-host-migrant-children-separated-families/.

India TV. 2015. "#ProfileForPeace: Indians and Pakistanis Join Campaign to
Spread Message of Peace." October 24. https://www.indiatvnews.com/news
/india/profileforpeace-indians-and-pakistanis-campaig-message-of-peace
-55513.html.

Inside Edition. 2015. "Parking Lot Life Hack: Breaking the Code." CBS News,
February 11. https://www.insideedition.com/headlines/9695-parking-lot-life
-hack-breaking-the-code.

Itzigsohn, José. 2000. "Immigration and the Boundaries of Citizenship: The
Institutions of Immigrants' Political Transnationalism." *International Migration Review* 34(4): 1126–54.

Jaffrelot, Christophe, and Lawrence Louër. 2017. *Pan-Islamic Connections: Transnational Networks between South Asia and the Gulf.* London: Hurst.

Jamil, Uzma, and Cécil Rousseau. 2012. "Subject Positioning, Fear, and Insecurity in South Asian Muslim Communities in the War of Terror Context."
*Canadian Review of Sociology* 49(4): 370–88.

Jensen, Joan M. 1988. *Passage from India: Asian Indian Immigrants in North
America.* New Haven, CT: Yale University Press.

Joppke, Christian, and John Torpey. 2013. *Legal Integration of Islam: A Transat-
lantic Comparison.* Cambridge, MA: Harvard University Press.

Joseph, Craig, and Karen Keyworth. 2010. "A Question of Identity." *Islamic Horizons* 39(2) (March/April): 43–48.

Kapoor, Kanupriya, and Al-Zaquan Amer Hamzah. 2015. "Thailand, Malaysia May Set Up Camps for Influx of Boat People." Reuters, May 12. https://www.reuters.com/article/asia-migrants/thailand-malaysia-may-set-up-camps-for-influx-of-boatpeople-idUSKBN0NX0FN20150512.

Kassam, Raheem. 2016. "BBC Scrubs 'Ali' from Munich Killer's Name on TV, in Articles, and on Social Media." Breitbart, July 23. https://www.breitbart.com/london/2016/07/23/bbc-scrubs-muslim-name-ali-munich-killer-article/.

Katz, Jonathan, and Richard Pérez-Peña. 2015. "In Chapel Hill Shooting of 3 Muslims, a Question of Motive." *New York Times*, February 11.

Kearns, Erin, Allison Betus, and Anthony Lemeaux. 2017. "Why Do Some Terrorist Attacks Receive More Media Attention than Others?" *Justice Quarterly*, March 7. https://papers.ssrn.com/sol3/papers.cfm?abstract_id=2928138.

Keay, John. 2004. *India: A History*. London: Harper Collins.

Khan, Yasmin. 2008. *The Great Partition: The Making of India and Pakistan*. New Haven, CT: Yale University Press.

Kibria, Nazli. 1998. "The Racial Gap: South Asian American Racial Identity and the Asian American Movement." In *A Part, Yet Apart*, edited by Lavina Dhingra-Shankar and Rajini Srikanth, 69–78. Philadelphia: Temple University Press.

Kibria, Nazli. 2011. *Muslims in Motion: Islam and National Identity in the Muslim Diaspora*. New Brunswick, NJ: Rutgers University Press.

Kim, Ann H., and Michael J. White. 2010. "Panethnicity, Ethnic Diversity and Residential Segregation." *American Journal of Sociology* 115(5): 1558–96.

Kishi, Katayou. 2016. "Anti-Muslim Assaults Reach 9/11 Era Levels, FBI Data Show." Pew Research Center, November 21. https://www.pewresearch.org/fact-tank/2016/11/21/anti-muslim-assaults-reach-911-era-levels-fbi-data-show/.

Koenig, Matthias. 2005. "Incorporating Muslim Migrants in Western Nation-States: A Comparison of the United Kingdom, France, and Germany." *Journal of International Migration and Integration* 6(2): 219–34.

Kraut, Alan M. 2004. "Foreign Bodies: The Perennial Negotiation over Health and Culture in a Nation of Immigrants." *Journal of American Ethnic History* 23(2): 3–22.

Kurien, Prema. 2001. "Religion, Ethnicity, and Politics: Hindu and Muslim Indian Immigrants in the United States." *Ethnic and Racial Studies* 24(2): 263–93.

Kurien, Prema. 2004. "Multiculturalism, Immigrant Religion, and Diasporic Nationalism: The Development of an American Hinduism." *Social Problems* 51(3): 362–85.

Kurien, Prema. 2010. "Religion, Ethnicity and Politics: Hindu and Muslim Indian Immigrants in the United States." *Ethnic and Racial Studies* 24(2): 263–93.

Kurien, Prema, 2016. "Race, Religion, and the Political Incorporation of Indian Americans." *Journal of Religious and Political Practice* 2(3): 273–95.

Lachman, Samantha. 2016. "Why Bernie Sanders' Comments on the Israeli-Palestinian Conflict Are Historic." *Huffington Post*, April 15. https://www.huffpost.com/entry/bernie-sanders-hillary-clinton-israel_n_57114f60e4b0060ccda353ab.

Lamont, Michèle, and Virág Molnár. 2002. "The Study of Boundaries in the Social Sciences." *Annual Review of Sociology* 28: 167–95.

Landau, Noa, and Jack Khoury. 2018. "Israel: Gaza March 'Dangerous' Provocation, Hamas to Blame for Any Violence." *Haaretz*, March 29.

Landler, Mark, and Gardiner Harris. 2018. "Trump, Citing Pakistan as a 'Safe Haven' for Terrorists Freezes Aid." *New York Times*, January 4.

Leidig, Eviane Cheng. 2016. "Why Trump Is Winning Over American Hindus." *U.S. News*, October 26.

Leiken, Robert S., and Steven Brooke. 2007. "The Moderate Muslim Brotherhood." *Foreign Affairs* 86(2): 107–21.

Leonard, Karen. 1994. *Making Ethnic Choices: California's Punjabi Mexican Americans.* Philadelphia: Temple University Press.

Levin, Brian. 2016. "Study: In Wake of Terror, Anti-Muslim Crimes Escalate." *Huffington Post*, December 18. https://www.huffpost.com/entry/study-in-wake-of-terror-a_b_8838670.

Levitt, Peggy. 1998. "Social Remittances: Migration Driven Local-Level Forms of Cultural Diffusion." *International Migration Review* 32(4): 926–48.

Levitt, Peggy. 2001. *The Transnational Villagers.* Berkeley: University of California Press.

Levitt, Peggy. 2004. "Transnational Migrants: When 'Home' Means More than One Country." Migration Policy Institute, October 1. http://www.migrationpolicy.org/article/transnational-migrants-when-home-means-more-one-country.

Levitt, Peggy. 2007. *God Needs No Passport: Immigrants and the Changing American Religious Landscape.* New York: New Press.

Lichtblau, Eric. 2015. "Crimes against Muslim Americans and Mosques Rise Sharply." *New York Times*, December 17.

Lichtblau, Eric. 2016. "FBI Steps Up Use of Stings in ISIS Cases." *New York Times*, June 8.

Lichterman, Paul. 2008. "Religion and the Construction of Civic Identity." *American Sociological Review* 73: 83–104.

Liu, Zhaoyang. n.d. "American Anti-Catholicism in the 1920s." Re-Imagining Migration. https://reimaginingmigration.org/american-anti-catholicism-in -the-1920s/. Accessed April 1, 2019.

LoBianco, Tom, and Jeremy Diamond. 2016. "Why Bernie Sanders Skipped Pro-Israel Conference." CNN, March 21.

Love, Erik. 2017. *Islamophobia and Racism in America*. New York: New York University Press.

MACLC (The Muslim American Civil Liberties Coalition), CLEAR (The Creating Law Enforcement Accountability and Responsibility), and AALDEF (The Asian American Legal Defense and Education Fund). 2013. *Mapping Muslims: NYPD Spying and Its Impact on American Muslims*. Long Island City, NY: CUNY School of Law.

Mamdani, Mahmood. 2002. "Good Muslim, Bad Muslim: A Political Perspective on Culture and Terrorism." *American Anthropologist* 104(3): 766–75.

Mandaville, Peter. 2011. "Transnational Muslim Solidarities and Everyday Life." *Nation and Nationalism* 17(1): 7–24.

Manik, Julfikar Ali, Geeta Anand, and Ellen Barry. 2016. "Bangladesh Attack Is New Evidence that ISIS Has Shifted Its Focus beyond the Mideast." *New York Times*, July 2.

Manzoor, Sarfraz. 2015. "Can We Drop the Term Moderate Muslim? It's Meaningless." *Guardian*, March 16.

Marans, Daniel. 2018. "Michigan Lawmaker Suggests Muslim Candidate Faces Hurdles Due to His Faith." *Huffington Post*, July 15.

Markel, Howard, and Alexandra Minna Stern. 2002. "The Foreignness of Germs: The Persistent Association of Immigrants and Disease in American Society." *Milbank Quarterly* 80(4): 757–88.

Mas, Ruth. 2010. "Transnational Politics: Recent Accounts of Muslims in France." *Journal of Middle East Women's Studies* 6(2): 123–32.

Massey, Douglas, Rafael Alarcón, Jorge Durand, and Humberto González. 1987. *Return to Aztlan: The Social Process of International Migration from Western Mexico*. Berkeley: University of California Press.

Masud, Tareque. 2002. *The Clay Bird*. Movie, 95 minutes. Studio: Milestone Video. https://www.youtube.com/watch?v=UJ7snUtgKx4.

Mathew, Biju, and Vijay Prashad. 2000. "The Protean Forms of Yankee Hindutva." *Ethnic and Racial Studies* 23(3): 516–34.

Mazrui, Ali A. 2004. "Muslims between the Jewish Example and the Black Experience: American Policy Implications." In *Muslims' Place in the American Public Square*, edited by Zahid H. Bukhari, Sulayman S. Nyang, Mumtaz Ahmed, and John L. Esposito, 117–44. Walnut Creek, CA: Altamira Press.

McCoy, Terrence. 2014. "Michelle Obama's #BringBackOurGirls Picture Sparks Criticism of American Drone Strikes." *Washington Post*, May 15.

McKirdy, Euan, and Madison Park. 2017. "Joel Osteen Says Church Has Opened Doors to Flood Victims." CNN, August 30.

Medina, Jennifer. 2011. "Charges against Muslim Students Prompt Debate over Free Speech." *New York Times*, February 9.

Mekhennet, Souad, Griff Witte, and William Booth. 2016. "Munich Officials: Gunman Acted Like a 'Deranged Person' but Had No Ties to Terror Groups." *Washington Post*, July 23.

Metcalf, Barbara D. 2009. *Islam in South Asia in Practice*. Princeton, NJ: Princeton University Press.

Mishra, Sangay K. 2016. *Desis Divided: The Political Lives of South Asian Americans*. Minneapolis: University of Minnesota Press.

Mogahed, Dalia, and Azka Mahmood. 2019. "American Muslim Poll 2019: Predicting and Preventing Islamophobia." Institute for Social Policy and Understanding, May 1. https://www.ispu.org/american-muslim-poll-2019-predicting-and-preventing-islamophobia/.

Moore, Jack. 2017. "How the ISIS Attacks in Paris Changed Europe and Fueled a New Nationalism." *Newsweek*, November 13.

Mudde, Cas. 2016. "The Brussels Attacks and the New Normal of Terrorism in Western Europe." *Huffington Post*, March 22. https://www.huffpost.com/entry/the-brussels-attacks-and_b_9521360.

Murdock, Sebastian, and Melissa Jeltsen. 2017. "Muslims Opening Their Doors to Flood Victims: 'We Feel and Suffer the Same.'" *Huffington Post*, August 30. https://www.huffpost.com/entry/muslims-opening-their-doors-to-flood -victims-we-feel-and-suffer-the-same_n_59a6e953e4b00795c2a341b9.

Mustafa, Sabir. 2013. "Hefazat-e-Islam: Islamist Coalition." BBC News, May 6. http://www.bbc.com/news/world-asia-22424708.

Napoli, Philip M. 2003. *Audience Economics: Media Institutions and the Audience Market*. New York: Columbia University Press.

Naudet, Gédéon. 2018. *November 13: Attack on Paris*. Netflix documentary series, 55 minutes. https://www.netflix.com/title/80190097.

NBC News. 2015. "Suspect's Wife: Shooting of Students Not Related to Race or Religion." February 11.

Nir, Sarah Maslin, and Michael Gold 2019. "An Outbreak Spreads Fear: Of Measles, of Ultra-Orthodox Jews, of Anti-Semitism." *New York Times*, March 29.

Ose, Erik. 2015. "Why the Chapel Hill Shooting Was More Hate Crime than 'Parking Dispute.'" *Huffington Post*, February 18. https://www.huffpost.com /entry/why-the-chapel-hill-shooting-hate-crime_b_6681968.

Pape, Robert. 2016. "A New Normal for Europe." *Boston Globe*, March 22.

Parvaz, D. 2016. "Afghans Weigh in on U.S. Presidential Candidates." Al Jazeera, November 7.

Patel, Faiza, and Meghan Koushik. 2017. "Countering Violent Extremism." *Brennan Center for Justice*. New York: New York University School of Law.

Paul, Sonia, and Mansi Choksi. 2016. "How Donald Trump Ended Up at a Bollywood-Theme Hindu Rally in New Jersey." Public Radio International, October 20. https://www.pri.org/stories/2016-10-19/how-donald-trump-ended -bollywood-themed-hindu-rally-new-jersey.

Pearlman, Jonathan. 2015. "Who Are the Rohingya Boat People?" *Telegraph*, May 21.

Perez, Evan, Shimon Procupecz, Catherine E. Shoichet, and Tim Hume. 2016. "Omar Mateen: Angry, Violent, 'Bigot' Whole Pledged Allegiance to ISIS." CNN, June 14.

Peters, Jeremy W. 2016. Among Donald Trump's Biggest U.S. Fans: Hindu Nationalists." *New York Times*, October 14.

Petersen, Marie Juul. 2012. "Islamizing Aid: Transnational Muslim NGOs after 9.11." *Voluntas* 23: 126–55.

Pew Research Center. 2007. "Muslim Americans: Middle Class and Mostly Mainstream." May 22. https://www.pewresearch.org/2007/05/22/muslim -americans-middle-class-and-mostly-mainstream/.

Pew Research Center. 2011. "Muslim Americans: No Signs of Growth in Alienation or Support for Extremism." August 30. https://www.pewforum.org/2011 /08/30/muslim-americans-no-signs-of-growth-in-alienation-or-support-for -extremism/.

Pew Research Center. 2015. "The Future of World Religions: Population Growth Projections, 2010–2050." April 2. https://www.pewforum.org/2015/04/02 /religious-projections-2010-2050/.

Pew Research Center. 2017. "U.S. Muslims Concerned about Their Place in Society, but Continue to Believe in the American Dream." July 26. https://www .pewforum.org/2017/07/26/findings-from-pew-research-centers-2017-survey -of-us-muslims/.

Pew Research Center Global Attitudes and Trends. 2011. "U.S. Image in Pakistan Falls No Further Following bin Laden Killing." June 21. https://www .pewresearch.org/global/2011/06/21/u-s-image-in-pakistan-falls-no-further -following-bin-laden-killing/.

Pew Research Center Global Attitudes and Trends. 2012. "Pakistani Public Opinion Ever More Critical of US: 74% Call America an Enemy." June 27. https://www.pewresearch.org/global/2012/06/27/pakistani-public-opinion -ever-more-critical-of-u-s/.

Pew Research Center Global Attitudes Project. 2003. "Views of a Changing World: How Global Publics View War in Iraq, Democracy, Islam and Governance, and Globalization." June 3. https://www.pewresearch.org/global /2003/06/03/views-of-a-changing-world-2003/

Pew Research Center Religion and Public Life. 2019. Religious Landscape Survey. https://www.pewforum.org/religious-landscape-study/state/mississippi/.

Phillips, Brian J. 2015. "This Is Why the Paris Attacks Have Gotten More News Coverage than Other Terrorist Attacks." *Washington Post*, November 16.

Portes, Alejandro, Luis E. Guarnizo, and Patricia Landolt. 1999. "The Study of Transnationalism: Pitfalls and Promise of an Emergent Research Field." *Ethnic and Racial Studies* 22(2): 217–37.

Powell, Kimberly A. 2011. "Framing Islam: An Analysis of U.S. Media Coverage of Terrorism since 9/11." *Communication Studies* 62(1): 90–112.

Prashad, Vijay. 1998. "Crafting Solidarities." In *A Part, Yet Apart*, edited by Lavina Dhingra-Shankar and Rajini Srikanth, 105–26. Philadelphia: Temple University Press.

Prashad, Vijay. 2000. *The Karma of Brown Folk*. Minneapolis: University of Minnesota Press.

Prashad, Vijay. 2012. *Uncle Swami: South Asians in America Today*. New York: New Press.

Rabasa, Angel, Cheryl Benard, Lowell H. Schwartz, and Peter Sickle. 2007. *Building Moderate Muslim Networks*. Center for Middle East Public Policy. Santa Monica, CA: RAND Corporation.

Rana, Junaid. 2011. *Terrifying Muslims: Race and Labor in the South Asian Diaspora*. Durham, NC: Duke University Press.

Raphelson, Samantha. 2018. "Muslim Americans Running for Office in Highest Numbers since 9/11." *MPR News*, July 18.

Rashid, Ahmad. 2012. *Pakistan on the Brink: The Future of America, Pakistan, and Afghanistan*. London: Allen Lane.

Rashid, Qasim. 2011. "Will the Moderate Muslims Please Stand Up?" *Huffington Post*, February 3. https://www.huffpost.com/entry/will-the-real-moderate-mu_b_817600.

Read, Jen'nan Ghazal, and John P. Bartkowsky 2000. "To Veil or Not to Veil? A Case Study of Identity Negotiation among Muslim Women in Austin, Texas." *Gender and Society* 14(3): 397–417.

Reuters. 2018. "Pakistan to Send Troops to Saudi Arabia to Train and Advise." February 16.

Riaz, Ali. 2010. "The Politics of Islamization in Bangladesh." In *Religion and Politics in South Asia*, edited by Riaz Ali, 45–70. New York: Routledge.

Ripley, Will. 2016. "How Did a Socialist Kibbutz Influence Bernie Sanders?" CNN, February 10. https://www.cnn.com/2016/02/09/politics/bernie-sanders-kibbutz-volunteer-israel/index.html.

Rizvi, Ali A. 2014. "An Open Letter to Moderate Muslims." *Huffington Post*, October 6. https://www.huffpost.com/entry/an-open-letter-to-moderat_b_5930764.

Rogers, Katie, and Sheryl Gay Stolberg. 2018. "Trump Resisting a Growing Wrath for Separating Migrant Families." *New York Times*, June 18.

"The Rohingya Boat Crisis: Why Refugees Are Fleeing Burma." 2015. *The Week*, May 21. http://www.theweek.co.uk/63745/the-rohingya-boat-crisis-why-refugees-are-fleeing-burma.

Romero, Luis A., and Amina Zarrugh. 2017. "Islamophobia and the Making of Latinos/as into Terrorist Threats." *Ethnic and Racial Studies* 41(12): 2235–54.

Rubin, Alissa J. "French 'Burkini' Bans Provoke Backlash as Armed Police Confront Beachgoers." *New York Times*, August 24.

Said, Edward. 1979. *Orientalism*. New York: Vintage Books.

Salahuddin, Patricia. 2016. "Constructing Muslim Identity in the Classroom." *Islamic Horizons* 45(2) (March/April): 30–31.

Santana, Maria. 2014. "Ebola Fears Spark Backlash against Latino Immigrants." CNN Politics, October 12. http://www.cnn.com/2014/10/10/politics/ebola -fears-spark-backlash-latinos/index.html.

Selod, Saher. 2018. *Forever Suspect: Racialized Surveillance of Muslim Americans in the War on Terror*. New Brunswick, NJ: Rutgers University Press.

Semple, Kirk. 2015a. "'I'm Frightened': After Attacks in Paris, New York Muslims Cope with a Backlash." *New York Times*, November 25.

Semple, Kirk. 2015b. "Young Muslim Americans Are Facing the Strain of Suspicion." *New York Times*, December 14.

Sengupta, Somini, and Henry Fountain. 2018. "The Biggest Refugee Camp Braces for Rain: 'This Is Going to Be a Catastrophe.'" *New York Times*, March 14.

Shaheen, Jack G. 2001. *Reel Bad Arabs: How Hollywood Vilifies a People*. New York: Olive Branch Press.

Shams, Tahseen. 2015. "Bangladeshi Muslims in Mississippi: Impression Management Based on the Intersection of Religion, Ethnicity, and Gender." *Cultural Dynamics* 27(3): 379–97.

Shams, Tahseen. 2017. "Mirrored Boundaries: How Ongoing Homeland-Hostland Contexts Shape Bangladeshi Immigrant Collective Identity Formation." *Ethnic and Racial Studies* 40(4): 713–31.

Shams, Tahseen. 2018. "Visibility as Resistance by Muslim Americans in a Surveillance and Security Atmosphere." *Sociological Forum* 33(1): 73–94.

Shams, Tahseen. 2020. "Successful yet Precarious: South Asian Muslim Americans, Islamophobia, and the Model Minority Myth." *Sociological Perspectives* (forthcoming).

Shane, Scott. 2016. "Saudis and Extremism: 'Both the Arsonists and the Firefighters.'" *New York Times*, August 25.

Silva, Derek M. D. 2017. "The Othering of Muslims: Discourses of Radicalization in the *New York Times*, 1969–2014." *Sociological Forum* 32(1): 138–61.

Smith, Michael Peter, and Matt Bakker. 2008. *Citizenship across Borders: The Political Transnationalism of El Migrante.* Ithaca, NY: Cornell University Press.

Smith, R. C. 2003. "Diasporic Memberships in Historical Perspective: Comparative Insights from the Mexican, Italian, and Polish Cases." *International Migration Review* 37(3): 722–57.

Sohi, Seema. 2014. *Echoes of Mutiny: Race, Surveillance and Indian Anticolonialism in North America.* New York: Oxford University Press.

Southern Poverty Law Center. 2016. "Intelligence Report: Backlash." https://www
.splcenter.org/fighting-hate/intelligence-report/2016/backlash.

Soysal, Yaesmin Nuhoglu. 1994. *Limits of Citizenship: Migrants and Postnational Membership in Europe.* Chicago: University of Chicago Press.

Spencer, Robert. 2016. "BBC Scrubs Munich Killer's Muslim Name." Jihad Watch, July 24. https://www.jihadwatch.org/2016/07/bbc-scrubs-munich-killers
-muslim-name.

Spielhaus, Riem. 2010. "Media Making Muslims: The Construction of a Muslim Community in Germany through Media Debate." *Contemporary Islam* 4: 11–27.

Stack, Liam. 2016. "American Muslims under Attack." *New York Times*, February 15.

Stancill, Jane, Jay Price, and Anne Blythe. 2015. "Chapel Hill Killings Reverberate around the World." *News and Observer*, February 11.

Statistics Canada. 2017. "Police-Reported Hate Crimes, 2015." June 13. http://www
.statcan.gc.ca/daily-quotidien/170613/dq170613b-eng.htm?HPA=1.

Sullivan, Margaret. 2016. "Are Some Terrorism Deaths More Equal than Others?" *New York Times*, April 2.

Sussman, Tina. 2015. "Islamic State Presence in the U.S. Is 'the New Normal,' FBI Director Says." *Los Angeles Times*, November 19.

Tannenbaum, Michal. 2007. "Back and Forth: Immigrants' Stories of Migration and Return." *International Migration* 45(5): 147–75.

Telles, Edward, and Vilma Ortiz. 2008. *Generations of Exclusion: Mexican Americans, Assimilation, and Race.* New York: Russell Sage Foundation.

Tharoor, Ishaan. 2010. "WikiLeaks: The Saudi's Close but Strained Ties with Pakistan." *Time*, December 6. http://content.time.com/time/world/article
/0,8599,2035347,00.html.

Tharoor, Ishaan. 2017. "The World's 'Most Friendless People' Are under Assault Yet Again." *Washington Post*, August 31.

Troianovsky, Anton, Christopher Alessi, and William Wilkes. 2016. "Munich Gunman Had Interest in Mass Shootings, No Apparent Islamic State Ties." *Wall Street Journal*, July 23.

Uddin, Sufia M. 2006. *Constructing Bangladesh: Religion, Ethnicity, and Language in an Islamic Nation*. Chapel Hill: University of North Carolina Press.

UNICEF. 2018. "Rohingya Crisis." May 24. https://www.unicef.org/emergencies /bangladesh_100945.html.

United Nations. 2013. "Trends in International Migrant Stock: Migrants by Destination and Origin." Department of Economic and Social Affairs, Population Division. UN Database (POP/DB/MIG/Stock/Rev.2013).

University of Texas Libraries. 2008. "Map: Middle East and Asia." https://legacy .lib.utexas.edu/maps/middle_east_and_asia/txu-oclc-247232986-asia_pol _2008.jpg.

van der Veer, Peter. 2002a. "Colonial Cosmopolitanism." In *Conceiving Cosmopolitanism*, edited by R. Cohen and S. Vertovec, 165–80. Oxford: Oxford University Press.

van der Veer, Peter. 2002b. "Transnational Religion: Hindu and Muslim Movements." *Global Networks* 2(2): 95–109.

von Tunzelmann, Alex. 2007. *Indian Summer: The Secret History of the End of an Empire*. New York: Picador.

Waldinger, Roger. 2015. *The Cross-Border Connection: Immigrants, Emigrants, and Their Homelands*. Cambridge, MA: Harvard University Press.

Waldinger, Roger, and David FitzGerald. 2004. "Transnationalism in Question." *American Journal of Sociology* 109(5): 1177–95.

Warikoo, Niraj. 2016. "Young Arab-American Muslim Voters Helped Fuel Sanders' Win." *Detroit Free Press*, March 8.

Wax-Thibodeaux, Emily, and Abigail Hauslohner. 2017. "'Helping Is a Total No-Brainer': Houston-Area Mosques Open Their Doors as Shelters." *Washington Post*, September 1.

Whine, Michael. 2007. "Islamic Organizations on the Internet." *Terrorism and Political Violence* 11(1): 123–32.

Wilkie, Christina. 2016. "Donald Trump: Americans Who Do Not Report Their Suspicious Neighbors Should Be 'Brought to Justice.'" *Huffington Post*, June 13. https://www.huffpost.com/entry/donald-trump-orlando-san-bernardino_n _575f1802e4b0e4fe51435eb2.

Williams, Rhys H., and Gira Vashi. 2007. "The *Hijab* and American Muslim Women: Creating the Space for Autonomous Selves." *Sociology of Religion* 68(2): 269–87.

Wilson, Christopher, and Alexandra Dunn. 2011. "Digital Media in the Egyptian Revolution: Descriptive Analysis from the Tahrir Data Sets." *International Journal of Communication* 5: 1248–72.

World Bank. 2014. "Bangladesh." http://data.worldbank.org/country/bangladesh.

Wright, Rebecca. 2017. "'The Rohingya Alan Kurdi': Will the World Take Notice Now?" CNN, September 13.

Wuthnow, Robert, and Stephen Offutt. 2008. "Transnational Religious Connections." *Sociology of Religion* 69(2): 209–32.

Wynbrandt, James. 2004. *A Brief History of Saudi Arabia*. New York: Checkmark Books.

Yildiz, Ali Aslan, and Maykel Verkuyten. 2013. "We Are Not Terrorists: Turkish Muslim Organizations and the Construction of a Moral Identity." *Ethnicities* 13(3): 359–81.

Yilmaz, Ihsan. 2010. "Transnational Islam." *European Journal of Economic and Political Studies* 3: 1–5.

Yourish, Karen, Derek Watkins, Tom Giratikanon, and Jasmine C. Lee. 2016. "How Many People Have Been Killed in ISIS Attacks around the World." *New York Times*, July 16.

Zeitz, Josh. 2015. "When American Hated Catholics." *Politico Magazine*, September 23. https://www.politico.com/magazine/story/2015/09/when-america-hated-catholics-213177.

Zhou, Min, and Carl Bankston III. 1998. *Growing Up American: How Vietnamese Children Adapt to Life in the United States*. New York: Russell Sage Foundation.

Zong, Jie, and Jeanne Batalova. 2016. "Asian Immigrants in the United States." *Migration Policy Institute*, January 6. http://www.migrationpolicy.org/article/asian-immigrants-united-states.

Zubaida, Sami. 2004. "Islam and Nationalism: Continuities and Contradictions." *Nations and Nationalism* 10(4): 407–20.

# Index

Note: Page numbers in *italics* indicate illustrations.

## GLOBALIZATION
### IN EVERYDAY LIFE

As global forces undeniably continue to change the politics and econo-mies of the world, we need a more nuanced understanding of what these changes mean in our daily lives. Significant theories and studies have broadened and deepened our knowledge on globalization, yet we need to think about how these macroprocesses manifest on the ground and how they are maintained through daily actions.

*Globalization in Everyday Life* foregrounds ethnographic examination of daily life to address issues that will bring tangibility to previously abstract assertions about the global order. Moving beyond mere il-lustrations of global trends, books in this series underscore mutually constitutive processes of the local and global by finding unique and informative ways to bridge macro- and microanalyses. This series is a high-profile outlet for books that offer accessible readership, inno-vative approaches, instructive models, and analytic insights to our understanding of globalization.

*Beauty Diplomacy: Embodying an Emerging Nation*
Oluwakemi M. Balogun
2020